Complex Predicates in Modern Persian

Complex Predicates in Modern Persian
A Functional Characterization

Zari Saeedi

SHEFFIELD UK   BRISTOL CT

Published by Equinox Publishing Ltd.

UK: Office 415, The Workstation, 15 Paternoster Row, Sheffield, South Yorkshire
     S1 2BX

USA: ISD, 70 Enterprise Drive, Bristol, CT 06010

www.equinoxpub.com

First published 2016

British Library Cataloguing-in-Publication Data
A catalogue record for this book is available from the British Library.

ISBN-13 978 1 78179 218 6 (hardback)

Library of Congress Cataloging-in-Publication Data
Saeedi, Zari.
Complex predicates in modern Persian: a functional characterization / Zari Saeedi.
Includes bibliographical references and index.
ISBN 978-1-78179-218-6 (hb)
1. Persian language–Verb. 2. Persian language–Verb phrase. 3. Persian language–
Syntax. 4. Predicate (Logic). I. Title.
PK6299.S35 2016
491'.5556–dc23
                          2015031047

Typeset by BBR, Sheffield
Printed and bound in Great Britain by Lightning Source

Contents

Tables

Tables of prepositional NJs in Appendix B

Acknowledgements

I would like to acknowledge my deepest sense of appreciation and indebtedness to Professor John Saeed, the former Head of the School of Linguistic, Speech and Communication Sciences at Trinity College, Dr. Brian Nolan, the Head of Department of Informatics, Professor David Singleton and Dr. Jeffrey Kallen at the School of Linguistics, Speech and Communication Sciences and Professor Philip Jagger at the School of Oriental and African Studies, University of London, without whose valuable comments the fulfilment of this book, which is based on my research during my PhD studies at Trinity College, would have been impossible.

Abbreviations

AAJ	Argument adjunct
ACC	Accusative
ACS	Accessible
ACV	Active, Activated
Adj.	Adjective
ADJCP	Adjectival Complex Predicate
ADJLVC	Adjectival light verbal construction
ADJNJ	Adjectival Nuclear Juncture
ADJU	Adjunct
Adv.	Adverb
ADVCP	Adverbial Complex Predicate
ADVLVC	Adverbial light verbal construction
ADVNJ	Adverbial Nuclear Juncture
Adv. Suffix	Adverbial Suffix
ARG	Argument
ASP	Aspect
AUX.	Auxiliary
CP	Complex Predicate
DCA	Direct Core Argument
DEF	Definite(ness)
DEIC	Deictic
DOM	Direct Object Marker
DUR	Durative (progressive)
FUT	Future
HPSG	Head-driven Phrase Structure Grammar
IMP	Imperative
Ind. Art.	Indefinite article
Ind. M.	Indefinite marker
INF	Infinitive
Intran	Intransitive
LDP	Left-detached position
LEX	Lexeme
LFG	Lexical-Functional Grammar
Lit.	Literal meaning
LS	Logical structure
LSC	Layered Structure of the Clause

LV	Light verb
LVC	Light verbal construction
NASP	Nominal Aspect
NCP	Nominal Complex Predicate
Neg.	Negative
NEG	Negation
NI	Noun incorporation
NJ	Nuclear Juncture
NLVC	Nominal light verbal construction
NMP	Non-Macrorole
NNJ	Nominal Nuclear Juncture
NOM	Nominative
NP	Noun phrase
NPIP	NP-Initial Position
NUC	Nucleus
NUM	Number
NV	Non-verbal
OP	Operator
PCP	Prepositional Complex Predicate
Pl.	Plural
PLVC	Prepositional light verbal construction
PNJ	Prepositional Nuclear Juncture
PoCS	Postcore slot
POSS	Possessive
PP	Prepositional phrase
PPART	Past participle
PrCS	Precore slot
PRED	Predicate
Prep.	Preposition
PRO	Pronoun
PRO$_{REL}$	Relative Pronoun
Pron. Filler	Pronunciation filler
PRSPET	Present perfect
PSA	Privileged Syntactic Argument
PV	Preverbal
QNT	Quantifier
RDP	Right-detached position
REF	Referential NP
RRG 3 P.P.A.	Role and Reference Grammar 3 Place Predicate Analysis

S	Sentence
Sg.	Singular
SOV	Subject-object-verb
SUBL	Sublative
Suf.	Suffix
TAM	Tense, aspect, mood
TNS	Tense
Tran	Transitive
VP	Verbal phrase

1

Aims and Scope of the Study

1.1 Objectives

Complex predicates have always been of a challenging nature for linguists, especially for those who are interested in working on Persian, or Farsi, one of the oldest recorded Indo-European languages with 2500 years of written history (Khanlari, 1979), which employs a large number of complex verb constructions in forming propositions. These constructions in Persian consist of two elements, a preverbal and a verbal element, which combine together to form a complex predicate and act as a single lexical unit. There are four identified types of the preverbal elements of nouns, adjectives, adverbs and prepositional phrases that possess the capability of conjoining with the verbal or light verbal constituent (Saeedi, 2009a, 2009b, 2010, 2012). The light verb in such constructions as *narahæt kærdæn* 'make sad' (Lit.: 'sad make'), which consists of the adjectival element *narahæt* 'sad' and the light verb *kærdæn* 'make', is in fact the impoverished form of the full/heavy verb and plays part of the predicating role of the whole construction. The behaviour of such complex predicates in Persian has given rise to interesting questions to which the few earlier research studies carried out on these constructions have failed to provide comprehensive answers. The questions centrally concern the relative contribution of each of the preverbal and verbal elements to the event and argument structure of the whole complex, namely, the impact of each element in determining the syntactic valency-transitivity status and the semantic-thematic roles of the construction, the amount of contribution of each component in the Aktionsart class or aspectual properties of the predicate, and the degree of lightness of the verbal element, i.e. whether it is completely or partially bleached.

In this book an attempt has been made to provide an answer to the above questions by investigating the semantic morphosyntactic interface of Persian complex predicates within Role and Reference Grammar (RRG) (Van Valin and LaPolla, 1997; Van Valin, 2005), which as will be discussed, provides an insightful way of capturing the various linguistic properties of these Persian Complex Predicates (CPs) or Nuclear Junctures (NJs) (in RRG's terms). Basically, this book follows two aims: a descriptive aim and a theoretical one. In terms of description, a more comprehensive analysis than hitherto available of these constructions will be provided, employing such RRG tools as the layered structure of the clause (LSC), logical structure (LS) and the nexus-juncture relation and constructional schema. This book is, in fact, the first study to provide a comprehensive and detailed account of the full range of the adjectival and prepositional types of Persian light verbal constructions (LVCs). In addition, it is the first book on the RRG analysis of these constructions in Persian. To fulfil the theoretical aim a unified account of the range of light verbal complex predicates (distinguished in this research study) through the framework of RRG will be provided. An important aim is to show that among existing linguistic theories, RRG benefits from a more comprehensive linking architecture, which enables it to characterize the complex predicates of a number of language systems including Modern Persian (Farsi). As will be discussed later in this study, the linking procedure of RRG provides an interface between the semantic structure in which the predicate is a unit and the syntactic structural representation, which allows such syntactic characteristics as discontinuity, i.e. the intervention of some constituents between the preverbal and verbal elements.

According to RRG, the distinction between the lexical and syntactic phenomena can be characterized on the basis of the system linking semantics and syntactic representation provided by Van Valin and LaPolla (1997) and Van Valin (2005). By examining the RRG linking system it becomes clear that by manifesting and linking the lexical/semantic features along with the syntactic realization of linguistic phenomena, RRG depicts an account of the linkage between the lexical and syntactic characteristics of such constructions as complex predicates. In fact, the RRG linking system between the syntactic functions and the lexical decompositional parameters makes it possible to obtain a better understanding of the Persian nuclear juncture constraints.

1.2 Research methodology and scope

As mentioned above, the present study is concerned with investigating nuclear junctures in Persian, Farsi, which is classified below as presented in Figure 1.1 (from Baldi, 1983).

Persian has been categorized into old, middle and modern languages and this study focuses on the standard variety of modern Persian used by educated Tehran speakers both male and female within the age range of 20–50. In this study the Persian orthography, which has similar alphabets as Arabic, has been romanized. In Persian the canonical word order is subject-object-verb

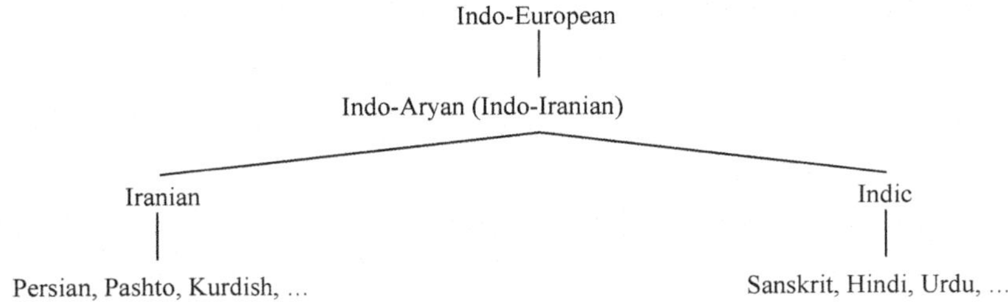

Figure 1.1 Partial Persian genetic tree diagram.

(SOV), there is no gender and case distinction, but person and number can be identified; adverbs can appear in various positions and adjectives follow the noun they modify. Individual word orders and specific features of the language under study will be provided in each related subsequent chapter. Even though the researcher of this study is a native Tehran speaker, an attempt has been made to access a variety of informants embodying different forms of the written and spoken contexts to increase the reliability of the findings. The main data sources used in the present research include media, newspapers, books, recorded authentic conversations, emails, and online databases for Persian examples. One of the sources for data collection was *Hamshahri Corpus* as an online newspaper accessible from http://en.wikipedia.org/wiki/ Hamshahri_Corpus. The Hamshahri collection contains more than 160,000 articles covering subject categories: politics, city news, economics, reports, editorials, literature, sciences, society, foreign news, sports, etc. The size of the documents varies from short news (under 1 kilobyte) to rather long articles (e.g. 140 KB) with an average of 1.8 KB. The next data source was the Farsi Linguistic Database developed by Dr. S. M. Assi at the Institute for Humanities and Cultural Studies in Tehran, accessible at http://pldb.ihcs. ac.ir. This database comprises a selection of contemporary Modern Persian literature, formal and informal spoken varieties of the language and a series entries and word list. The present study also availed itself of the examples in the Bijankhan Corpus developed by Professor M. Bijankhan (1994) and Data Base Research at the University of Tehran. The data were collected from daily news and common texts covering 4300 subjects. This database contains 2.6 million manually tagged words with a tag set that contains 550 Persian part-of-speech tags and accessible at http://ece.ut.ac.ir/dbrg/Bijankhan/ DBRG/Hamshahri. The researcher also utilized Tehran native speakers' judgements to differentiate the (un)grammaticality of the constructions along with her own intuition. Although the study is not based on corpus-oriented generalizations, the researcher tried to use various data sources and informants to overcome the weaknesses of traditional data elicitation.

In this study four propositions were formulated as follows.

1. Persian light verbs are not completely bleached elements in these constructions as claimed by Karimi-Doostan (1997) and Vahedi-Langrudi (1996); the correct characterization is that they are semantically bleached with respect to event structure.
2. The preverbal constituents contribute differently, according to their grammatical category, to the semantic structure of the complex predicate.
3. The grammatical behaviour of these Persian LVCs is not a manifestation of some anomalous intermediate syntactic and lexical status as Megerdoomian (2001a) suggests by assigning them a 'dual' nature. Rather, these features can be accounted for within the framework of RRG. This is contrary to Goldberg's (2004) similar claim that the analysis of these constructions is problematic since they behave like a lexical phenomenon on the one hand and a syntactic one on the other.
4. A characterization of the nuclear junctures is best provided in a functional account that facilitates explanation at the semantic-lexicon-morphosyntactic interface.

1.3 Organization of the study

In order to fulfil the objectives of the study, namely, to provide a semantic and morphosyntactic analysis of Persian light verbal constructions, in Chapter 2 the literature on the complex predicates (nuclear junctures) that occur cross-linguistically is reviewed. This includes discussion of such constructions as *make an offer* in English, where a preverbal or nominal element (*an offer*) combines with the impoverished form of the verb (*make*) called a 'light verb' (Jespersen, 1954; Cattell, 1984) to build the type of Complex Predicate (CP) known as a light verbal construction (LVC). As will be shown, these are regarded as a type of Nuclear Juncture (NJ) in Role and Reference Grammar (RRG). This section of Chapter 2 discusses the three major types of complex predicates identified in the literature: noun incorporation, causative and light verbal constructions. In the second section of Chapter 2 (Section 2.2) Persian complex predicates are introduced, their lexical and syntactic properties will be discussed and some earlier analyses of them will be reviewed. In addition, the light and full forms of the same verbs will be contrasted by discussing argument structure and causativization.

In Chapter 3 the focus is on outlining a clear picture of the theoretical framework of Role and Reference Grammar, the theory adopted for the present study. To pave the way for the main analysis, and to highlight the RRG's approach to complex predicates, this chapter provides some background information regarding the organization of RRG, the syntactic representation including the Layered Structure of the Clause and the operator projection, the lexical and semantic representation, and the linking algorithm in RRG.

To provide the foundations for the descriptive analyses of Persian light verbal constructions, it is discussed that in Persian/Farsi four major types of Nuclear Junctures (NJs) can be distinguished (Saeedi, 2009a), i.e. the combination of noun, adjective, adverb and prepositional phrase with the light verb on the basis of the category of the preverbal elements. In this study these constructions have been referred to as nominal, adjectival, adverbial and prepositional, respectively. Since the focus of this book is on the adjectival and prepositional CPs, for each group of these constructions a number of diagnostic tests are applied in each related chapter to determine their aspectual properties. The tests of the identified types of NJs examined in Chapters 4 and 5 are placed in different Appendices, A and B respectively, to facilitate reference to these materials. That is, in each chapter only the results of the test application for the nuclear junctures under examination are included in the chapters. Chapter 4 is concerned with first type: adjectival light verbal constructions; that is, where the preverbal component is an adjective. In this chapter the adjectival complex predicates are discussed in terms of the type of the preverbal element or adjective and the light verbal component used in the data. The next analytical chapter of this book, Chapter 5, explores the prepositional light verbal constructions where a prepositional phrase combines with light verbs to form a nuclear juncture. Following the procedure in Chapter 4, the preverbal element (i.e. prepositional phrase) in Chapter 5 is classified into different groups to depict a more comprehensive picture of the interrelationship between these elements and such parameters as Aktionsart and event/argument structure: syntactic vs. semantic valency. For each of the mentioned analytical chapters (4 and 5) a large variety of data from the Persian examples were collected and the Layered Structure of the Clause or LSC (in RRG's terminology), the constructional schemas, nexus-juncture type and the logical structures of these sentences are presented.

2

Light Verbs in Persian

2.1 Complex predicates

In this chapter, an attempt has been made to provide an informal overview of light verbal constructions (LVCs) as one of the main subcategories of complex (compound or composite) predicates in modern Persian or Farsi, where the preverbal (PV) and verbal elements combine to make complex predicates or Nuclear Junctures (NJs) (as referred to in Role and Reference Grammar (RRG)). Complex Predicates (CPs) have been analyzed cross-linguistically from different perspectives. These constructions are of great theoretical interest because their analysis raises important questions about the interrelationship of morphology, syntax and lexicon. Before a more detailed discussion of light verbal constructions, some background information regarding the definition/formation of complex predicates is provided.

2.1.1 Complex predicates: definitions

The question of how complex predicates should be defined and analyzed has been a major topic of linguistics viewed from different perspectives for several decades. Investigating English composite predicate constructions, Cattell (1984) is probably one of the first scholars who helped to pave the way for future syntacticians to characterize these constructions. As Grimshaw and Mester (1988) indicate, ideas using complex predicate formation of various types have been developed for related English phenomena by Cattell (1984), Higgins (1974) and Jackendoff (1974). Cattell (1984), in the third chapter of his book, which is devoted to complex predicate analyses of English sentences, discusses structures such as the following.

(1) a. Harry made an offer of money to the police.
    b. Harry offered money to the police.

In the above example (1a) the expression *made an offer* is a complex predicate in English, which from a semantic point of view resembles the idea expressed in the single-word verb *offered*. Similarly, T. Mohanan (1990) provides the following two sentences from English to highlight the difference between a complex predicate and other predicates.

(2) a. Bill **made the claim** that unicorns are birds.
    b. Bill **disproved the claim** that unicorns are birds.

According to Mohanan, unlike the expression *made the claim* in (2a), the expression *disproved the claim* in (2b) is not comprehended as a single unit. Moreover, (2a) is semantically equivalent to the simple verb 'claim' while (2b) is not so. It was this intuition that led Cattell (1984) to call the expression in (2a) a complex predicate (T. Mohanan, 1997, p. 431). Mohanan argues that a complex predicate is formed when two semantically predicative elements unite to correspond to a single syntactic clause. As Mohanan maintains, in most South Asian languages, including Hindi which was the main focus of his analysis, nouns, adjectives, or non-finite forms of verbs, can join other verbs to form complex predicates or CPs. In general, a CP, Mohanan points out, can be defined as one in which two semantical elements jointly determine the structure of a single syntactic clause.

Complex predicate constructions have also been investigated within different theoretical frameworks. Baker (1997) claims that a CP as a semantically transparent term in syntactic theory simply refers to any predicate with semantic, syntactic or morphological complexity. He employs a generative Government and Binding Theory in his analysis in which a single inflectional domain is created by syntactic movement rules from a more articulated and complex underlying representation. In fact, by complex predicate, Baker means a single inflectional domain that is composed of two or more distinct morphemes, each of which bears at least one argument (in Baker's theory, argument structure is represented by 'theta (θ) grids'). The formation of CPs is expressed by Baker in terms of movement at phrase structure or head-to-head movement.

In his (1997) study, 'Complex predicates and agreement in polysynthetic languages', Baker tries to examine the relationship between these constructions and other typological properties of language. He identifies a typological class that he calls 'polysynthetic head-marking languages', which have productive noun incorporation as well as obligatory verb agreement with any nominals playing the role of subject or object. In these languages, he claims, CPs form a single word. Baker (1997, p. 270) provides the following example[1] from Nahuatl (Uto-Aztecan).

(3) Ni-mitz-cua-l-tia   in   nacat
     1st.Sg.SUB-2ndSg.OBJ-eat-X-CAUS   the   meat
     'I made you eat the meat.'

(X: represents the formative *-l-* which appears on a particular conjunction class of verbs.)

In (3) which represents causative CP in Nahuatl (as one of the polysynthetic languages), the causative morpheme, as Baker (1997) argues, does not attach directly to the verb root, but rather to the root plus the formative *-l-* which augments the stem of the verb. With the exception of this and a few other features of CPs that are specific to Nahuatl, there are, according to Baker, some common features or restrictions on the class of CPs among polysynthetic languages. The two main restrictions are: 1) the two theta-marking heads of a complex predicate must form a single morphological word, and 2) all the arguments involved in complex predicate constructions are arguments of one of the heads and the other head shares one or more of these arguments (Baker, 1997, p. 285). Since causative constructions are dealt with in another section (2.1.4), a more detailed discussion of these CPs is presented later in the present chapter.

Adopting a similar view to Baker's, Hale and Keyser (1997) maintain that many surface monomorphemic verbs in the lexicon are internally complex and, in fact, complex predicates are the norm rather than being special. Like Baker, Hale and Keyser believe that CPs are just types of complementation structures and that there is no need to adopt other mechanisms in addition to those in syntax.

According to Hale and Keyser (1997, p. 29), 'no ordinary verbal lexical item, for example, consists solely of a head and the associated category V. There is always more to a verb'. Each verb along with its morphological form and meaning, Hale and Keyser (1997) argue, presents a structure which reveals the syntactic relations within which the internal argument structures are formed, and since all the verbs presumably possess an internal argument they are all complex to that extent.

Alsina, Bresnan and Sells (1997) define complex predicates as predicates which are composed of more than one word or morpheme and are multi-headed; each of the grammatical elements contributes part of the information associated with a head. Basing his analysis of Romance causatives on a Lexical-Functional Grammar (LFG) approach, Alsina (1993) maintains that the CPs in Romance languages must be formed in the syntax, and not in the lexicon. The following example provided by Alsina (1997, p. 222) illustrates a causative CP in Catalan, which according to Alsina is formed in syntax, rather than in lexicon.

(4) a. La Maria fa   [[$_V$ riure] i   [$_V$ plorar]] el   nen.
     Maria   makes laugh   and cry   the boy
     'Maria is making the boy laugh and cry.'

In the above example the verbs *riure* and *plorar,* as Alsina (1997) argues, are well-formed lexical items that occupy X0 positions in the syntax. The constructions like (4a) above are generally known as 'indirect causatives' (Shibatani and Pardeshi, 2002). In (4a) these two predicates are coordinated and, in fact, the noun phrase (NP) *el nen* satisfies the cause argument structure of both verbs. According to Alsina, this coordination procedure indicates that the complex predicates formation in Romance causatives takes place in syntax.

To cope with examples like (4a) Alsina (1993) develops a predicate composition process combining distinct argument structures in the syntax. Arguing for a more abstract representation, Alsina does represent some semantic information directly at argument structure and follows Dowty's system of proto-roles in representing the arguments (Butt, 1995). In general, Butt (1995, p. 133) describes Alsina's approach as achieving a medium between the traditional use of θ-role labels, and Grimshaw's (1990) and T. Mohanan's (1990) proposals that no semantic information whatsoever is encoded at argument structure.

Alsina (1997) compares causative constructions in Chichewa (Bantu) and Catalan (Romance) and argues that the two languages are basically similar with regard to their argument structures. Their difference lies in the idea that in Chichewa one single word represents the predicate of a causative construction, while in Catalan the causative construction predicate (as in 4a) is represented by two words. Alsina (1997, p. 209) provides the following example to illustrate causative construction formation in Chichewa.

(4) b. Njōvu   i-na-sék-éts-a   afīsi
     elephant S-PAST-laugh-CAUS hyenas
     'The elephant made the hyenas laugh.'

Unlike Catalan (example 4a), Chichewa, as Alsina (1997) points out, employs one word or lexical item to form causative construction. As exemplified in

(4b) above, *inasékétsa* represents a causative verb in Chichewa in which *sék* 'laugh' and *éts* 'cause' form one word as the causative verb.

Alsina's (1997) proposal is that whether CPs are formed in the lexicon or in the syntax has no effect on the valence or argument structure and that this difference can affect only the wordhood of these constructions (Alsina, Bresnan and Sells, 1997). This, as Alsina and colleagues (1997, p. 7) further point out, is evidence that contrary to the position of LFG and most lexicalist theories, predicatehood does not coincide with morphological integrity. It also highlights the need for a modification in these theories so that CPs can form either in the lexicon or in the syntax. Alsina's (1997) proposal is directed toward the problem of CP formation in syntax within the LFG framework. According to Alsina and co-workers (1997), in Alsina's proposal the operation responsible for forming complex predicates is predicate composition, which takes predicate information of two sister nodes in order to yield the predicate information borne by the mother node. Since the predicate information of the two (i.e. sister nodes vs. mother node) are not the same, the subcategorization information (or f-structure information as it is referred to in LFG) between phrase structure node and its head cannot be shared.

Investigating Permissive and Instructive complex predicates in Urdu language and selecting an LFG framework similar to Alsina's for her analysis, Butt (1997) defines complex predicate formation at a level distinct from that of phrasal construction. In fact, she maintains that two predicates can only form a complex predicate when their argument structures can combine and form a simple f-structure. Butt also claims that a Permissive construction in the Urdu language forms a simple predicate since it has one subject or one object, while Instructive sentences must have a complex f-structure and therefore do not meet the condition to form a complex predicate. An example of each is provided below from Andrews and Manning (1999), who claim that the Urdu complex predicate proves the existence of such a phenomenon as complex predicates, and that they occur not only with structures similar to XCOMPs but also to complex verbs.

    (5) Instructive:

        Anjum ne   Saddaf ko   citt ii   lik -ne   ko
        kah-aa
        Anjum Erg. Saddaf Acc. letter.F(NOM) write-INF Acc
        say-PERF.Ma.Sg.
        'Anjum told Saddaf to write a note.'

(6) Permissive:
    Anjum   ne   Saddaf ko   citt ii   lik -ne
    d-ii
    Anjum Erg Saddaf Acc letter.F(NOM) write-INF
    give-PERF.Fe.Sg.
    'Anjum let Saddaf write a note.'

Butt (1995, p. 36) also provides the following illustrative examples of the Instructive constructions (7) and Permissive complex predicates (8) in Urdu.

(7) anjum=ne   saddaf=ko   haar   banaa-ne
    di-yaa
    Anjum.F=Erg Saddaf.F=Dat necklace.M=Nom make-INF.OBJl
    give-PERF.Ma.Sg.
    'Anjum let Saddaf make a necklace.'

(8) anjum=ne   saddaf=ko   haar
    banaa-ne=ko   kah-aa
    Anjum.F=Erg Saddaf.F=Dat necklace.M=NOM
    make-INF.OBJl=Acc say-PERF.Ma.Sg.
    'Anjum told Saddaf to make a necklace.'

(In Butt's examples above '=' is a symbol for showing the place where an affix is attached to the verb.)

According to Butt (1995), the verb *banaa-ne* 'make' and the finite verb *di-yaa* 'let' in (7) behave as a single construction and as a result act as a complex predicate. In contrast, the verb *banaa-ne-ko* 'make' and *kah-aa* 'say' in (8) do not function as one single unit and cannot be considered as a complex predicate construction. The differences between (7) and (8) include the use of the clitic *ko* on the infinitive verb *banaa-ne* and the difference in the finite verbs used in the two examples. Therefore, as Butt indicates, unlike the Instructive constructions (such as 8), the Permissive sentences (as in (7)) are examples of complex predicates in the Urdu language. In other words, although the Instructive and Permissive constructions in Urdu apparently seem to be two types of complex predicates, according to Butt (1995), they are quite different with regard to argument structure, since the two predicates of the Permissive function as a single predicate, are structurally a simple clause, and as a result are complex predicates. The Instructive, on the other hand, has a matrix verb that takes an embedded complement, is complex in terms of argument structure, and, consequently, cannot function as a complex predicate (Butt, 1995, p.43).

In fact, Butt (1995, p. 108) assigns complex predicates the following characteristics.

- The argument structure is complex (two or more semantic heads contribute arguments).
- The grammatical functional structure is that of a simple predicate. It is flat: there is only a single predicate (a nuclear PRED) and a single subject.
- The phrase structure may be simple or complex. It does not necessarily determine the status of the complex predicate.

For some linguists, for example, Ackerman and Lesourd (1997), complex predicates raise issues for the boundary between the lexicon and syntax. According to Ackerman and Lesourd, the existence of analytic predicates like the causatives of Catalan or the preverbal and verbal (PV V) complexes of Hungarian, as in (9) below, presents a fundamental challenge to assumptions of lexicalist syntactic theories.

(9) Az anya   rá   kiáltott   a   gyereknek / a   gyerekre
    the mother onto shouted   the   child-Dat/the   child-SUBL
    'The mother shouted at the child.'

(In Ackerman and Lesourd's example above SUBL stands for sublative.)

In (9) the preverbal element *rá* 'onto' occurs with the verb *kiáltott* to form a complex predicate that, according to Ackerman and Lesourd (1997), displays a lexical semantics, case-government pattern and grammatical function array different from those of a simple predicate in Hungarian.

Complex predicates composed of preverbal and verbal elements, they point out, occur in a large number of languages and a preverbal component can be a particle, a prefix or a proclitic element; the preverbal element can also be bounded or unbounded. According to Ackerman and Lesourd (1997), the complex predicate construction is a familiar synthetic morphological object and is formed as a zero-level syntactic category when the preverbal component is a bound element (a prefix), whereas the predicate composition is an analytic or phrasal one when it is unbounded. They further remark that the formation of complex predicates is the result of the collocations of independent lexical elements and, in fact, the diachronic development of the preverbal element is the main cause of its various types.

As observed so far, complex predicates have been investigated and looked at from different angles by linguists. Some scholars such as Alsina (1997) and Butt (1995) claim that CPs are formed by syntactically independent elements and that we need a predicate composition mechanism that is different from the usual types of complementation to bring together the argument structures of these elements (Alsina, Bresnan and Sells, 1997, p. 1). Others, such as Hale and Keyser (1997) and Baker (1997), maintain that there is no need for any mechanisms beyond those in syntax and that CPs are types of complementation (Alsina, Bresnan and Sells, 1997, p. 2). Still others take complex predicate formation to be a morpholexical operation. It is also observed that the domain of complex predicates is likely to include a wide range of constructions. In the following section, however, the discussion is confined to three important constructions, namely, noun incorporation, causative constructions and light verbs.

2.1.2 Noun incorporation

A complex predicate is sometimes formed through the combination of a noun with a verb, which is referred to as *noun incorporation*. Noun incorporation, Mithun (1984) maintains, is perhaps the most nearly syntactic of all morphological processes. As Mithun further states, noun incorporation can combine two syntactically associated constituents, i.e. nouns and verbs (Ns and Vs), and is much more productive than causativization and nominalization because it can join two potentially open sets, namely noun and verb stems, rather than focusing on one group of morphemes and a limited number of affixes (Mithun, 1984). Consider the following sentences provided by Mithun from Oceania (Oceanic family of languages).

(10) a. Ngoah kohkoa oaring-kai
          I   grind   coconut-these
          'I am grinding these coconuts.'
    b. Ngoah ko   oaring
          I   grind coconut
          'I am coconut-grinding.'

As is observed in (10a), the object *oaring-kai* 'coconut-these' is independent from the verb of the sentence. In contrast, in (10b) the verb (V) *ko* 'grind' and the object (N) *oaring* 'coconut' combine with each other to make a complex predicate in Oceanic. In fact, as Mithun (1984, p. 849) argues, in (10b) the verb *ko* and its direct object *oaring* are simply juxtaposed to form an especially tight bond, although the verb and the noun *oaring* are phonologically two independent items. According to Mithun, in (10b) as a result of noun incorporation operation, the object (N) *oaring* loses its syntactic status as an argument and the integrated VN unit acts as an intransitive predicate rather than transitive (as in (10a)). This compounding process also has a semantic effect since it turns the two separate semantic items into a whole unified component (Mithun, 1984).

Spencer (1995) defines the canonical type of noun incorporation (NI) as the one in which the verb incorporates its direct object but not its subject. As Spencer notes, Baker's (1988) theory of noun incorporation is based on Chomsky's (1986) theory of syntax and NI is the result of the syntactic rule Move-Alpha applying to the head of the direct noun phrase. Noun incorporation in Baker's theory, according to Spencer (1995), adjoins the noun to the verb root (an instance of head-to-head movement) and this leaves a trace of category N zero, which must be properly governed by the compounded noun. According to Baker's interpretation of Chomsky's theory, this is possible only if the NP from which incorporation occurs is a complement to the verb (cf. Spencer, 1995, p. 441).

In short, the fundamental issue in analyzing complex predicates formed through noun incorporation is whether it is viewed as essentially a lexical phenomenon or a syntactic one. Some linguists such as Rosen (1989) indicate that there are two types of noun incorporation processes that are both lexical by nature, while others like Baker (1988) have argued that noun incorporation is basically a syntactic process. This issue will be addressed from a Role and Reference Grammar perspective later in this work.

2.1.3 Causative constructions

Another major type of complex predicate that has received a great deal of attention is the causative construction. A distinction is made here, in the usual way, between the semantic notion *causative* and the grammatical notion *causative construction*. The latter implies the occurrence of more than one lexical item (word or morpheme). This identification also recognizes a parallel between related non-causative and causative constructions. Typically, this involves motivated and consistent differences in argument structure. As Comrie (1976, cited in Saksena, 1982, p. 21) notes:

> A given causative verb will be expected to have one more noun phrase argument than the corresponding non-causative verb, since in addition to the subject and object, if any, of that verb, there will be a noun phrase expressing the person or thing that causes, brings that action.

Not only does a causative construction involve a causer-causee relationship, it can also represent lexical, morphological and syntactical information, on the basis of which three types of causative constructions have been recognized. Along with the lexical, morphological and syntactical information, causative constructions, Song (1996) believes, may even involve pragmatics.

The causative can be shaped either in a monoclausal or a multiclausal form. Andrews and Manning (1999, p. 115) illustrate the latter in the following example from English.

(11)   The farmer is making him plough the field.

Andrews and Manning (1999) also provide another example from Italian causative verbs as follows.

(12)   Paolo   lo   farà   scrivere   a   Piero.
       Paolo   it   make.FUT.3ʳᵈ.Sg.   write.INF   to   Piero
       'Paolo will make Piero write it.'

According to Andrews and Manning (1999, p. 26), sentences like (12) in Italian represent those complex predicates in which 'a light verb and its apparent complement actually combine in such a way as to share the same array of grammatical relations.' The term they use to refer to the phrase structure complement of the light verbs in cases such as Italian causative verbs is 'pseudo-complement'. By this, Andrews and Manning mean a complement which is a semantic argument, but with regard to the level of f-structure it is not considered as a separate clause nucleus.

However, in some languages monoclausal morphological causative constructions, as some linguists such as Baker (1988) claim, may have an underlying biclausal structure. In some other types of causatives, similar to the ones analyzed by Comrie (1976) in French, the element bearing causation is embedded with the verb and forms a single unit while the causative verb acts as an independent lexical element. The French example as provided by Comrie is as follows.

(13)   Je   ferai   lire   le   livre   à   Nicole.
       I   make+FUT   read   the   book   IOBJ   Nicole
       'I will make Nicole read the book.'

As is clear from the above example, in French causatives the elements of [V cause], i.e. *ferai* and [V effect] *lire,* are adjacent to each other but they act as two independent lexical verbs.

Baker (1988) also claims that from the case marking patterns of simple ditransitive verbs in a specific language, the properties of the morphological causatives in that language can be predicted and that these constructions can be formed only from unaccusative verb roots. Baker exemplifies this phenomenon using an example (14) from Mohawk (Northern Iroquoian) language.

(14)   Uwari   t-a-yu-ahsv-ht-e'   ne   a'share'
       Mary   Cis- -Fe.Sg.SUB-fall-CAUS-PUNC   NE   knife
       'Mary made the knife fall.'

(According to Baker (1988) NE in Mohawk is a pronominal particle whose exact meaning and distribution is unclear.)

In (14) the counterparts for 'made … fall' form a causative complex predicate which according to Baker forms a single word or inflectional domain. That is, in Mohawk the verb *ahsv* 'fall' is basically an intransitive verb to which the causative morpheme *ht* is attached to form a causative CP. In fact, as Baker maintains, polysynthetic languages including Mohawk do not have causatives of transitive verbs, where the matrix verb alone θ-marks the causer-agent, and the embedded verb alone θ-marks a cause-agent or a goal (Baker, 1997, p. 285).

As shown in Sections 2.1.1, 2.1.2 and 2.1.3, complex predicates can be defined and formed on the basis of the elements comprising the whole construction and can be formulated through different operations. Among the most important forms of CP constructions, noun incorporation and causative constructions have been discussed so far. The next section (2.1.4) is devoted to analyzing another important type of these predicates called light verb constructions.

2.1.4 *Light verbal constructions*

Light verbal constructions are a form of complex predicate where the verb is thematically incomplete; hence, 'light' to use the term from Jespersen (1954) and Cattell (1984), and it is, in fact, the semantically bleached version of a corresponding full verb. In this study, 'light verbs' can be defined as the impoverished form of the full/heavy verbs and can be considered as a significant linguistic phenomenon since these complex predicates, as will be discussed in Section 2.3.1, cross the boundary between lexicon and syntax. An examination of the literature on this construction shows that the type of complement taken by the light verb varies cross-linguistically. It may be a non-verbal element such as a noun or a verbal noun, an adjective, an adverb, or a prepositional phrase; it may be another verb as in serial complex predicate constructions.

Grimshaw and Mester (1988) and S. Rosen (1989) examined the Japanese verb *suru* and the predicate-argument complex associated with this verb, which they describe as thematically incomplete or 'light'. Grimshaw and Mester (1988, p. 206) illustrate the phenomenon in (15a), where *suru* is used with a direct object NP as well as in (15b), which represents *suru* behaviour in noun incorporation and the nominal element AISEKI (the direct object NP) is not case-marked:

(15) a. John-wa   Bill-to   AISEKI-o   shita
        John-Top   Bill-with   table-sharing-Acc   suru-PAST
        'John shared a table with Bill.'
     b. John-wa   Bill-to   AISEKI   shita
        John-Top   Bill-with   table-sharing   suru-PAST
        'John shared a table with Bill.'

(In the above examples, Grimshaw and Mester use capitals to highlight the NP in the complex predicate construction.)

In the examples, *aiseki* 'table-sharing' forms a complex predicate with the light verb *suru* and is the head of the direct object NP and θ-marks 'John' and 'Bill'. While *suru* remains thematically incomplete or light, it subcategorizes and case-marks the direct object NP but it cannot assign it a theta role. Another example Grimshaw and Mester (1988) use to discuss the Japanese light verb *suru* is the following.

(16)   America-ga   200-neu-mae-ni   Igirisu-kara
        DOKURITSU-o   shita
        America-NOM   200-years-ago-at   England-from
        independence-Acc   suru-PAST
        'America became independent of England 200 years ago.'

In (16), *dokuritsu-o* and *shita* make the complex predicate in which *dokuritsu-o*, as the noun that occurs with *suru,* can possess any number or type of argument structure. In other words, the nouns with which *suru* occurs, according to Grimshaw and Mester, can themselves have any number of arguments and any type of argument structure. *Suru* is a transitive verb and assigns the accusative case. Grimshaw and Mester claim that *suru*'s direct object is not an argument and it is the *suru* itself that assigns the case to a transparent NP which bears the accusative case marker *-o. Suru,* they claim, functions as a bearer of verbal inflection for the clause and as a case assigner, allowing the noun in its direct object to assign θ-roles in a verbal context. Combining an NP with *suru* turns the head noun into the functional equivalent of a verb (Grimshaw and Mester, 1988, p. 211). In fact, the basis for their claim that *dokuritsu* is not an argument, as Bresnan (1982) points out, originates from the Lexical Functional Grammar treatment of raising to object/exceptional case marking. This raising operation comes from the idea that the verb is analyzed as taking a direct object that is not related to any of its arguments (Bresnan, 1997). *Suru,* according to them, is similar to the 'do' of English Do Support. 'Do' in English bears inflection but does not impose selectional restrictions. The main difference between 'do' and *suru,* they claim, lies in the fact that *suru* is transitive and can join or combine NPs for assigning θ-role, while 'do' is intransitive in English and must combine with another verbal element.

In short, Grimshaw and Mester (1988) claim that *suru* subcategorizes and case-marks a direct object NP, without assigning it a theta (θ)-role. They propose an operation they call 'Argument Transfer', which is the operation responsible for θ-marking in the formation of a *suru* complex. In fact, the nominal θ-marker lends part of its arguments to the argument structure of the light verb, in this case *suru* and turns it into a θ-marker. Therefore, the head of the object NP and the *suru,* Grimshaw and Mester point out, can act as θ-markers and the 'transfer' operation does not integrate the two elements and their argument structure into a unified whole as is generally referred to in the construction of complex predicates.

In Romance languages, Andrews and Manning point out, there is one type of light verbal construction in which these verbs take a phrase structure complement, which look like ordinary VP complements but in fact share the same sort of grammatical relations (Andrews and Manning, 1999). (Since the related examples provided by Andrews and Manning were discussed in the causative section (2.1.3), they are not discussed here.) Unlike Rosen (1989), Grimshaw and Mester (1988), who believe that light verbs have no roles in the argument structure of sentences, Butt (1995), T. Manning (1997) and Alsina (1993), treat light verbs as constructions contributing to the argument structure of complex predicates. Butt, for instance, claims that light verbs cannot be empty at least with respect to the complex predicate subject and maintain that they do contribute to the argument structure of these constructions.

As noted by Andrews and Manning (1999) there is a tradition within Transformational Grammar of describing light verbs as 'reanalysis' and 'restructuring' verbs. These terms, according to Andrews and Manning (1999, p. 27), cover a number of structures including causatives, perception and motion predicates (Rizzi, 1982; Burzio, 1986). Within this tradition, Rizzi (1982) and Burzio (1986) provide analyses of light verbs or what they call restructuring constructions in Italian. According to Rizzi (1982, p. 5), the restructuring rule in Italian syntax which is governed by modals, aspectual and motion verbs reanalyzes a terminal substring Vx ^{2}(P) V as a single verbal complex, hence automatically transforming the underlying bisentential structure into a simple sentence. Rizzi illustrates the above feature of restructuring constructions in (17) and Figure 2.1 (Rizzi's tree diagram is based on generative grammar).

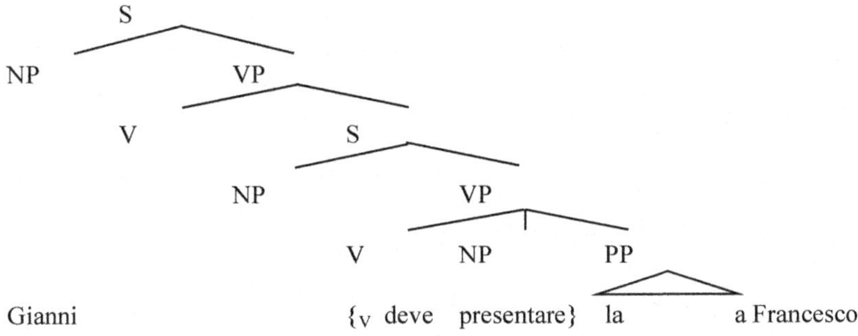

Figure 2.1 Restructuring (light verbal) constructions in Italian.

(17) Gianni deve   presentare la a Francesco.
      Gianni should/must present   it to Francesco.
      'Gianni should/must present it to Francesco.'

In (17) the embedded subject NP, Rizzi argues, is a trace or pronoun (PRO) and, in fact, restructuring can reanalyze the terminal substring included in the braces as a single verbal complex (V) (Rizzi, 1982, p. 5). Rizzi points out that if restructuring is applied to (17), it yields the simple structure (18a), which in turn changes to (18b); that is, the clitic pronoun moves to the first lexical verb as the main verb of the complex predicate and makes a light verbal construction.

(18) a. Gianni [$_V$ deve presentare] la a Francesco.
      b. Gianni la deve presentare a Francesco.

Similarly, Burzio (1986) maintains that the best-known characteristic of restructuring constructions is that objects of the complement verb cliticize to the main verb, as Burzio exemplifies in (19) as follows.

(19) Giovanni lo vuole leggere.
      Giovanni it wants to read
      'Giovanni wants to read it.'

In (19) the verb *vuole* 'want' and its infinitival complement *leggere* 'to read' appear to form a single unit after the object of the complement verb *lo* 'it' cliticizes to the main verb *vuole*.

In Relational Grammar light verbs are characterized as a process of 'clause union' (Aissen and Perlmutter, 1976, 19983; Perlmutter and Postal, 1983) in which heavy verbs (phrases) combine with one or two light verbs. As a matter of fact, Relational Grammar, as Perlmutter and Postal (1983) state, has a large class of distinct 'structural' grammatical relations. Perlmutter and Postal (1983, p. 84) provide the following example from French clauses to illustrate this point.

(20) a. J'ai envoyé la machine à Marie.
          'I sent the machine to Marie.'
      b. J'ai envoyé la machine à Paris.
          'I sent the machine to Paris.'

According to structural or Transformational Grammar, (20a) and (20b) would both be analyzed as having prepositional phrase constitutions of either the clause as a whole or of some verbal phrase (VP) or VP-like subconstituent (Perlmutter and Postal, 1983). In contrast, Relational Grammar analyzes the two sentences quite differently; that is, Marie in (20a), Perlmutter and Postal (1983) indicate, bears one primitive grammatical relation to the clause, namely, an indirect object relation, while in (20b) Paris, on the other hand, bears a 'directional relation' which is distinct from Marie's relation with the clause. In fact, in a Relational Grammar or Clause Union scheme the relational structures, Aissen (1983, pp. 72–73) maintains, associate a verb with a set of nominals and specify the relations borne by those nominals to the clause at that level of structure (a structure similar to one type of light verbal construction discussed in this section).

So far, an attempt has been made to provide some definitions of complex predicates and the way they have been dealt with within different theoretical frameworks. Then the pervasive types of complex predicates were confined to three major categorizations: noun incorporation, light verbs and causative constructions. Having provided some background information on each of these categories, the researcher shifts to the major concern of this chapter, complex predicates in modern Persian or Farsi, in the following section.

2.2 Persian complex predicates

In this section, what have traditionally been called 'compound verbs' in the literature on Persian is concentrated and the same terminology is used here. In these constructions a non-verbal element, which can be a noun, adjective, adverb or a prepositional phrase combines with the impoverished form of the verb (light verb) to act as a single predicate. As an example, consider *u qosse xord* 'he/she grieved' (Lit.: 'he/she grief ate') where the noun *qosse* 'grief' joins the light verb *xord* 'ate' to act as the predicate of the sentence. In fact, a thorough analysis of these verb types and their classifications is presented in Sections 2.2.1 and 2.2.2 to pave the way for the major analysis of light verbal constructions in Persian, which is the core concern of the present chapter. Section 2.2.1 (which can be called the earlier accounts of compound verbs) is devoted to analyzing these verbs and the way different scholars have classified them. Section 2.2.2 basically focuses on Dabir-Moghaddam's (1997) account of compound verbs in Persian. He divides Persian compound verbs into two major groups, i.e. 'Combination vs. Incorporation', each of which is further classified into a number of subcategories. Megerdoomian's (2002) and Karimi-Doostan's (1997) studies along with Dabir-Moghaddam's classification have been considered as the basis of a more detailed discussion of the types of Persian compound verbs included later in the present section since their analyses are among the most recent ones.

2.2.1   Earlier analyses of compound verbs

According to Tabaian (1979), verbal phrases in Persian are traditionally divided into simple and 'compound' or 'composite' verbs. Any verbal phrase that contains only a verbal root is a simple verb, and the verbal phrases that contain either a prefix plus a verbal root, or a nominal plus either a regular verbal root or an auxiliary verb, are compound verbs (Tabaian, 1979). Among earlier works that deal with Persian compound verbs is Lazard's (1957) categorization. Lazard (1957) divides compound verbs in Persian into three different types.

1. The first type consists of a preverb and a verb.
2. The second is formed with the Persian auxiliaries *kærdæn, šodæn* and *budæn*, and a noun (this group can further be divided into two subcategories:
   a. the nominal part is a noun which can be an action, abstract, or a concrete noun; and
   b. the nominal part is an adjective or an adverb).
3. The third refers to the verbal phrases formed by incorporating the object into the verb.

As most of Lazard's categories overlap with other scholars' categorization (including Lambton's (1984) and Dabir-Moghaddam's (1997), which are dealt with in the following sections), a more detailed discussion of his categorization of the Persian compound verbs does not seem to be necessary here.

According to Rastorgueva (1964), the main Persian compounds that are formed with the auxiliary *kærdæn* and *šodæn* fall into two categories.

1. All the transitive verbs that consist of a substantive plus *kærdæn* or one of its stylistic variants (e.g. *saxtæn* 'make').
2. All the intransitive verbs that consist of a substantive with *šodæn* or one of its variant forms (e.g. *gæštæn* 'become/get').

Tabaian (1979) identifies three distinct types of structures involved in Persian compound verbs.

1. The first group of verbal constructions, he claims, are those which are formed with the addition of the prefixes *baz* 'again', *bær* 'upon, over', *dær* 'in', *vær* 'side', *piš* 'front', *pæs* 'back', *sær* 'over' and *færa* 'up' to a verbal root.
2. The second group of verbal constructions, according to Tabaian, are those which include a complement (direct or indirect object) and a simple verb, that is, the metaphoric verb phrases in which simple verbs like *xordæn* 'eat', *zædæn* 'strike, hit' and *bordæn* 'carry' occur with a noun, as Tabaian (1979) states, also belong to this type of verbal construction.
3. The third and final group of compound verbs, described by Tabaian, is that in which the auxiliary verbs *kærdæn* 'to make', *šodæn* 'to get', *budæn* 'to be' and *daštæn* 'to have' are combined with a nominal.

Persian compound verb types have been studied by some other linguists. Discussing the semantic structure of the verb phrase in Persian, Bashiri (1981) classifies the verbs into 'absolute verbs' and 'modal verbs' and provides the following definitions of the two verb types.

> Absolute verbs are the ones that 'are not susceptible to modification' and 'have a decided semantic core'. Modal verbs are those that 'point to the modes of existence, action or change in a person or an object. As such, these verbs are fluid and are manipulated by the content of their modifying noun.'
>
> (Bashiri, 1981)

Zand (1991), devoting his PhD dissertation to an aspectual analysis of Persian intransitive verbs, divided these verbs into 'deadjectival/achievement, denominal/activity, or plain verbs' depending on their synchronic morphology. As Zand (1991) claims, the deadjectival and the denominal verbs differ in their aspectual properties, which encompass semantic differences of these groups of verbs. Also, the thematic roles as well as the derivational system of deadjectival and denominal verbs, he points out, are justified on the basis of the inherent aspectual properties of the intransitive verbs. In his examination of these verb types, Zand presents the effect of causativization on the aspectual properties of Persian deadjectival and denominal verbs. Zand claims that causativization can charge the aspectual properties of denominal verbs but it has no effect on deadjectival verbs.

Having examined the earlier analyses of Persian complex predicates in the present section (2.2.1), the researcher now moves to the next section, which discusses the more recent studies including Dabir-Moghaddam's paper on these constructions.

2.2.2 Dabir-Moghaddam's analysis

As was mentioned before, Persian compound verb types have also been investigated by Dabir-Moghaddam (1997), who categorized them as 'Combination' and 'Incorporation'. He classifies the combination type verbs into five groups as follows.

1. The adjective + auxiliary group in which three types of auxiliary verbs have been distinguished:
    a. the stative auxiliary *budæn* 'be', for example, *delxor budæn* 'to be annoyed',
    b. the inchoative auxiliary *šodæn* 'become', (e.g. *delxor šodæn* 'become annoyed'), and
    c. the causative auxiliary *kærdæn* 'make', (e.g. *delxor kærdæn* 'to annoy').

    'The compound verbs formed via (a)–(c) above constitute an open set.'

2. The noun + verb group in which the most important verbs used in this type of compound verb formation are: *kærdæn* 'do' (e.g. *tæh-did kærdæn* 'threat', Lit.: 'threat do'); *zædæn* 'strike' (e.g. *ney zædæn* 'play the flute', Lit.: 'flute strike'); *dadæn* 'give' (e.g. *dæst dadæn* 'shake hand', Lit.: 'hand give'); *gereftæn* 'take' (e.g. *pæs gereftæn* 'regain', Lit.: 'back take'); *kešidæn* 'draw' (e.g. *færyad kešidæn* 'shout', Lit.: 'shout draw'); *daštæn* 'have' (e.g. *dust daštæn* 'like', Lit.: 'friend have'); *xordæn* 'eat' (e.g. *qosse xordæn* 'grieve', Lit.: 'grief eat'). All the compound verbs in this category, according to Dabir-Moghaddam, are intransitive.

3. The prepositional phrase + verb group in which the verbs may be either transitive or intransitive (e.g. *be yad daštæn* 'remember', Lit.: 'to rememberance have').

4. The adverb + verb group (e.g. *færa gereftæn* 'acquire', Lit.: 'beyond take'). The (in)transitivity condition is the same as in 3 above.

5. Past participle + passive auxiliary group in which past participles of
    the verbs are combined with the passive auxiliary *šodæn* to form pas-
    sive verbs.

The second major type of compound verb formation, distinguished by Dabir-
Moghaddam (1997), is 'Incorporation' which has further been subcategorized
as: (1) direct object incorporation, and (2) prepositional phrase incorporation.
  According to Dabir-Moghaddam, the direct object in Persian sometimes
loses its grammatical endings such as the indefinite marker *-i,* the postposition *-ra,* the plural suffix or the possessive pronominal suffix and is incorporated with the verbal element to form an intransitive verb. Item (21a) below
contains an independent direct object that is incorporated in (21b).

(21) a. bæčče-ha qæza-eš-an-ra   xor-d-ænd
         child-pl   food-his/her-pl-Do eat-Past-they
         'The children ate their food.'
      b. bæčče-ha qæza xor-d-ænd
         'The children ate their food.'
                                                    (Dabir-Moghaddam, 1997)

As referred to above, the second subcategory of incorporation type is the
one in which some prepositional phrases that act as location adverbs incorp-
orate with the verb to form a compound, although, after incorporation, as
Dabir-Moghaddam maintains, the preposition disappears. He provides the
following examples.

(22) a. bæčče be zamin   xor-d-ø
         child to ground   eat-Past-Ma./Fe.
         'The child fell to the ground.'
      b. bæčče zamin xor-d-ø
         'The child fell down.'

Incorporation, or specifically noun incorporation (NI), as one of the formation processes of compound verbs, has also been discussed by Ghomeshi and
Massam (1994). Referring to Mithun's (1984) four point classification of
noun incorporation, they point out that Persian has only Mithun's type I noun
incorporation in that it does not allow an oblique argument to be advanced
into the case position vacated by the incorporated noun, it is not used to background known information, and it cannot be accompanied by a more specific

object NP. According to them, the Persian phenomenon seems to form a subject of a very productive form of compounding whereby a verb is combined with other lexical categories (Ghomeshi and Massam, 1994, p. 184).

2.3 Persian light verbs

As analyzed in the general background discussion of complex predicates in the present chapter, the verbal element in the domain of compound, composite or complex verb-predicates is sometimes referred to as a light verb, a phenomenon which has been examined from different perspectives by a number of researchers. Ghomeshi (2002) maintains that modern Persian complex predicates have a compositional interpretation, as in (23) below, or an idiomatic reading, as in (24). These elements cannot be considered to be fixed lexical units, since several elements may intervene between the non-verbal (NV) and the light verb (LV). They also provide interesting problems for a number of existing theories: for example, they are problematic for an analysis based on syntactic incorporation in the sense of Baker (1988) since: (a) NV is separable from LV, (b) NV is not necessarily an X0, and may appear with a specifier and a modifier, and (c) NV ranges over different categories (Ghomeshi, 2002).

(23) a. be donya amædæn
to world coming
'to be born'
b. pæs dadæn
back giving
'to return'

(24) a. chane zædæn
chin hitting
'to negotiate'
b. dæst ændaxtæn
hand throwing
'to mock'

A key analytical decision is whether to treat the preverbal element as an argument of the verbal element. A number of linguists such as Barjasteh (1983), Vahedi-Langrudi (1996), Dabir-Moghaddam (1997) and Ghomeshi and Massam (1994) maintain that in complex predicate constructions of Persian the preverbal component does indeed act as an argument of the verbal element. Others (e.g. Mohammad and Karimi, 1992) treat Persian light verbs as semantically empty or bleached elements and claim that the preverbal element lends its argument to the light verb. Karimi-Doostan (1997) points out that the verbal elements or light verbs affect the aspectual information of the complex predicate constructions but not their argument structure. Karimi-Doostan (1997) claims that each of the preverbal and verbal elements in these constructions has a thematic role and is incorporated at the logical function. Megerdoomian (2002), however, maintains that it is the preverbal component that contributes the substantive aspects of the predicate and the light verb bears the event information of complex predicate construction.

In Persian the preverbal element, or what Goldberg (1996) refers to as 'the host' combined with a light verb can be of different categories. The preverbal element, Megerdoomian (2001c) points out, provides the substantive information to the complex predicate and affects the internal arguments of the verbal predicate, while light verbs affect the presence of the external argument.

As mentioned before, Persian light verb complex predicates have not been analyzed in depth and some limited studies have been carried out on these constructions. The only major work devoted to the study of the light verb and its categories is by Karimi-Doostan (1997) who divides light verbs into Stative and Dynamic light verbs and subcategorized the latter as Transition and Initiatory light verbs, as shown in Table 2.1. The Transition light verbs, as one type of dynamic group, appear in telic and bounded verb phrases referring to events in which a patient argument is affected or undergoes a change of state (Karimi-Doostan, 1997). The change of state of the argument seems to bound the event structure of the verbal phrases (VPs). Initiatory light verbs,

Table 2.1 Types of light verbs in Persian (Karimi-Doostan, 1997; cited in Megerdoomian, 2002, p. 83)

Stative LV	Dynamic LV	
	Transition LV	**Initiatory LV**
daštæn	xordæn 'eat'	zædæn 'hit, strike'
'have'	šodæn 'become'	dadæn 'give'
	amædæn 'come'	bæxšidæn 'offer, forgive'
	gereftæn 'catch, take'	aværdæn 'bring'
	ræftæn 'go'	kešidæn 'pull'
	didæn 'see'	bordæn 'take, carry'
	kærdæn 'do'	gozaštæn 'put'
	yaftæn 'find'	kærdæn 'do, make'

unlike the transition verbs, may allow light verb constructions with atelic or unbounded readings and may refer to events in which an entity initiates an action. Initiatory light verbs, he claims, appear with external arguments, while transition light verbs usually do not possess an unbounded reading and their subject corresponds to an internal argument. Karimi-Doostan believes that the light verb should be treated as an underspecified lexical entry, and that it does not contain any information regarding the argument structure. It does, on the other hand, bear an aspectual role that is fused in the lexicon with the argument structure provided by the preverbal element.

According to Karimi-Doostan (1997), the light verbal constructions made with such light verbs as *xordæn* 'eat' (in Table 2.1) have the feature of [+telic], since this light verb *xordæn* 'eat' belongs to the transition (in his terms) type of LVs. One of the examples he provides for this light verb is *Ali gul xord* (Lit.: 'Ali deception eat') 'Ali was deceived'. According to his categorization of light verbal constructions (LVCs), the LVC *gul xord* above possesses an unbounded reading. In this study, however, this claim is challenged and it is shown that different light verbs including *xordæn* 'eat', for instance, can have different aspectual properties based on the specific type of the preverbal elements. As an example, consider the example provided in Saeedi (2009a, p. 93), where the same light verb (*xordæn* 'eat') combines with an action noun (*qute* 'plunge') having the aspectual feature of [–telic] (contrary to Karim-Doostan's claim), which indicates that it belongs to the activity verb type with an unbounded interpretation. More detailed discussion of Karimi-Doostan's analysis will be provided in the subsequent chapters.

After reviewing the studies carried out on Persian light verbal constructions, it can be summarized that on the basis of the kind of the preverbal element used with the verbal parameter or the light verb (LV) in these constructions, they can generally be categorized into four major types (Saeedi, 2009a), i.e. the combination of noun, adjective, adverb and preposition (prepositional phrase (PP)) with a light verb. The present study's major concern is to analyze the adjectival and the prepositional nuclear junctures which will be discussed in Chapters 4 and 5, respectively.

2.3.1 Nature of Persian light verbs

It has been argued in several accounts that Persian complex predicates, in general, and light verbal constructions, in particular, pose problems for grammatical theories because their behaviour crosses the boundaries between lexicon and syntax. Light verbs in Persian, as Goldberg (2004) puts it, act in some ways as a single word, and in other ways as more than one word. They form, she notes, a central part of the grammar of Persian and many other languages, including Hindi, Japanese and Hungarian (Goldberg, 2004). So far, there has been no comprehensive theoretical analysis of these constructions explaining why it has sometimes been claimed that they have a hybrid nature. The researcher argues against this view, and will propose a unified RRG account of these constructions, which supports the idea that they are not problematic. However, for the moment, in the following sections (2.3.1.1 and 2.3.1.2) the main lexical and syntactic properties of Persian light verbs that have been adduced to support this view are summarized.

2.3.1.1   Lexical properties of Persian LVs

Some researchers such as Barjasteh (1998) and Goldberg (1996) among others believe that light verbal/complex predicate constructions in Persian are formed in the lexicon. Some of the main lexical properties of complex predicate/light verbal constructions analyzed by a number of researchers (Karimi-Doostan, 1997; Mergerdoomian, 2002; Goldberg, 2004) are as follows (where the examples are mostly the writer's own).

First, complex predicate constructions can have the same argument structure as their single heavy verbs. Consider the following examples.

> (25)   a.   u   bæraye   movæfæqiyyæt   kušid
>   He/She   for   success   try.Past.3rd.Sg.
>   'He/She tried for success.'
>   b.   u   bæraye   movæfæqiyyæt   kušeš   kærd
>   He/She   for   success   try   do.Past.3rd.Sg.
>   'He/She tried for success.'

In (25a) above the verb *kušid* 'tried' is used as a full/heavy predicate taking one argument (*u* 'he/she'), and in (25b) the light verbal form of this verb, i.e. *kušeš kærd* 'tried' (Lit.: try did), also takes one argument (*u* 'he/she').

Secondly, another lexical property of Persian light verbs is that these constructions can be used to form adverbs and adjectives (Goldberg, 1996; Karimi-Doostan, 1997; Megerdoomian, 2002). Also, through a nominalization process adding the morpheme *-æn* to the past stem of the complex predicate, Gerundive nominals are formed, and by adding the morpheme *-ænde* to the present stem of the verbal element, Agentive nominals are formed. Example (26) represents Gerundive nominal and (27) Agentive nominal constructions.

(26)   swogænd xord-æn-e in   færd   mohem   æst
        oath   eat.-Inf.-Ez this   person   important   is
        'This person's swearing is important.'

(27)   færa gereftæn   færa-gir-ænde-gan
        up   take.Inf   ──────────▶   up-verb stem-Suf.-Pl.
        'learn'   'learners'

In some cases, light verbs are used for adjectival formation (Karimi-Doostan, 1997; Megerdoomian, 2002; Goldberg, 2004); that is, the particle -*e* is added to the past stem of the verb part of the construction to form a participial adjective (28), and the suffix -*i* is added to the infinitive form of the verb to make an adjective (29). Megerdoomian illustrates these phenomena in the following examples.

(28)   lebas-ha-ye xošk=šod.e
        dress-Pl.-ez dry=become.PPART
        '(the) dried clothes'

(29)   in   kelid   peyda=šodæn-I   n-ist
        this   key   found=become-Suf.   Neg.-is
        'This key is not to be found.'

Another apparent lexical property of these constructions in Persian is the formation of manner adverbials by combining the suffix -*an* with the present stem of the verbal element (30).

(30)   man sorfe=kon-an   be bimarestan   ræftæm
        I   cough=do-Suf.   to hospital   go.Past.1st.Sg.
        'I went to hospital while (I was) coughing.'

Another reason or property which has caused some scholars (e.g. Ghomeshi and Massam, 1994; Dabir-Moghaddam, 1997) to claim that complex predicate formation is a lexical process is the stress pattern of the compounds; that is, the primary stress usually falls on the preverbal element, which seems to be treating these constructions as a unified element (31).

(31)   tæhdid kærdæn
        threat   do
        'to threaten'

2.3.1.2 Syntactic properties of Persian LVs

According to some researchers (e.g. Vahedi-Langrudi, 1996; Karimi-Doostan, 1997; Megerdoomian, 2002; Goldberg, 2004), Persian complex predicates and light verbs in particular also exhibit some typically syntactic behaviour. Elements such as certain morphemes, auxiliaries (or modals) as well as nouns (direct objects), as Megerdoomian (2002) points out, may separate the preverbal and verbal elements, which seems counter to the lexical analyses discussed in the previous section. Certain preverbal elements in the complex can undergo modification, coordination and relativization operations, and either element of a complex predicate may also be gapped in some constructions. Inflectional prefixes such as the negative affix *ne-* or *-næ*, the imperative and subjunctive prefix *be-,* the progressive or durative *mi-* (*mi* + present stem for present progressive and *mi* + past stem for past progressive) and the imperative negative prefix *mæ-* all attach to the verbal component in complex predicates, thus intervening between the two parts (Megerdoomian, 2002, p. 63). The example (32) is related to the use of *næ-* and (33) to the use of *mi-*.

(32) u   hæmsær-æš-ra   tælaq   næ-dad
      He   wife-Poss.3rd.Sg.-DOM   divorce   Neg.-give.Past.3rd.Sg.
      'He did not divorce his wife.'

(33) qosse xordan   qosse=mi-xor-im
      grief   eat   ⟶   grief=DUR-eat.1st.Pl.
      'I grieved.'   'We grieve.'

Direct objects, too, can intervene between the two elements of complex predicates, acting as the complement of the preverbal element. The following example (34) is cited from Mergerdoomian (2002).

(34) setayeš-e æli-ro   kærdæm
      praise-Ez Ali-DOM   do.Past.1st.Sg.
      'I praised Ali.'

In Persian, as mentioned before, the auxiliary can intervene between the internal elements of a complex predicate. As is shown in (35), the future tense auxiliary *xastæn* 'want', which bears the number and agreement features, can occur between the constituents of complex predicates.

(35)   u   šoma-ra   seda   xah-æd   zæd
       He/She   you-OM   call   want-Past.3rd.Sg.   strike.Past.3rd.Sg.
       'He/She will call you (your name)'.

As mentioned before, the elements of CPs such as *swogænd xordæn* 'take an oath/swear' (in the examples (36a–e) below) can also be modified by adjectives as in (36a) (where the adjective *mohem* 'important' separates the two parts) or by determiners such as *in* 'this' (preceding the preverbal element) accompanied with the Direct Object Marker (DOM)(-*ra*) attached to the preverbal part as in (36b), relativized by *ke* 'that' as in (36c), focused on by the WH-question words (such as *če* 'what') preceded before the preverbal element as in (36d), and coordinated by *væ* 'and', for instance, as in (36e) below:

(36)   a.   in   færd   swogænd-e   mohem-i   xord.
            this   person   oath-Ez   important-Ind.M.   ate
            'This person took an important oath.'
       b.   in   færd   in   swogænd-ra   xord.
            this   person   this   oath-DOM   ate
            'This person took such an oath.'
       c.   swogænd-i   ke   in   færd   xord   mohem   bud.
            oath-Ind.M.   that   this   person   ate   important   was
            'The oath that this person took was important.'
       d.   in   færd   če   swogænd-i   xord.
            this   person   what   oath-Ind.M.   ate
            'What oath did this person take?'
       e.   in   færd   swogænd   væ   qæsæm   xord.
            this   person   oath   and   swearing   ate
            'This person took an oath and swearing.'

These syntactic behaviours are a problem for lexical analyses of light verbs according to traditional views of the distinction between lexical and syntactic rules.

2.3.2   Distinguishing categories of verbs

In order to make a clear-cut distinction between light verbs and other grammatical categories which, as observed in the literature on Persian complex predicates, have created some confusion, in this section four categories of verbs (heavy lexical verbs, light verbs, auxiliary verbs and the copula *budæn* 'be') are distinguished on the basis of their grammatical behaviour. It is argued that in Persian these elements have different behaviours with respect to a number of factors including predication, assigning argument structure, carrying function features and contributing to semantic content. To begin with, a distinction is made between light verbs and auxiliary verbs.

2.3.2.1   Light verbs vs. auxiliaries

In the present section, the behaviour of the main auxiliaries in Persian: *xastæn* 'want' (*xah* as the stem of the verb), *budæn* 'be' and *daštæn* 'have' are compared with that of the light verbs. Consider the following examples.

(37) u   an   ketab-ra   xah-æd   nevešt.
      he/she   that   book-DOM   want.AUX.-3rd.Sg.   write.Past.3rd.Sg.
      'He/She will write that book.'

(38) u   an   ketab-ra   nevešte   bud.
      he/she   that   book-DOM   write.PPART   be.AUX.Past.3rd.Sg.
      'He/She had written that book.'

(39) u   an   ketab-o (ra)   dare   mi-nevis-e.[2]
      he/she   that   book-Dom   have.AUX.   DUR-write.Pres-3rd.Sg.
      'He/She is writing that book.'

As is clear from the above examples, the auxiliaries have different functions in the given sentences; that is, the auxiliary *xastæn* 'want' acts as a future auxiliary, *budæn* 'be' as a past perfect auxiliary, and finally *daštæn* 'have' as a progressive/durative auxiliary verb. In fact, being an auxiliary is not the only role these four words can play, i.e. they can sometimes behave as a heavy verb, light verb or copula in different contexts. Consider (37′) below, which is the same sentence as in (37) above with a different use of *xastæn* 'want' (as the first auxiliary mentioned above).

(37′) u   an   ketab-ra   mi-xah-æd.
       he/she   that   book-DOM   DUR-want.Pres.-3rd.Sg.
       'He/She wants that book.'

In (37′) above, *xastæn* 'want' behaves as a full/heavy verb contrary to its auxiliary usage in (37). In order to clarify the difference between the auxiliary form of *xastæn* 'want' in (37) and its full/heavy function, compare the semantic content of *xastæn* in these two sentences ((37) and (37′)). In (37) *xastæn* functions as 'will'; that is, it just carries the future auxiliary feature with no extra semantic information, while *xastæn* in (37′) acts as a full predicate meaning 'want' carrying the main semantic load as the predicate of the whole proposition. The grammatical distinction is clear: as the main lexical verb in (37) *xastæn* is prefixed by the durative aspectual morpheme *mi-*, while in (37′), as an auxiliary verb, it is itself a tense-aspect marker.

The next Persian auxiliary mentioned in this section is *budæn* 'be' (shown in (38) above), which can function as a copula as exemplified in (38′) below.

> (38′) u   nevis-ænde bud.
>   he/she write-Suf.   be.Past.3rd.Sg.
>   'He/She was (a) writer.'

In (38′) above, *budæn* 'be' is a copula joining the subject of the sentence *u* 'he/she' to its complement and it is just a grammatical word carrying person and number features with no semantic information. Also, consider the following sentence for the last auxiliary (given in (39) above), namely, *daštæn* 'have'.

> (39′) u   an   ketab-ra   dar-æd.
>   he/she that book-DOM have.Pres.-3rd.Sg.
>   'He/She has that book.'

> (39′′) u   be an   ketab niyaz   dar-æd.
>   he/she to that book   need (noun) have.Pres.-3rd.Sg.
>   'He/She needs that book.'

As mentioned before, *daštæn* 'have' acts as an auxiliary in (39), while in (39′) above, *daræd* 'has' as the inflected form of *daštæn* 'have' acts as a full/heavy verb, and in (39′′) the same word (*daræd*) functions as a light verb which is a complex predicate or light verbal construction along with the nominal element *niyaz* 'need'. In fact, *daštæn* 'have' in Persian behaves like the verbs 'be' or 'do' in English where they can be an auxiliary, full/heavy predicate or a copula. Consider 'do', for instance, which acts as full/heavy verb in such sentences as *Mary does it*, as an auxiliary in *Mary doesn't read*, or as a light verb in *Mary does a favour*. In (39) *daštæn* 'have' (or *dare* as the inflected form of *daštæn*) as an auxiliary is just a grammatical word carrying the person/number and the progressive features of the sentence without adding to the semantic information. On the contrary, in (39′) *daštæn* (or *daræd* as the inflected form of *daštæn*) behaves as a full predicate which means 'have' or 'possess' and bears the main semantic load as the only predicate of the sentence. Also, in (39′′) *daštæn* 'have' (or *daræd* as the inflected form of *daštæn*) functions as a light verb playing the role of the predicate along with the nominal element *niyaz* 'need', and the semantic content is carried by the two elements of the complex predicate (the preverbal/nominal element *niyaz* 'need' and the light verbal element *daræd* (*daštæn*) 'has').

As far as the Persian auxiliaries are concerned, the three main auxiliaries (*xastæn* 'want', *daštæn* 'have', *budæn* 'be'), unlike light verbs, are incapable of having a predicating role in conjunction with non-verbal elements.[3] That is, they always take another verb as their complement and if the auxiliaries *xahæd* 'will' (Lit.: want) in (37), *bud* 'was' in (38) and *dare* 'has' in (39) remain in these sentences while the full verbs (i.e. *nevešt* 'wrote' in (37), *nevešte* 'written' in (38) and *mi-nevis-e* 'is writing' in (39)) are omitted from the examples in (37)–(39), the sentences are ill-formed, having no semantic information regarding their predicate. As a matter of fact, the main function of auxiliaries is carrying the TAM (tense, aspect and mood) features, as presented in (37)–(39) above.

The second main difference between auxiliaries and light verbs is that light verbs, unlike auxiliaries, are capable of assigning argument structure. Consider the examples in (40) and (41) below, where a light verb is combined with an adjective (*šokke* 'shocked'):

(40) u   šokke   šod.
      he/she   shocked   become.Past.3rd.Sg.
      'He/She became shocked.'

(41) an hadese   u-ra   šokke   kærd.
      that accident he/she-DOM   shocked   make-Past.3rd.Sg.
      'That accident made him/her shocked.'

That is, if the light verb *šod* 'became' in (40) above is replaced with another light verb, namely, *kærd* 'made' (*kærdæn* 'make' is the infinitive form) in (41), the argument structure of the sentence changes. In (40) there is one macrorole (*u* 'he/she') which is the actor of the sentence, and the verb of the sentence (*šod* 'became') with the logical structure BECOME **šokke′** (u) is Macrorole-intransitive (M-intransitive). That is, on the basis of the number of macroroles this verb has taken (which is one) it can be said that it is M-intransitive. In (40) the M-intransitivity of the verb coincides with its S-intransitivity, which refers to the number of the Syntactic arguments. On the contrary, by changing the light verb in (40) from *šod* 'became' to *kærd* 'made' in (41), the logical structure of the light verb changes (**do'** (*hadese*, ø) CAUSE [BECOME **šokke'** (*u*)]) and it takes two macroroles that are actors (the agent-like argument *hadese* 'accident' and the patient-like argument *u* 'he/she'). By contrast, auxiliaries are not capable of assigning argument structure or causativity and, as was presented in sentences (37)–(39) above, even though different auxiliaries have been used in these sentences, there is no difference between their argument structures: they all have two arguments (*u* 'he/she' and *ketab* 'book') and are bivalent considering the fact that the full/heavy verb (*neveštæn* 'write') is the same in all the examples (37)–(39). This indicates that in auxiliary constructions it is the main verb that assigns the argument structure of the predication. The auxiliary does not assign argument structure.

In sum, the present section further supports the idea discussed earlier that light verbs in combination with adjectives function differently from auxiliaries. Even though the light verbs such as *daštæn* 'have' (which is dealt with in the nominal light verbs section) and *šodæn* 'become' do have similar auxiliary counterparts and sometimes have similar characteristics, i.e. they can both take verbal complements, nonetheless, unlike auxiliaries, light verbs are not completely semantically bleached elements and, as discussed here and will be discussed in more detail later in this study, they may contribute to a number of semantic parameters including aspect information, argument structure and causativity. Furthermore, different types of light verbs (i.e. initiatory vs. transition in Karimi-Doostan's (1997) terminology) can correspond to different types of arguments (internal/external). By comparison, there is no such a relationship between auxiliary and argument types. In general, the difference between auxiliaries and light verbs in Persian, as discussed above, centres around the syntactic (their syntactic functions such as carrying TAM features by auxiliaries) vs. lexical/semantic (such as contributing to semantic information and predication) variables. A similar distinction has been identified for other Indo-Aryan languages with light verbs (e.g. Butt and Geuder, 2001). A more detailed discussion of the lexical and syntactic properties of each type of Persian light verbal constructions has been presented at the end of each related chapter and in the final chapter (6) of this study. In the next section the categorical distinction between light verbs and full/heavy verbs will be discussed.

2.3.2.2   Light verbs and full/heavy verbs

With the exception of a few light verbs (such as *daštæn* 'have'), which have
the same auxiliary counterparts, the majority of Persian light verbs introduced
in this chapter do not have an equivalent auxiliary form. On the other hand,
most of the light verbs discussed in this study do have heavy lexical verb
counterparts. As an example, consider the full/heavy verb *gereftæn* 'take/
catch' which has a light verb counterpart with the same form. The following
sentences show the full verb (42) and the light verb (43) uses of *gereftæn*
'take/catch' in Persian.

> (42)   u   tup-ra   æz   dust-æš   gereft.
>   he/she   ball-DOM   from   friend   take/catch.Past.3rd.Sg.
>   'He/She took the ball from his/her friend.'

> (43)   dæst-e   u   dærd   gereft.
>   hand-Ez   he/she   pain   take/catch.Past.3rd.Sg.
>   'His/Her hand ached.'

As mentioned above, *gereft* 'took/caught' as the inflected form of *gereftæn*
'take/catch' acts as a full/heavy verb in (42) and as a light verb in (43). The
light verb *gereft* 'took/caught' in (43) combines with the noun *dærd* 'pain' and
forms the nuclear juncture *dærd gereft* 'ached' (Lit.: pain take/catch); that is,
the two elements of the preverbal and the light verbal behave as the predicate,
while in (42) *gereft* 'took/caught' is the only predicate of the sentence.

In general, there are a number of differences between light verbs and full/
heavy verbs with regard to some parameters such as: selectional restrictions;
ra- insertion; modification by adverbs; and argument structure, which are
discussed below.

Selectional restrictions

One of the important differences between full/heavy verbs and light verbs
is that the former (full verbs) impose selectional restrictions on the semantic features of the argument in the sentence, while the latter (light verbs)
are not capable of semantically restricting the arguments independently of
the preverbal element. In other words, if the internal argument (object) *tup*
'ball' of the sentence in (42) above is replaced by *ehsas-at* 'feelings' (Lit.:
feeling-Pl.) in (42′) below, the sentence becomes anomalous due to the fact
that the presence of the full verb *gereft* 'take/catch' semantically restricts

some characteristics on the object as something to be caught (taken) and the word *ehsas-at* 'feelings' does not meet the semantic requirement for this verb.

>(42′) *u   ehsas-at-ra   æz   dust-æš   gereft.
>   he/she feeling-Pl.-DOM   from friend   take/catch.Past.3rd.Sg.
>   'He/She took the feelings from his/her friend.'

(Note: The asterisk before the example sentence in (42′) denotes its ungrammaticality.)

Compare this with the replacement of the preverbal element *dærd* 'pain' in (43) above with *yad* 'learning' in (43′) below which is semantically ill-formed; that is, even though the light verb *gereft* 'take/catch' is the same in (43) and (43′), the change in the preverbal element (from *dærd* 'pain' to *yad* 'learning') causes the example in (43′) to be anomalous.

>(43′) *dæst-e   u   yad   gereft.
>   hand-Ez he/she   learning   take/catch.Past.3rd.Sg.
>   'His/Her hand learned.'

In fact, and as the examples in (43) and (43′) present, the light verb by itself does not have the capability of imposing some semantic restrictions on the arguments of the sentences and it is the preverbal element which determines the semantic features or characteristics of the complements. This is in contrast with the full form of the verb, where it can independently impose some semantic restrictions.

Direct object marker *-ra* insertion

As mentioned before, it is possible for the internal argument of the full/heavy verb to be followed by the Direct Object Marker (DOM) *-ra* as presented in (42) above, where *tup* 'ball' as the internal argument of the full verb *gereft* 'took/caught' is followed by *-ra*. By contrast, the insertion of this DOM for the preverbal element *dærd* 'pain' in (43) makes the sentence ill-formed (**dæst-e   u dærd-ra   gereft.* 'His/Her hand ached' (Lit.: hand-Ez   pain-ra took/caught)). In other words, the nominal preceding (and combining with) the light verb is not functioning as its object, as is the case with the corresponding full or heavy verb.

Modification by adverbs

Unlike full/heavy predicates, light verbs are not capable of being preceded and modified by adverbs independently of their preverbal elements. Consider the use of the adverb *bešeddæt* 'severely' in the following examples ((42´´) and (43´´)), which are the same sentences as (42) and (43) above.

> (42´´) u   tup-ra   æz   dust-æš   bešeddæt gereft.
>   he/she ball-DOM from friend-his/her severely   take/catch.
>   Past.3rd.Sg.
>   'He/She took the ball from his/her friend severely.'

> (43´´) *dæst-e   u   dærd bešeddæt gereft.
>   hand-Ez he/she pain   severely   take/catch.Past.3rd.Sg.
>   'His/Her hand ached severely.'

As is clear from the above examples, the full/heavy verb *gereft* 'took/caught' in (42´´) may be immediately preceded and modified by the adverb *bešeddæt* 'severely', while the light verb form of *gereft* 'took/caught' in (43´´) may not. Of course, by placing the adverb before the whole nuclear juncture (*bešeddæt dærd gereft*) the sentence will be acceptable. In other words, with heavy lexical verbs the adverb may intervene between the verb and its complement; with light verbs the adverb may not. It can only occur before the whole LVC.

Argument structure

In Persian *gereft* 'took/caught' as a full/heavy verb behaves as a trivalent predicate (as shown in (42) above), while the use of this predicate as a light verb (given in (43)) functions differently. Consider (43) above, where the light verbal form of the same verb (*gereft* 'took/caught') is used with one argument (*dæst-e u* 'his/her hand'), making the sentence monovalent and intransitive. That is, the behaviour of the light verbal form of the verb *gereft* in (43) is not the same as that of the full/heavy form with regard to transitivity status and assigning the number of arguments.

The differences discussed in this section can be taken as being diagnostic of the grammatical difference between light and heavy verbs.

2.3.2.3   Light verbs and copula *budæn*

Light verbs, as a subcategory of nuclear junctures, behave differently from the Persian copula *budæn* 'be', where the combination of the adjective and the copula, as postulated in RRG, cannot form a complex predicate. Unlike the light verbs *kærdæn* 'do/make' and *šodæn* 'become', the copula verb *budæn* 'to be' when used with adjectives does not affect the transitivity/intransitivity status, does not contribute to the argument structure and semantic content of the sentence, and has no role in assigning aspectual information. As the following example (44) represents, the copula verb *bud* 'was' used with an adjective is a stative verb that attributes the adjective *æsæbani* 'angry' to Ali. While *šod* 'became' in (45) indicates an inchoative/unaccusative status for the construction.

(44)   Ali   æsæbani   bud.
      Ali   angry   be-Past.3ʳᵈ.Sg.
      'Ali was angry.'

(45)   Ali   æsæbani   šod.
      Ali   angry   become-Past.3ʳᵈ.Sg.
      'Ali became angry.'

In (44), *bud* 'was' is a copula since it has no predicating role on its own; it actually functions as a linking device between 'Ali' and the adjective *æsæbani* 'angry', i.e. it attributes the adjective (*æsæbani* 'angry') to 'Ali'. As a matter of fact, the adjective *æsæbani* 'angry' is the predicating element of the sentence regarding the distinction Napoli (1989, p. 20) makes between modifying and predicating adjectives. The copula verb *bud* 'was', unlike the light verb *šod* 'became' in (45), bears no semantic load and is a grammatical word that carries the tense and indicates the person and number. In other words, light verbs are capable of contributing to valency or Aktionsart (aspect), while copulas, as pointed out by Van Valin (personal contact), have no roles in any of these parameters. In fact, even the omission of copulas in sentences may have no influence on their substantive meaning. In some languages such as Arabic or Russian (as in *Ali uchitjelj* 'Ali is a teacher' (Lit.: 'Ali teacher')), a copula is not used in similar sentences and the predicative adjective or noun (as in *uchitjelj* 'teacher' in the above sentence) fulfils the predicating role of the propositions. As mentioned before, according to RRG the only role copulas have is carrying TAM features, with no impact on the aspectual properties or the valency of the arguments. By comparison, the light verb *šod* 'became' (as in (45) above) contributes to the accusative inchoative aspect of the constructions. In other words, it assigns 'Ali' an internal argument role, indicating that something made 'Ali' angry. This also suggests that *šodæn* 'become' (as the infinitive form of *šod* 'became') in

Persian is not an auxiliary but a light verb, since auxiliaries are not capable of assigning a particular type of argument. It is not a copula either since, contrary to Mahootian's (1997) claim, copulas are semantically empty from the semantic point of view, while light verbs such as *šodæn* 'become', as discussed earlier, do contribute to the aspectual information and are not completely semantically bleached constituents.

Also, in Persian the copula used for identificational constructions (e.g. *Ali moællem æst* 'Ali is a teacher') and attributive forms (e.g. *Ali šad æst* 'Ali is glad') has the same logical structure, i.e. **be'** (x, [**pred'**]). In fact, in Persian the copula *budæn* 'be', when used with an adjective, does not contribute to the semantic information of the sentence it appears in, i.e. the copula carries the person and number (as well as negation) and is a semantically empty constituent.

As pointed out by Gustavsson (1976, p. 16), who carried out an analysis of the copula *byt* combined with adjectives in modern Russian, the copulative function (such as marking tense, mood, gender, number and person) is the only meaning copula has.

Moreover, Pustet (2003) points out that copulas are neither meaningful, nor can they function as predicate on their own. In the meantime, copulas are not usually capable of contributing to aspectual information. As discussed in Sections 2.3.2.1–2, although light verbs, like copulas, do not have an independent predicating role by themselves, they add to the semantic information of the construction and contribute to the aspectual structure of the whole complex predicate.

The investigations of the present study have identified the same list of light verbs provided by Karimi-Doostan (1997). There may be other possible light verbs but these have not featured in the data of this study. Therefore, this list presented below (46) is used to illustrate the discussion. Since this list is used repeatedly in this study and there is a need to make references to the aspectual properties and the (in)transitivity status of the full/heavy form of these verbs, the Aktionsart type and the (in)transitivity reading of their full independent form is presented in parentheses in front of each verb. Note that since the verb *šodæn* 'become' has no full independent form, as discussed in Section 2.3.2 of this chapter, no Aktionsart type has been provided for this verb in the list.

(46)

Verb	Aktionsart type	Verb	Aktionsart type
-xordæn 'eat'	(Activity-tran.)	-daštæn 'have'	(State-tran.)
-šodæn 'become'	(Intrans./Inchoative LV), No full form	-kærdæn 'do/ make'	(Activity-tran.)
-amædæn 'come'	(Accomplishment-intran.)	-gereftæn 'take/ catch'	(Achievement-tran.)
-ræftæn 'go'	(Accomplishment-intran.)	-didæn 'see'	(Achievement-tran.)
-zædæn 'hit/ strike'	(Activity-tran.)	-dadæn 'give'	(Achievement-tran.)
-bæxšidæn 'offer/forgive'	(Achievement-tran.)	-aværdæn 'bring'	(Accomplishment-tran.)
-kešidæn 'pull'	(Activity-tran.)	-bordæn 'take/ carry'	(Accomplishment-tran.)
-gozaštæn 'put'	(Achievement-tran.)	-yaftæn 'find'	(Achievement-tran.)

2.3.3 *Causativization*

Although full verbs in Persian, Karimi-Doostan (1997) maintains, can be causativized by adding the morpheme *-an(i)dæn* to the present stem of the verb, light verbal constructions do not undergo this morphological process of causativization easily. By comparing the examples in (47) and (48), the difference between full and light predicates with respect to causativization becomes more transparent.

(47)   Full (heavy) verbs:
      a. pušidæn 'put on, wear'
         puš-(Pr. Stem) + -andæn   ⟶ pušandæn 'cause to put on'
      b. fæhmidæn 'understand'
         fæhm-(Pr. Stem) + -andæn ⟶ fæhmandæn 'cause to understand'

(48)   Light verbs:
      a. kærdæn 'do'
         kon-(Pr. Stem) + -andæn ⟶ *konandæn 'cause to do'
      b. yaftæn 'Find'
         yab-(Pr. Stem) + -andæn ⟶ *yabandæn 'cause to find'
                          (Karimi-Doostan, 1997, p. 88)

As was shown in (48a) and (48b), cited from Karimi-Doostan, *kærdæn* and *yaftæn* are two light verbs that do not yield to causativization as a morphological process. Indeed, when these two verbs are used in their full forms, which are exactly the same as their light use, *kærdæn and yaftæn* still cannot undergo this process, i.e. they cannot be causativized. According to Karimi-Doostan (1997), light verbs are incapable of undergoing causativization operation independently. In my view, however, this is not the case for all light verbs and there are light verbs that possess this capability. Consider the following light verbs in Persian.

(49)   a. xordæn 'to eat'
            xor-(Verb Stem) + -andæn   ⟶   xorandæn 'cause to eat'
       b. kešidæn 'to draw'
            keš-(Verb Stem) + -andæn   ⟶   kešandæn 'cause to draw'

As observed in (49), the light verbs *xordæn* and *kešidæn* are causativized by adding the suffix *-andæn* to the stem of the two verbs and they are grammatical, i.e. the two verbs are capable of undergoing causativization operation.

2.4 Conclusion

In this chapter, light verbal constructions as one type of complex predicates in modern Persian (Farsi) have been investigated informally. The chapter began by discussing definitions of complex predicates in the grammatical literature. Then three important types of complex predicate, i.e. noun incorporation, causative verbs and light verbal constructions, were discussed and a number of examples from different languages were provided for each. The next section (2.2) was devoted to Persian, which employs a wide range of light verbs with a great linguistic importance since these structures characterize a number of lexical as well as syntactic features that provide some evidence for the unified theory of language. The advocates of this theory postulate that the components of linguistic phenomena should not be dealt with as separate entities; rather, they should be looked at as a whole. Although light verbs are similar to full verbs in that they carry tense and aspect, with regard to their semantic content, they are impoverished elements, i.e. they are not full predicates. In this study, however, light verbal constructions or complex predicates in Persian are categorized on the basis of the type of the preverbal elements used in the constructions, in order to determine the amount of contribution each element provides in these structures, since, as mentioned before, different kinds of adjective, noun, adverb and prepositional phrase conjoin the verbal or light verbal elements to form complex predicates. The motivation behind this is that there is no detailed comprehensive research study based on this kind of categorization in Persian. These light verbal constructions are the major concern of the formal discussions in Chapters 4 and 5. Having provided some general/informal background information on light verbal constructions, the researcher can now move on to the main focus of the next chapter, which is the theoretical framework adopted in this study to analyze these constructions in Persian.

Notes

1. Note that all the examples cited in the present chapter remain in the transcription or orthographies provided in the original sources.
2. Note that *-o* attached to *ketab* 'book' in (39) is the less formal form of the direct object marker *-ra*.
3. Karimi-Doostan (1997, p. 92), making a similar point, asserts that auxiliaries are not capable of participating in the formation of the light verbal constructions.

3

Theoretical Framework

3.0 Introduction

In the second chapter, light verbal constructions (LVCs) in Modern Persian (Farsi) were explored and the reader was provided with an informal overview of these constructions as one of the major subcategories of complex (compound or composite) predicates. In the present chapter, Role and Reference Grammar (RRG) as the framework that is believed to be appropriate to capture the nature of Persian complex predicates in general, and light verbal constructions in particular, is introduced. Some studies (e.g. Toratani's 2002 analysis of compound verbs in Japanese, which will be discussed later in this chapter) have employed Role and Reference Grammar to analyze a number of complex (compound) predicate types. As will be observed, an important proposal is that the Interclausal Relations Hierarchy (Van Valin and LaPolla, 1997; Van Valin, 2005), which maps the morphosyntactic relations into the semantic ones, is an important tool in the analysis of these constructions. This chapter basically outlines the framework of Role and Reference Grammar and looks at the way simple and complex sentences are analyzed within this theory.

3.1 Role and Reference Grammar: background

It is commonplace to identify two broad traditions among grammatical theories: formal and functional; see for example Newmeyer (1998) and Croft (1995, 1999). The formal theories are usually characterized as sharing a 'commitment to characterizing form independently of meaning and function' (Newmeyer, 1998, p. 7). According to Newmeyer, the leading example of this approach is Chomsky's 'generative enterprise' (for an example, see Chomsky, 1982). Functional theories, on the other hand, seek to define language as a system of communication, where meaning and function influence, or in a stronger version motivate or determine, linguistic structure. Two major functional theories are Functional Grammar (Dik, 1991) and Systemic Functional Grammar (Halliday, 1994). Some observers, including Newmeyer and Croft in the works cited above, have classified theories on a continuum between formal and functional, with Role and Reference Grammar being identified as a functional approach, but with an interest in formalizing the description of linguistic rules and representations.

The first version of Role and Reference Grammar (RRG) theory was developed by Van Valin and Foley (1980) on the basis of Fillmore's (1963) Case Grammar, which was basically a semantically oriented theory in which the purely syntactic features of sentence (S), noun phrase (NP), verbal phrase (VP) and prepositional phrase (PP) were replaced by the semantic elements such as 'Agent', 'Patient', 'Instrument', 'Locative' and 'Benefactive'. Van Valin and Foley, who were in fact Fillmore's students, elaborated his thoughts into a new and more comprehensive model of language analysis, which they referred to as RRG. Role and Reference Grammar theory was later modified by Van Valin and LaPolla (1997) and Van Valin (2005). The following section aims at presenting an introduction of this theory and providing a descriptive picture of its theoretical principles for analyzing linguistic phenomena.

3.2 Organization of RRG

In Role and Reference Grammar, the grammatical structures are employed to express meaning in context, and in fact language takes place in a social environment in which syntactic features of language interact with semantics and pragmatics. As Van Valin and Foley (1984, p. 16) note, the name of this theory derives from the emphasis on the interaction of Role (semantic) and Referential (pragmatic) features in grammatical systems. According to the latest version of RRG (Van Valin, 2005, p. 1), there are three main representations in this theory:

1. a representation of the syntactic structure of sentences which refers to the formal representation of linguistic elements;
2. a semantic representation which focuses on the meaning aspect of language; and
3. an information representation, or what is also referred to as 'Focus' structure, which corresponds to the functions of a communicative situation.

Another important element of Role and Reference Grammar is the set of rules that connects the semantic and syntactic representations and this is called the 'Linking Algorithm'. In relating these two types of representations, discourse and pragmatics act as two determining elements. Figure 3.1 summarizes the

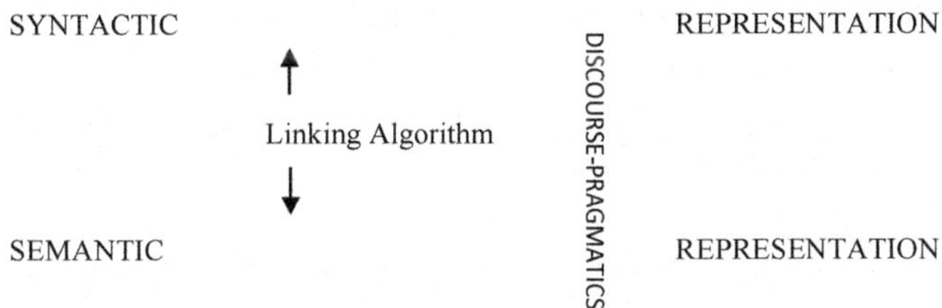

Figure 3.1 Organization of the Role and Reference Grammar (RRG) (Van Valin, 2005, p. 2).

relation of these factors. In Sections 3.3 and 3.4 the two types of representations in RRG theory, namely syntactic and semantic representations, which are the main concern of the present study, are discussed respectively in brief.

3.3 Syntactic representation

According to Van Valin (2005) (as the latest published version of RRG), every theory of clause structure should deal with two crucial issues: relational vs. non-relational structures. The former is related to the predicate-arguments relations and the latter to the hierarchical organization of phrases, clauses and sentences, which in RRG is referred to as the Layered Structure of the Clause (LSC). This layered structure (which is dealt with in the following section) is concerned with: (a) the contrast between predicates and non-predicating elements, and (b) the contrast between arguments and non-arguments (Van Valin, 2005).

3.3.1 Layered structure of the clause

Van Valin and LaPolla (1997) make a clear distinction between the universal and non-universal dimensions of the conception of clause structure units, which they refer to as the Layered Structure of the Clause (LSC). As mentioned earlier, this layered structure, which was originally proposed by Foley and Van Valin (1984) and later developed by Van Valin (1993), is concerned with two crucial contrasts, i.e. the predicate/non-predicating element contrast and the argument/non-argument contrast, both of which are found in all languages, regardless of whether they have free or fixed word order, are configurational or non-configurational, head-marking or dependent marking (Van Valin, 2005). Therefore, the basic constituent parameters of the clause, including the **nucleus,** the **core** and the **periphery,** are universal, too. The nucleus contains the predicate (usually the verb) of the clause or the sentence, the core houses the nucleus and the arguments of the predicate, and finally the periphery, which refers to the non-arguments of the predicate, houses adjunct temporal and locative modifiers of the core. Figure 3.2 summarizes the relation between the components of the clause structure in the following example (1).

(1) Mary typed the letter yesterday in her office.

Furthermore, there are semantic units underlying the syntactic components of the layered structure of the clause. This semantic foundation of LSC is presented in Table 3.1.

These hierarchical units have no dependence on the relation of immediate dominance or linear precedence; consequently, if the rules of a particular language allow, these units are not the only elements which may occur in a simple or a single-clause sentence; that is, there are two other positions in which other components can be housed, namely, **precore slot** (PrCS) and **postcore slot** (PoCS). The former refers to the position in which question words occur in a sentence (e.g. Do you like this fruit?) and the fronted element (e.g. This fruit, I like). And the latter appears in some verb final languages such as Dhiveli (Indo-Aryan) (Cain and Gair, 2000). Moreover, in some languages some elements may appear in two other positions detached from the main units of the sentence, i.e. **left-detached position** (LDP) vs. **right-detached position** (RDP). As Van Valin (2005) maintains, LDP is a location (not obligatory) in which sentence-initial elements (mostly adverbials) are set off from the clause by a pause such as: *Yesterday, I got a new book from the library.* The RDP refers to the position of a post-clausal element in a right-dislocation construction such as the one provided by Van Valin: *I know them, those boys.* What is important

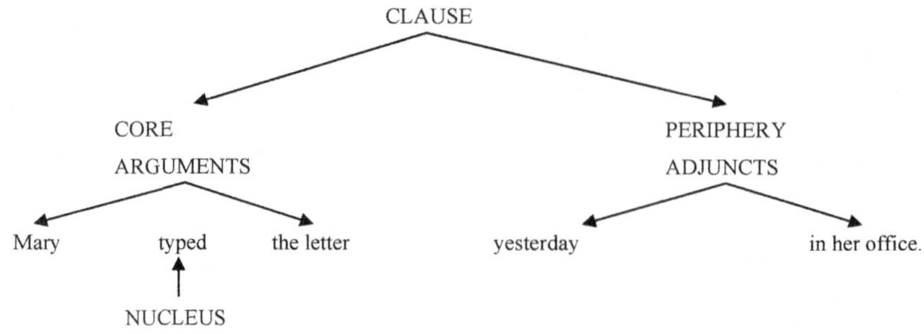

Figure 3.2 Components of the Layered Structure of the Clause (LSC).

Table 3.1 Semantic foundation of the syntactic units of LSC (Van Valin and LaPolla, 1997, p. 27)

Semantic element(s)	Syntactic units
Predicate	Nucleus
Argument in semantic representation of predicate	Core argument
Non-arguments	Periphery
Predicate + arguments	Core
Predicate + arguments + non-arguments	Clause (= core + periphery)

to note here is that a distinction should be made between the universal and non-universal components of the layered structure of the clause. In RRG theory, nucleus, core and periphery are the universal constituents of the layers in languages and the PrCS, PoCS, LDP and RDP are the non-universal parameters of the elements in a simple sentence. Another crucial difference between the universal and non-universal aspects of the layered structure of the clause is that the former are all semantically motivated, while the latter are pragmatically motivated or at least are associated with constructions which have strong pragmatic conditions on their occurrence (Van Valin and LaPolla, 1997).

In general, RRG (Van Valin, 2005, p. 12) introduces a general schema of a projection grammar representation of the LSC, originally provided by Johnson (1987), to capture the differences of linguistic variations. In RRG this formalization, termed by Johnson (1987) himself as 'projection grammar', is schematized in Figure 3.3. This general schema consists of two parts: the top part is called 'constituent projection' and the bottom part the 'operator

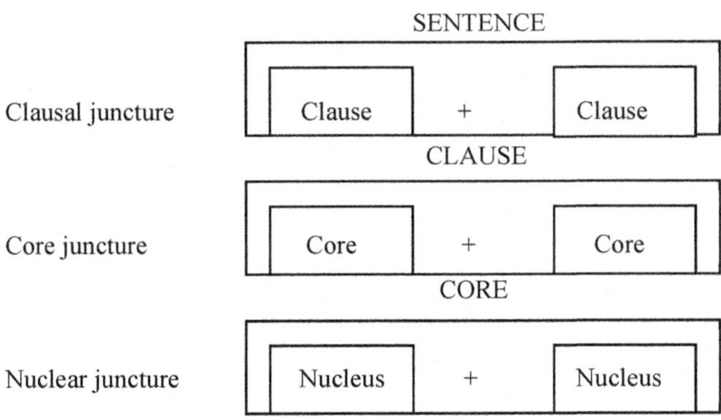

Figure 3.3 Types of juncture.

projection', which are joined through the nucleus as the central parameter in the layered structure of the clause. The scope of the operator in the operator projection is shown by the component that is the target of the arrow (Van Valin and LaPolla, 1997).

As observed in this section, RRG theory has developed a system of layered structures for analyzing the simple sentences in a given language. But of course not all the sentences in a language are simple and the theory provides the analytical machines to investigate complex structure. These will be addressed in the next section.

3.3.2   Complex sentences

Role and Reference Grammar has also developed a very distinct and comprehensive framework specifically designed for complex sentences. The two crucial issues that every linguistic theory, including RRG, should deal with in terms of complex sentences are the elements involved and the relations among these elements. According to RRG, the components of the layered structure of the clause are, in fact, the involved units in complex sentences that are similar to those in simple sentences, namely, nucleus, core and clause. And the relations among these elements in complex sentences are characterized through 'coordination', 'subordination' and 'cosubordination'. All these relations involve three important levels: Juncture, Nexus and Interclausal levels in complex sentences. The first level (juncture) corresponds to the clausal vs. subclausal component building the complex sentences; the second level of nexus deals with the syntactic relationship between the units in juncture; and the last level is concerned with the semantic relationship between the units in the juncture. Figure 3.3 presents the types of juncture (Van Valin, 2001a). As presented in Figure 3.3, clausal juncture embodies multiple clauses which form one sentence, in core juncture multiple cores form one clause, and nuclear juncture makes one core by combining multiple nuclei. Table 3.2 and Figure 3.3 schematize these three types of junctures in RRG and the way the units in the layered structure of the clause form different junctures.

Table 3.2 Juncture types

Juncture types	Schematic representation
Nuclear juncture	[CORE ... [NUC PRED] ... + ... [NUC PRED] ...]
Core juncture	[CLAUSE ... [CORE ...] ... + ... [CORE ...] ...]
Clausal juncture	[SENTENCE ... [CLAUSE ...] ... + ... [CLAUSE ...] ...]

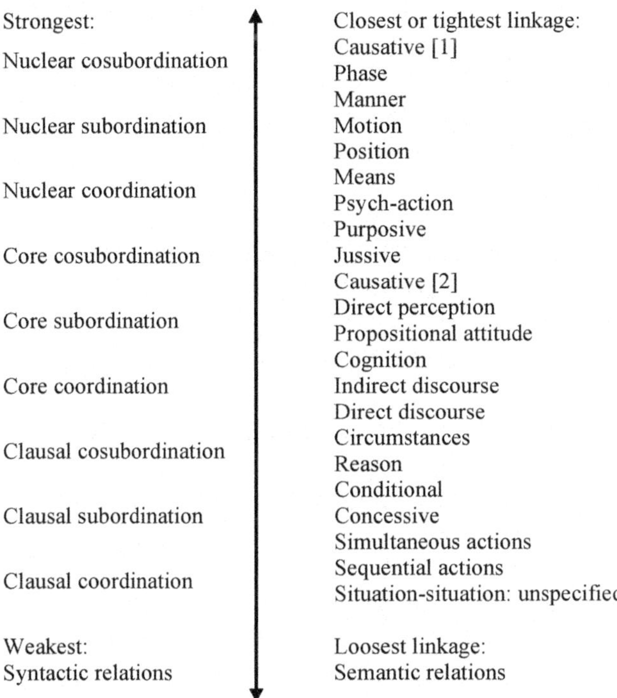

Figure 3.4 Interclausal relations hierarchy.

According to Van Valin and LaPolla (1997), coordination is concerned with the joining of two or more units of equal status, subordination deals with the embedding of one unit in another, where this embedded unit usually is not the independent main clause and acts as a modifier (as in adverbial subordinate clauses) or as an argument (as in complementation). Cosubordination involves the cases where two elements, although sharing an operator at the relevant level of juncture, are structurally independent.

All the relations of the three types of juncture yield nine possible juncture-nexus types. Van Valin (2005) illustrates these relation types, which are presented in Figure 3.4. The examples in (2) from English represent some juncture-nexus types provided by Van Valin and LaPolla (1997).

(2) English juncture-nexus combination:
    a. Max seemed tired.   Nuclear cosubordination
       Vince has wiped the table clean.

b. Ted tried to open the door. Sam sat playing the guitar.	Core subordination
c. Louisa told Bob to close the window. Fred saw Harry leave the room.	Core coordination
d. To wash the car today would be a mistake. Chris regretted Kim's dating Pat.	Core subordination
e. Pat ran down the hall laughing loudly. Leslie drove to the store and bought some beer.	Clausal cosubordination
f. Kim persuaded Dana that Casey had lost. Pat went to the party after he talked to Chris.	Clausal subordination
g. Anna read for a few minutes, and then she went out.	Clausal coordination

Toratani's (2002) analysis of Japanese compound verbs is a recent study within the RRG framework. In part of her dissertation, she examined non-phase (non-aspectual) compounds looking for the juncture-nexus type of these constructions. As a result of her analysis, she finds out that these compounds in Japanese appear in two types of constructions: (a) core cosubordination (e.g. *-nare* 'get need to'), and (b) core subordination (e.g. *-sugi* 'excessively'). Toratani (2002) also argues that phase verbs (i.e. aspectual verbs) in Japanese appear in two types of structures, namely, nuclear cosubordination (e.g. *-owe* 'finish') and core subordination (e.g. *-das* 'begin').

In general, regardless of the type of sentences in determining the layered structure of the clause in the syntactic representation of RRG, i.e. regardless of whether the sentence is simple or complex, each layer of the LSC may employ a number of elements which are referred to as Operators and are discussed in detail below.

3.3.3 Operators projection

In English, auxiliary verbs are used to change the sentences into question form. These auxiliary verbs do not belong to either of the categories nucleus, core or periphery; rather, they are the grammatical elements which modify different layers of the clause. In other words, auxiliary verbs, for example, are the tense operators that modify the clausal elements. Each of the categories

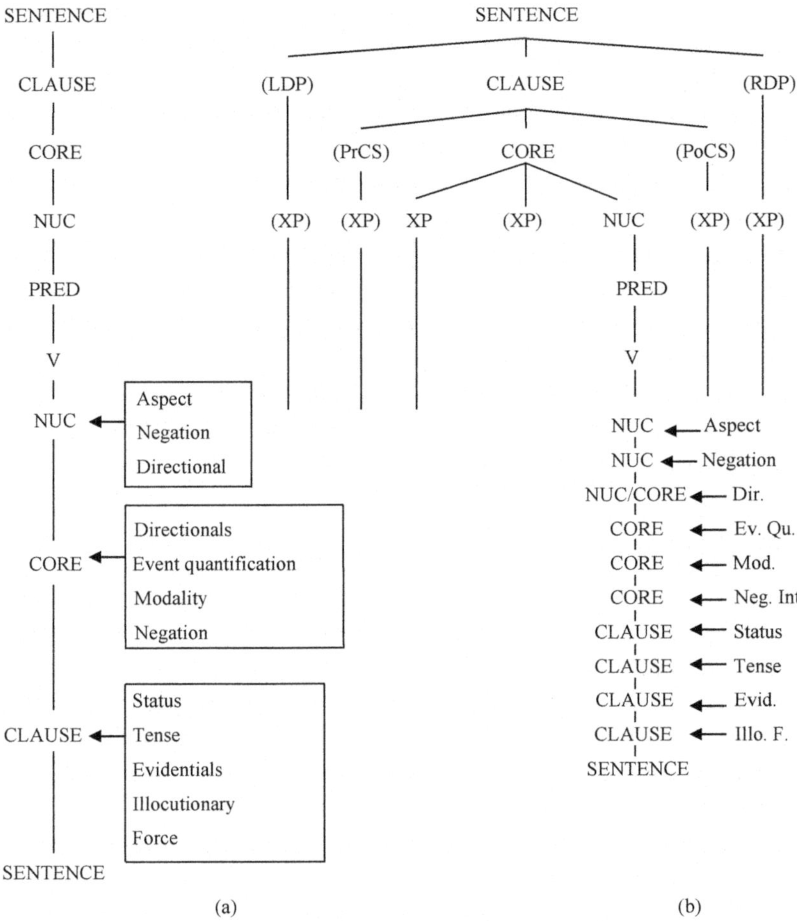

Figure 3.5 LSC with constituent and operator projections.

of nucleus, core and periphery has a number of operators which modify them. The list of these operators provided in Van Valin (2005) is presented in Figure 3.5. In fact, Figure 3.5 schematizes both constituent and operator projections.

3.4 Lexical representation and semantic roles

As Van Valin (2005) points out, RRG is a lexicalist theory and the system of lexical representation that a theory takes advantage of has a crucial role in the type and nature of the grammatical generalizations, since these generalizations are stated both in the syntax and in the lexicon. In RRG theory, the lexical entries for verbs are on the basis of logical structures (LSs) and its nominal representation is on the basis of the nominal qualia proposed in Pustejovsky (1995). In this theory, it is believed that only idiosyncratic information should form the foundation of lexical entries for verbs, with as much as possible derived from general lexical principles or rules. In RRG, a distinction has been made between lexical and syntactic phenomena in terms of the linking procedure; that is, if LSs, the arguments therein, or the mapping between LSs and macroroles (the semantic roles such as 'actor' and 'undergoer', which are discussed later in this chapter) are affected by a phenomenon, it is referred to as lexical (e.g. causativization, regardless of whether it is morphologically unmarked as in English or marked as in Turkish and Chicewa); if the phenomenon corresponds to the mapping between macroroles and the syntactic representation, it is referred to as a syntactic phenomenon (e.g. WH-question formation as in English) (cf. Van Valin, 1993).

3.4.1   Verb classes: Aktionsart

Since a theory of verb classes forms the building block of any lexical representation, RRG takes the Aktionsart ('form of action' in German) classes of verbs proposed by Vendler (1967) and Dowty's (1979) representational scheme as the starting point in developing verb classes. Aktionsart classification, originally introduced by Vendler (1957 [1967]), focuses on the inherent temporal properties of verbs and has been categorized into four major groups: states, achievements, accomplishments and activities. According to Van Valin and LaPolla (1997), each of the four main Aktionsart categories, which is the basis of the analysis in this study, can be related to one of the state-of-affairs types proposed by them as follows.

(3) **State-of-affairs type**   **Aktionsart type**
    Situation   State
    Event   Achievement
    Process   Accomplishment
    Action   Activity
                            (Van Valin and LaPolla, 1997, p. 92)

As Van Valin and LaPolla (1997, p. 92) maintain, the above Aktionsart types, which RRG claims to be universal, can be defined in conjunction with three features, [±static], [±punctual] and [±telic]. These features, Van Valin and

LaPolla (1997) state, 'refer to whether the verb has an inherent terminal point or not', and they can be summarized as follows.

(4) **Aktionsart type**   **Related features of each type**
    State   [+static], [–telic], [–punctual]
    Activity   [–static], [–telic], [–punctual]
    Accomplishment   [–static], [+telic], [–punctual]
    Achievement   [–static], [+telic], [+punctual]

In order to determine the Aktionsart type of a verb or predicate within the RRG framework, Van Valin and LaPolla (1997, p. 94) suggest a number of tests, which are a modified form of those originally proposed by Dowty (1979). Even though these tests are to be valid cross-linguistically, still there may be a need to modify some of them for a number of languages in order to match them to their specific linguistic systems. In the following sections, these tests or, if required, their modified forms are applied to the individual Persian light verbs (under examination in Chapters 4 and 5) to determine their Aktionsart class.

In RRG, the first test suggested to check the stativity (i.e. whether the verb is [–static] and codes a 'happening' or it is [+static] coding a 'non-happening') of a verb is its capability to occur with a progressive aspect. This test, as Van Valin and LaPolla (1997) maintain, works only in languages where there is a progressive aspect and is applicable to accomplishment and activity verbs, but is not effective for states and achievements. Persian, unlike English, 'does not have a distinct progressive aspectual form … but it has an imperfect aspect that is marked by the prefix *mi-*' (Rezai, 2003, p. 92). According to Vahidian and Emrani (2000), this prefix is not an indicator of progressive aspect in Persian. That is, there is no morphological marker on the verb to show the progressive aspect; rather, this role is indicated through some grammaticalized expressions. Mahootian (1997) remarks that the auxiliary *daštæn* 'to have' followed by the main action verb expresses progressive aspect in both present and past. Also, Karimi-Doostan (1997) uses the same auxiliary verb (*daštæn* 'to have') in his study to differentiate stativity from non-stativity. Dabir-Moghaddam (1998) proposes the two expressions *dær hale* 'in process of' and *mæšqu-le* 'in process of', which can co-occur with the progressive verbs. In fact, as Kahnemuyipour (2001) notes, in Persian there are some periphrastic constructions that can be used to identify the progressive aspect of the verbs.

In this study, the expression *dær hal-e* 'in process of' is used to determine the Aktionsart type of the light verbs, since the writer of this book agrees with Rezai (2003) in the sense that the auxiliary verb *daštæn* (which has sometimes been referred to as the progressive auxiliary in Persian) in some linguistic environments acts as near future and not progressive aspect, as in the sentence *færda bæradær-æm dare miyad Tehran* 'Tomorrow my brother is going to come to Tehran' (Lit.: tomorrow-brother-1st. Sg.-has.AUX-come-Tehran). In the following exemplified forms of the nominal light verbal constructions with the expression *dær hal-e* 'in process of', this phrase appears before the infinitive form of the nominal light verb, which in turn is followed by the suitable form of a copula. In Persian there is no fixed word order, but it is often the case that when this expression is added to the sentence, some elements in the sentence need to be scrambled; that is, the expression *dær hal-e* 'in process of' followed by the infinitive form of the light verbal complex predicate or Nuclear Juncture (NJ) appear after the privileged syntactic argument (subject), and the (suitable inflected form of) copula comes at the end of the sentence.

The second test suggested by Van Valin and LaPolla (1997) corresponds to the verb's ability to co-occur with adverbs such as 'vigorously', 'actively' and 'dynamically', which code dynamic action (Van Valin and LaPolla, 1997; Van Valin, 2005). As the adverbs speak for themselves, this test is an indicator of a [−static] or [±dynamic] feature; therefore, it does not work with state, achievement and accomplishment verbs. The Persian adverbs which are adopted and used interchangeably here and also have the same meaning as 'vigorously', 'actively' and 'dynamically' are *fæalane* 'actively' and *ba qodræt* 'vigorously'.

The third test addresses the verb's capability to appear in sentences with adverbs such as 'slowly' or 'quickly' called 'pace adverbs' (Van Valin and LaPolla, 1997), and is applicable to [−static] verbs and makes a distinction between the two verb features of [+punctual] and [−punctual]. This test works with accomplishment and activity verbs, but not with states and achievement. The Persian 'pace adverbs' used here are *besoræt* 'quickly' and *aheste* 'slowly', the latter, Van Valin and LaPolla (1997) note, being necessary for achievement. In this study, these two adverbs are applied interchangeably, with the exception of achievement verbs for which the use of the adverb *aheste* 'slowly' is necessary and state verbs for which this adverb is sometimes preferable. Therefore, for those Persian verbs that are more likely to be of these types this adverb has been used.

The next (fourth) test examines whether the verb occurs with the duration adpositional phrase 'for an hour' expression (Van Valin and LaPolla, 1997), which indeed identifies the verb's telicity, i.e. if the verb has a bounded or unbounded interpretation. Focusing on the property of temporal duration, this test indicates that, unlike achievements (having the [+punctual] feature), states, accomplishments and activities (possessing the [–punctual] property) do have temporal duration in time (Van Valin and LaPolla, 1997). In Persian, the expression *bæraye yek sæt* 'for an hour' is used to determine if an event continued for a certain amount of time.

The last (fifth) test introduced by Van Valin and LaPolla (1997) to characterize the telicity of the verb is the use of the expression 'in an hour'. This test works only with accomplishments and examines whether the verb has the feature [+telic]. The verb or the predicate is bounded, i.e. the event begins at a specific point in time and finishes at a certain time. The Persian expression used for this test is *dær yek sæt* 'in an hour' for the same sentences above.

Along with the lexical representation and Aktionsart classes discussed above, in RRG theory some semantic roles have also been distinguished which are discussed below.

3.4.2   Lexical entries for verbs

In RRG lexical entries are considered to be a crucial parameter in determining the grammatical behaviour of a lexical item. According to Van Valin and LaPolla (1997), 'the logical structure of the verb is the heart of its lexical entries' and if the verb is compatible with the principles listed in (5) (Van Valin and LaPolla, 1997, p. 152) below, there is no need to specify the thematic relation or transitivity.

(5)   Default macrorole assignment principles:
    a. Number: the number of macroroles a verb takes is less than or equal to the number of arguments in its logical structure.
       1. If a verb has two or more arguments in its LS, it will take two macroroles.
       2. If a verb has one argument in its LS, it will take one macrorole.
    b. Nature: for verbs which take one macrorole.
       1. If the verb has an activity predicate in its LS, the macrorole is actor.
       2. If the verb has no activity predicate in its LS, the macrorole is undergoer.

The following lexical entries are presented in (6) for a number of English verbs (Van Valin, 2005, pp. 46–7). Since the focus of this study for Persian verbs is on the four major Aktionsart types of state, achievement, accomplishment and activity verbs, only the logical structures of those examples which are related to these types are schematized below.

(6) a. STATES
Pat is a fool.   **be'** (Pat, [**fool'**])
Max shattered the cup.   **shattered'** (cup)
Kim is in the library.   **be-in'** (library, Kim)
Dana saw the picture.   **see'** (Dana, picture

  b. ACTIVITIES
The children cried.   **do'** (children, **cry'** (children)])
Carl ate pizza.   **do'** (Carl, [**eat'** (Carl, pizza)])

  c. ACHIEVEMENTS
The window shattered.   INGR **shattered'** (window)
The balloon popped.   INGR **popped'** (balloon)

  d. ACCOMPLISHMENTS
The snow melted.   BECOME **melted'** (snow)
Mary learned French.   BECOME **know'** (Mary, French)

3.4.3 Semantic roles

The 'specific semantic roles' (thematic relations) and the 'generalized semantic roles' (semantic macroroles: actor, undergoer) are the two major types of semantic roles in Role and Reference Grammar theory. In both these types of roles, the logical structures of the verb classes play a central role in the semantic representation of lexical entries. In general, the first type of semantic roles, the 'specific semantic roles' or the thematic roles, refers to the 'semantic relation between a predicate and its arguments which express the participant roles in the state of affairs denoted by the verb, ... thematic relations in RRG are linguistic entities that is they are part of natural language semantics, while participant roles are not; they are properties of status of affairs in the world' (Van Valin and LaPolla, 1997, p. 113). Adopting Jackendoff's (1976) proposal, RRG defines the thematic relations with respect to argument positions in logical structures instead of listing the thematic relations in a verb's lexical entry. Since from all the classes of verbs only two of them, namely, states and activities, define thematic relations, and in fact these two are the main building blocks of other types, the verb classes are categorized into state vs. activity verbs and a set of subcategories is introduced for each (Van Valin and LaPolla, 1997) as presented in Table 3.3.

Table 3.3 Definition of argument position in terms of argument position

I. State verbs		
a. Single argument		
1. State or condition	**broken'** (x)	x = PATIENT
2. Existence	**exist'** (x)	x = ENTITY
b. Two arguments		
1. Pure location	**be'-loc'** (x, y)	x = LOCATION, y = THEME
2. Perception	**hear'** (x, y)	x = PERCEIVER, y = STIMULUS
3. Cognition	**know'** (x, y)	x = COGNIZER, y = CONTENT
4. Desire	**want'** (x, y)	x = WANTER, y = DESIRE
5. Propositional attitude	**consider'** (x, y)	x = JUDGER, y = JUDGEMENT
6. Possession	**have'** (x, y)	x = POSSESSOR, y = POSSESSED
7. Internal experience	**feel'** (x, y)	x = EXPERIENCER, y = SENSATION
8. Emotion	**love'** (x, y)	x = EMOTER, y = TARGET
9. Attrib/ identificational	**be'** (x, y)	x = ATTRIBUTANT, y = ATTRIBUTE
II. Activity verbs		
a. Single argument		
1. Unspecified action	**do'** (x, ø)	x = EFFECTOR
2. Motion	**do'** (x, [**walk'** (x)])	x = MOVER
3. State motion	**do'** (x, [**spin'** (x)])	x = ST-MOVER
4. Light emission	**do'** (x, [**shine'** (x)])	x = L-EMITTER
5. Sound emission	**do'** (x, [**gurgle'** (x)])	x = S-EMITTER
b. One or two arguments		
1. Performance	**do'** (x, [**sing'** (x, (y))])	x = PERFORMER, y = PERFORMANCE
2. Consumption	**do'** (x, [**eat'** (x, (y))])	x = CONSUMER, y = CONSUMED
3. Creation	**do'** (x, [**write'** (x, (y))])	x = CREATOR, y = CREATION
4. Repetitive action	**do'** (x, [**tap'** (x, (y))])	x = EFFECTOR, y = LOCUS
5. Direct perception	**do'** (x, **see'** (x, (y))])	x = OBSERVER, x = STIMULUS
6. Use	**do'** (x, [**use'** (x, (y))])	x = USER, x = IMPLEMENT

The second type of semantic roles, the generalized semantic roles, refers to two major macroroles, i.e. **actor** and **undergoer**. In RRG theory, the old labels of 'subject' or 'object' have no place since according to this theory these terminologies refer to the syntactic relations rather than the semantic ones. In place of 'subject' RRG employs the notion of 'Privileged Syntactic Argument' (PSA), even though for most constructions PSA refers to the traditional subject. PSA can be of two types, namely, 'controller' and 'pivot'. Controllers may trigger verb agreement, as in 'The teacher has read the words', antecede a reflexive, or supply the interpretation for a missing argument in an adjacent unit, as in 'Chris wants to drink a beer', which can be semantically represented as:

(Chris$_i$ wants   [$_i$ to drink a beer]
CONTROLLER   PIVOT

(Van Valin, 2005, p. 95).

Pivots, Van Valin (2005) maintains, are canonically (but not exclusively) the missing argument in the constructions.

In RRG, the arguments filling the position of the object are characterized as 'direct or oblique core arguments' and there is, indeed, nothing in RRG which corresponds to direct or indirect object. With regard to the semantic roles, it should be noted that each of the actor (the most agent-like argument) and the undergoer (the most patient-like argument) contains a number of specific thematic relation. Figure 3.6 schematizes the relation between the logical structure argument positions and the macroroles (Van Valin, 2005, p. 126).

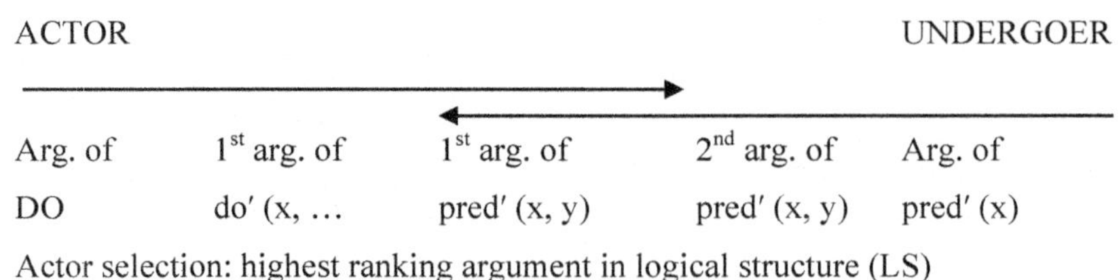

Figure 3.6 Actor-undergoer hierarchy (revised).

3.4.4 Linking algorithm

As shown in Figure 3.1, RRG has proposed a linking algorithm which maps the syntactic representation into the semantic one, and also the semantic representation into a syntactic one. Even though the two levels of representations, i.e. syntactic vs. semantic, are independent from each other and each level can map into the other one, these two processes of the bidirectional linking system, according to RRG, are not the same and are governed by a general constraint referred to as the completeness constraint (Van Valin, 2005, p. 129) stated below as (7).

> (7) Completeness constraint:
> All of the arguments explicitly specified in the semantic representation of a sentence must be realized syntactically in the sentence, and all of the referring expressions in the syntactic representation of a sentence must be linked to an argument position in a logical structure in the semantic representation of the sentence.

By 'explicitly specified' RRG means that 'the argument position in the logical structure is filled by a variable or a constraint; for it to be unspecified, it would be filled by "Ø" ' (Van Valin, 2005, p. 130), as in (8) below cited from Van Valin (2005).

> (8) a. Max loaded the minivan.
>   b. [**do'** (Max, Ø)] CAUSE [BECOME **be-in'** (minivan, Ø)]
>   b′. [**do'** (Max, Ø)] CAUSE [BECOME **be-in'** (minivan, the boxes)]

As is clear in (8), the logical structure of (8b) does not determine the second argument of **be-in'** and that is why the 'Ø' sign has been used, i.e. there is no second argument, while in (8b′) the second argument, i.e. 'the boxes', has been specified. As in the sentence in (8a) also the second argument has not been specified; only (8b) is a legitimate logical structure for this sentence due to the completeness constraint (Van Valin, 2005, p. 130).

3.4.4.1 Constructional schemas

Following Constructional Grammar, RRG introduces the notion of 'constructional schemas' (or what was referred to as 'constructional templates' in Van Valin and LaPolla, 1997), which contain syntactic, morphological, semantic and pragmatic information about the construction in question. Constructional schemas, RRG postulates, can capture not only the idiosyncratic and language-specific characteristics of constructions, but those shared properties of general grammar or cross-linguistic generalizations by virtue of their reference to general principles (Van Valin and LaPolla, 1997; Van Valin, 2005).

The important point to take into account before presenting these schemas is that in order to determine the syntactic features of any construction in question it is crucial to characterize the syntactic 'templates' which are stored in what is referred to as a 'syntactic inventory' presented in Figure 3.8 below. In RRG, it is postulated that the templates provide the constituent projection of the syntactic representation of a construction; therefore, there are templates for extracore positions (LDP, RDP, PrCS and PoCS) and core templates which fuse with each other. According to Van Valin (2005, p. 130), 'there are principles governing the selection of the appropriate core template'. Therefore, in the following part, first these principles for selecting the appropriate core templates (Van Valin, 2005, p. 130) are presented in (9), and then the syntactic templates (e.g. for English) and syntactic inventory are schematized in Figures 3.7 and 3.8, respectively.

(9) a. Syntactic template selection principle:
       The number of syntactic slots for arguments-adjuncts within the core is equal to the number of distinct specified argument positions in the semantic representation of the core.
    b. Language-specific qualifications of the principle in (a):
       1. All cores in the language have a minimum syntactic valence of 1.
       2. Argument-modulation voice constructions reduce the number of core slots by 1.
       3. The occurrence of a syntactic argument in the pre/postcore slot reduces the number of core slots by 1 (may override 1. above).

The point to mention here is that in all the layered structures of the clause (LSC), including the syntactic templates, the argument (ARG) node has been removed in the newest version of RRG, i.e. Van Valin (2005). In other words, in the previous versions of RRG (Van Valin and LaPolla, 1997), the NP is preceded by the ARG node, while in the revised/modified form ARG has been removed and indeed replaced by NP.

As mentioned before, determining the main syntactic features including selection of appropriate core templates from the syntactic inventory is just part of the linguistic information in the constructional schemas. That is, along with the syntactic representation these schemas provide morphological,

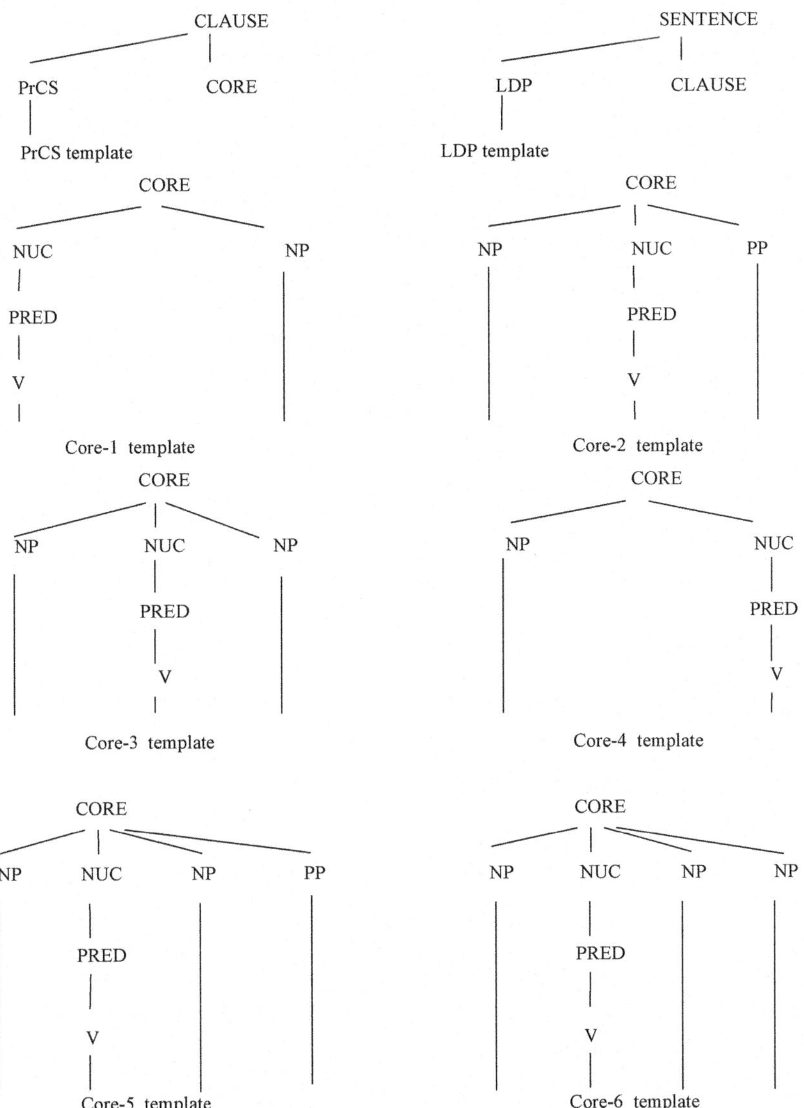

Figure 3.7 English syntactic templates (simplified) from the syntactic inventory (Van Valin, 2005, p. 15).

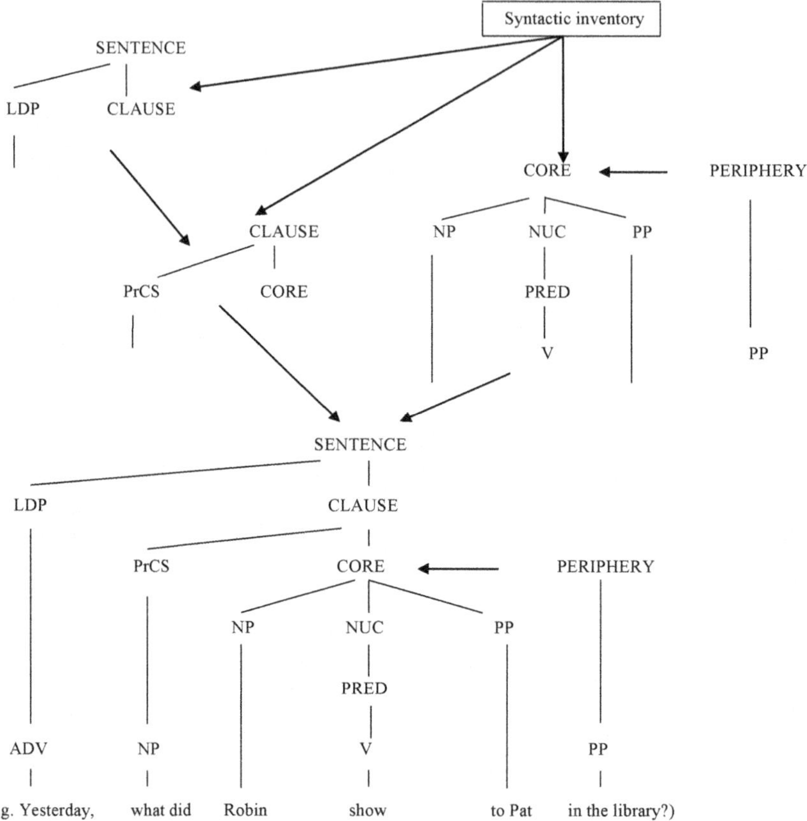

Figure 3.8 Combining syntactic templates from the syntactic inventory (Van Valin, 2005, p. 15).

semantic and pragmatic information. To exemplify these constructional sche-mas, Table 3.4 for the English passive (plain) is cited here from Van Valin (2005, p. 132), the main developer of RRG.

Focusing on the crucial role of the constructional schemas in bidirectional linking of syntax and semantics, Van Valin (2005) proposes a final form of the organization of RRG; an earlier revised form was presented at the begin-ning of this chapter in Figure 3.1. The final schematization of RRG organiza-tion is shown in Figure 3.9.

As mentioned before, constructional schemas have an important role in linking in both directions (Van Valin, 2005), i.e. from syntax to semantics and from semantics to syntax. Since in this study the linking procedure from

Table 3.4 Constructional schema for English passive (plain) (Van Valin, 2005, p. 132)

Construction: English passive (plain)

SYNTAX:
    Template(s): (3.6 b2)
    PSA: (4.15a, c2), Variable [± pragmatic influence]
    Linking: (4.43a)
    (4.43b): omitted or in peripheral *by*-PP
MORPHOLOGY:
    Verb: past participle
    Auxiliary: *be*
SEMANTICS:
    PSA is not instigator of state of affairs but is affected by it (default)
PRAGMATICS:
    Illocutionary force: unspecified
    Focus structure: no restrictions; PSA = topic (default)

PSA, privileged syntactic argument(s).

semantics to syntax is presented, only this linkage direction is discussed in the following section.

3.4.4.2 Linking from semantics to syntax

The latest modified linking procedure from semantics (logical structure) to syntax (layered structure of the clause) presented in Van Valin (2005, p. 136) has been spelled out in (10) below. In this linking procedure there are five major steps followed by some subcategories to capture language-specific variations.

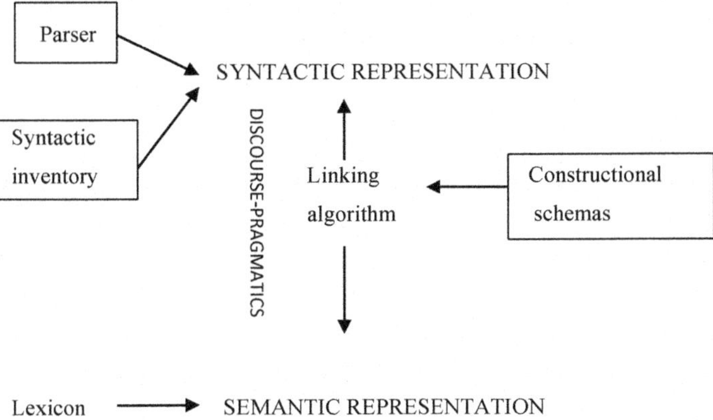

Figure 3.9 Organization of the Role and Reference Grammar (final).

(10)   Linking Algorithm: Semantics ⟶ Syntax
1. Construct the semantic representation of the sentence, based on the logical structure of the predicator.
2. Determine the actor and undergoer assignments, following the actor-undergoer hierarchy in Figure 3.6.
3. Determine the morphosyntactic coding of the arguments.
   a. Select the privileged syntactic argument, based on the privileged syntactic argument selection hierarchy and principles in (11) and (12).
   b. Assign the arguments the appropriate case markers and/or adpositions.
   c. Assign the agreement marking to the main or auxiliary verb, as appropriate.
4. Select the syntactic template(s) for the sentence following the principles in (9).
5. Assign arguments to positions in the syntactic representation of the sentence.
   a. Assign [−WH] argument(s) to the appropriate positions in the clause.
   b. If there is a [+WH] argument of a logical structure,
      1. assign it to the normal position of a non-WH argument with the same function, or
      2. assign it to the precore or postcore slot, or
      3. assign it to a position within the potential focus domain of the clause (default = the unmarked focus position).
   c. A non-WH argument may be assigned to the precore or postcore slot, subject to focus structure restriction (optional).
   d. Assign the [−WH] argument(s) of logical structure(s) other than that of the predicator in the nucleus to
      1. a periphery (default), or
      2. the precore or postcore slot, or
      3. the left- or right-detached position.

In (10) above, in step 3 it is mentioned that in order to determine the morpho-syntactic coding of the arguments the first is to select the Privileged Syntactic Argument (PSA), based on the privileged syntactic argument selection hierarchy and principles. The PSA hierarchy and principles are presented below in (11) and (12), respectively.

(11)   Privileged syntactic argument selection hierarchy:
arg. of DO > 1ˢᵗ arg. of **do′** > 1ˢᵗ arg. of **pred′** (x, y) > 2ⁿᵈ arg. of **pred′** (x, y) arg. of **pred′** (x)

(12)   Accessibility to privileged syntactic argument principles:
a. Accusative constructions: highest ranking direct core argument in terms of (11) (default).
b. Ergative constructions: lowest ranking direct core argument in terms of (11) (default).
c. Restrictions on PSA in terms of macrorole status:
1. Languages in which only macrorole argument can be PSA: German, Italian, Dyirbal, Jakaltek, Sama.
2. Languages in which non-macrorole direct core arguments can be PSA: Icelandic, Georgian, Japanese, Korean, Kinyarwanda.
d. Restrictions on PSA in terms of coding (Bickel, 2003):
1. Languages with case-sensitive PSA (e.g. English, German, Nepali, Maithili).
2. Languages with case-insensitive PSA (e.g. Belhare, Tibetan).

Figure 3.10 (Van Valin, 2005, p. 140) illustrates the linking diagram of an English sentence; that is, it presents the linking algorithm from semantics to syntax following the steps in (10). As is clear from Figure 3.10, the direction of the arrows shows that the linking procedure is from the semantic representation to the syntactic one; that is, the main semantic parameters, namely, the actor and undergoer are determined before the syntactic elements (NP, nucleus (NUC) or PP). In fact, the number besides these semantic/syntactic features indicates the order of steps (presented in (10)) taken in the linking algorithm from semantics to syntax. In the English sentence used in the Figure 3.10, *Sandy* is an actor, the NP *the flowers* is an undergoer, and *presented* is the active verb of the sentence. Also, in this type of linking algorithm (from semantics to syntax) the relationship between the logical structure of the sentence and the semantic/syntactic feature is clearly presented.

3.4.5   Valence, macroroles and transitivity

Role and Reference Grammar is one of the theories that make a clear distinction between syntactic and semantic concepts of valence, which refers to the number of the arguments a verb can take. The syntactic valence of a verb, Van Valin and LaPolla (1997) assert, corresponds to the number of overt

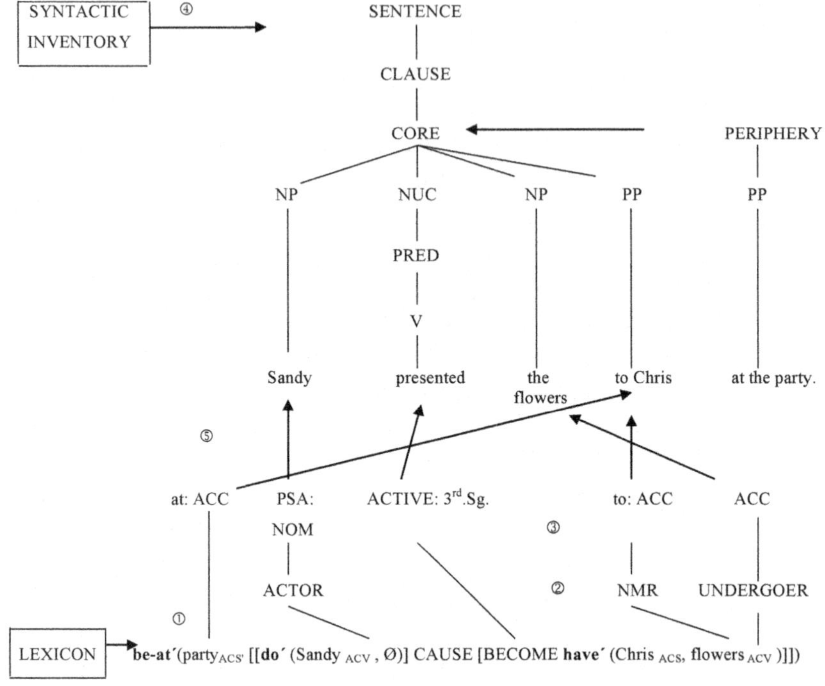

Figure 3.10 Linking diagram (from semantics to syntax) of an English sentence (abbreviation of all the steps). (ACC, Accusative; ACS, Accessible, ACV, Active, Activated; NMR, Non-Macrorole.)

morphosyntactically coded arguments a verb takes. The semantic valence is related to the number of semantic arguments a verb takes (Van Valin and LaPolla, 1997). In RRG, these two types of valence do not need to coincide. As an example, the verb *rain* in English, which usually takes the dummy subject *it,* has no semantic valence while it has one syntactic argument.

Unlike the traditional views, RRG does not equate the notion of syntactic valence with transitivity; rather, it postulates that transitivity is closely related to the number of macroroles a verb takes. In order to differentiate between the number of the syntactic valence and the number of the macroroles of a verb, RRG makes a distinction between the former, referred to as S-transitivity, and the latter as M-transitivity. In the case of the above example (*It rained*), *rain* is an M-atransitive verb with no macrorole ([MR0]) where its S-transitivity does not coincide with its M-transitivity, i.e. $It_{\varnothing}$ *rained* where $_{\varnothing}$ indicates that *it* is not a macrorole. Or in another example, *The man put the book on the table,* the verb *put* (INGR **do′** (x, [**predicate′**

(x) or (x,y)])) has three semantic arguments (the man, the book, the table) but it has two macroroles, an actor and an undergoer; therefore, this verb is M-transitive along with being S-transitive (M-transitivity coincides with S-transitivity for this verb). This can be presented as: The man$_{ACTOR}$ put the book$_{UND}$ on the table$_{\emptyset}$ ($_{UND}$ 'undergoer').

To provide the ground for the main analysis of the present research study, i.e. exploring Persian complex predicates or nuclear junctures (NJs) (as referred to in RRG) and to address the four propositions formulated in Chapter 1, these light verbal constructions, according to Saeedi (2009a), have been categorized into four major groups on the basis of the type of the preverbal element, namely, adjective, noun, adverb and prepositional phrase, two of which, i.e. the adjectival and prepositional NJs, are analyzed and discussed in the following chapters, respectively.

4

Adjectival Predicates

4.0 Introduction

The main aim of the present chapter is to provide a Role and Reference Grammar (RRG) analysis of the semantic and syntactic behaviour of another construction type where an adjective rather than a noun fuses with a light verb (LV), which is referred to here as an adjectival light verbal construction (LVC). It will be argued that RRG architecture allows us to capture LVCs' characteristics as nuclear junctures and provide a unified account of these constructions. To this end, first in Section 4.1 the representation of adjectives in RRG is discussed, and then Section 4.2 goes on to distinguish the attributive and predicative functions of adjectives in Persian. In Sections 4.3, 4.3.1 and 4.3.2 the types of light verbs and adjectives that can combine to form adjectival LVCs are discussed. Section 4.4 examines the aspectual/ Aktionsart of these constructions and Section 4.5 summarizes the findings of this chapter and analyzes the data regarding the event structure (4.5.1) and argument structure (4.5.2), and the adjectival and light verbal elements fusion and lexical-syntactic features are discussed in Section 4.5.3. The nexus-juncture linkage and the constructional schema for these LVCs are explored in Section 4.6. Finally, a summary of the adjectival LVCs' analysis is presented in Section 4.7.

The aim of this chapter (along with the other analytical chapter (5)) is to examine the four propositions (mentioned in Chapter 1). The first and second propositions are investigated by analyzing the event structure, Aktionsart/verb class and the argument structure of the adjectival Persian nuclear junctures, and the third and fourth propositions are scrutinized by examining the semantic and lexical features of these constructions. Along with this line of investigation for these two propositions, the writer will discuss how RRG accounts for the syntactic characteristics of the adjectival LVC in the final chapter (6).

A major focus of this chapter is to identify and correctly characterize the contribution made by the verb and its adjectival complement to the composite construction, the nuclear juncture. As discussed in Chapter 2, light verbs have been identified cross-linguistically as being impoverished in various semantic features, as compared with corresponding heavy lexical verbs, and to 'recruit', so to speak, the missing features from their complement in the formation of the complex predicate. This sharing or fusing of features is taken to be characteristic of this type of construction. The relative contribution of linguistic information from the light verb and its complement in these Persian adjectival LVCs is explored, and the discussion begins first by investigating in Section 4.4 the verb class, or the aspectual properties of the LVC. It begins with this aspect of the semantic content of these LVCs because, as observed in Chapter 3, it is crucial to the representation of clause structure in RRG. Section 4.4 contains a series of diagnostic tests to determine the aspectual properties of these constructions, and Section 4.5 summarizes and discusses the results of the analysis. On the basis of these findings, this section proposes logical structures for the various types of adjectival LVCs. Building on these, Sections 4.5.1 and 4.5.2 examine the amount of contribution of the two light verbal/adjectival elements to the event and argument structures (the syntactic vs. semantic valency). The lexical and syntactic properties of the adjectival LVCs are scrutinized in Section 4.5.3. Section 4.8 proposes constructional schemas for these nuclear junctures, which are the RRG templates summarizing their characteristics at all levels of representation.

4.1 Adjective types

Among the major classes of words, adjectives (along with adverbs) have proved difficult to characterize generally. One reason for this is that adjectives are not a universal word class, i.e. not all languages have a distinct group of words as adjectives. As Van Valin and LaPolla (1997, p. 28) point out, generative theories consider the two classes of noun [+N, −V] and verb [+V, −N] as the only universal categories from which the other two categories, i.e. adjectives and adpositions (adverbs), are derived, denoting the feature of [+N, +V] to adjectives and [−N, −V] to adpositions. Taking Lakhota as an example of a language which lacks the class of adjective, Van Valin and LaPolla (1997, p. 28) note:

> Lakhota ... shows no evidence of having a syntactic category of adjective.
>   There are, to be sure, words meaning 'tall', 'red', etc., but syntactically they either function as predicates, as in *ix?é-thaka ki* (rock-big the) 'the big rock' or they are compounded with the noun they modify, as in *ix?é-thaka ki* (rock-big the) 'the big rock'.

Modern Persian (Farsi), like English, has a distinct class of adjectives, which are not marked for person and number. Mahootian (1997) highlights the features of Persian adjectives, which can be used to identify them. According to her, adjectives in Persian do not show number marking, do not take determiners, do not take particles,[1] do not inflect for tense/aspect, mood, and cannot be preceded by superlative adjectives but can occur in superlative and comparative forms. Mahootian (1997) also points out that the adjectives belong to an open class and are modified by adverbs; they canonically occur before the verb and can appear as the first element in a compound verb, and they follow the nouns they attributively modify with an intervening morpheme called *ezafe* (see Samvelian, 2005, for *ezafe* constructions in Persian) (Mahootian, 1997, p. 133).

According to Payne (1997, p. 63), 'if a language has a morphosyntactically distinct class of adjectives, this group of words is typically used to express the following properties':

Age	(young, old, etc.)
Dimension	(big, little, tall, short, long, etc.)
Value	(good, bad)
Colour	(black, white, red, etc.)
Physical characteristics	(hard, heavy, smooth, etc.)
Shape	(round, square, etc.)
Human property	(jealous, happy, clever, wary, etc.)
Speed	(fast, slow, quick, etc.)

(Payne, 1997, p. 63)

As indicated by Thompson (1988) in his empirical study, there is typically a distinction between the predicating function of adjectives and their function of introducing new referents. Payne (1997) views the former function of adjectives as the prototypical function of verbs as predicators and the latter as the prototypical function of nouns as words that refer to entities. Napoli (1989) highlights the same distinction: claiming that adjectives can play two types of roles in the context they appear; they can act as a modifier or predicator. Referring to Williams' (1980) ideas about the possibility of multiple predicates, Napoli (1989) maintains that multiple predicates are possible in a single clause. She provides the following example from English, in which a single clause embodies two predicates, namely, a verb as *paint* and an adjective as *red*.

(1) We **painted** the barn **red**.

The sentence in (1) is analyzed as a single clause but there are two elements, i.e. the verb *paint* and the (colour) adjective *red*, which operate as the predicate of the sentence. In Napoli's term, *barn* is the only role player of the adjective *red* which is, in fact, its predicate. As mentioned above, Napoli (1989) differentiates between the predicating and modifying roles of adjectives and for the latter she provides the following sentence (2).

(2) We painted the **red** barn.

In (2), the adjective *red* is not part of the predicating mechanism, but rather it is a modifier of the noun *barn* since the result of painting the 'red barn', as Napoli indicates, may be that it turns out blue, as in the sentence below given by Napoli.

(3) We painted the **red** barn blue for a change.

Van Valin and LaPolla (1997) make the same distinction between predicative and attributive adjectives. Predicative adjectives, they claim, can assign arguments and possess a full layered structure, as with the word *proud* in (4) below provided by Van Valin and LaPolla (1997, p. 68). Attributive adjectives, on the other hand, have neither arguments nor a full layered structure (Van Valin and LaPolla, 1997).

(4) Robin is (very) **proud** of Pat.

Similar to the example in (1) given by Napoli (1989), Van Valin and LaPolla (1997, p. 531) illustrate the predicating role of the adjectives, again with the adjective *red*, in the example below and in Figure 4.1, showing its clause structure and associated semantic representation. Note that in Van Valin (2005) the argument (ARG) node has been replaced by its following node (e.g. noun phrase (NP), prepositional phrase (PP)) (i.e. [CORE [NP ...] [NUC ...] [NP ...]), but since some sentences in this study including the above example are cited from Van Valin and LaPolla (1997), in the corresponding Layered Structure of the clause (LSC) ARG has not been removed.

As shown in the layered structure of the sentence in (5) presented in Figure 4.1, the verb *paint* and the adjective *red* form a complex predicate or nuclear juncture (in RRG terms). That is, there are two nuclei both of which are followed by a (predicate) PRED node, indicating that the predicate of the clause is not a single element but rather two constituents, a verb and an

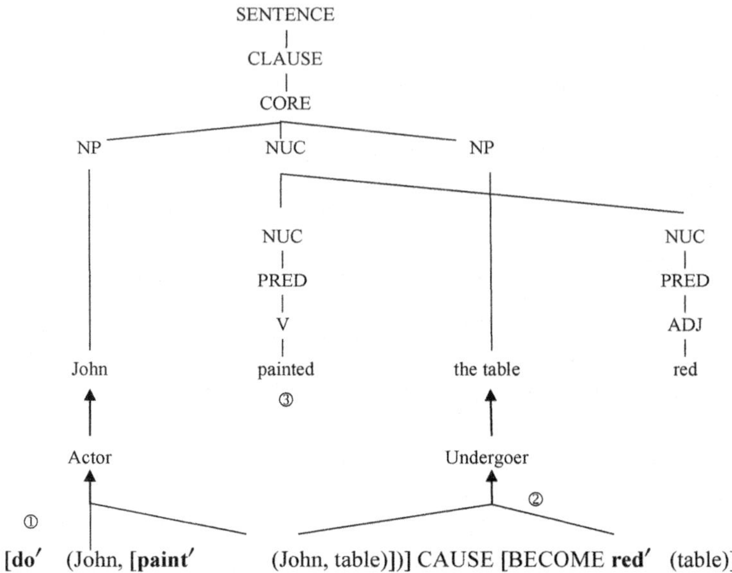

Figure 4.1 Linking from semantics to syntax in English nuclear juncture.

adjective. The adjective *red* is not modifying the undergoer or patient of the sentence, i.e. *table*; rather, it is predicating it, making the adjective a predicative one. There is one undergoer (*table*) and one actor (*John*), showing that the sentence is transitive. The S-transitivity coincides with M-transitivity; that is, the number of the syntactic arguments in the syntactic representation or the LSC of the sentence is equal to the number of semantic arguments in its semantic representation (two macroroles).

(5) John painted the table red.

4.2 Persian adjectives

Following this line of approach, the present study claims that adjectives in Persian function with regard to two crucial parameters: modification and predication. In Persian, the former role of adjectives is achieved when nouns follow them with an intervening *Ezafe* (as 'of' in English) as in (6) below; that is, adjectives in Persian follow the nouns they are modifying.[2] The latter predicating role is fulfilled when adjectives are followed by verbs and complete the meaning of the verb and, as a matter of fact, and as mentioned above, form an adjectival Nuclear Juncture (NJ). In Persian, the verbs that accompany and co-occur with adjectives (in a predicative role) are the copula *budæn* 'be' as in (7), the inchoative light verb *šodæn* 'become' as in (8) and the causative light verb *kærdæn* 'make' as in (9) below. Of these, the copula *budæn* 'be' is the only verb whose combination with the predicative adjective in Persian is not capable of forming a nuclear juncture. Thus, this study claims that adjectival LVCs (in Persian) are formed with the combination of an adjective with the light verbs *šodæn* 'become' and *kærdæn* 'make', as shown later in this study.

(6) pesær-e   šad
    boy-Ez (of)   glad
    'the glad boy'

(7) Ali   šad   bud
    Ali   glad   be-Past.3rd.Sg.
    'Ali was glad.'

(8) Ali   šad   šod.
    Ali   glad   become-Past.3rd.Sg.
    'Ali became glad.'

(9) Ali   dust-æš-ra   šad   kærd.[3]
    Ali   friend-his-DOM   glad   make-Past.3rd.Sg.
    'Ali made his friend glad.'

In (6) above, the human property adjective *šad* 'glad' follows and modifies the noun *pesær* 'boy'. The intervening morpheme *-e* represent the *ezafe* 'of' construction, which conjoins the noun *pesær* 'boy' to its adjective *šad* 'glad'. Therefore, the adjective in (6) is the modifier of the noun and has no predicating role. In (7), (8) and (9), however, the predicating role of the adjective is fulfilled in different degrees. In (7), the adjective *šad* 'glad' is followed by the copula *bud* 'was', which is the inflected form of the verb *budæn* 'be' and is semantically empty, indicating that the whole semantic predicating role is carried by the adjective in the sentence. Following Emonds (1985), Napoli (1989, p. 9) maintains that in adjective/copula constructions the adjective, and not the adjective + copula combination, is the predicate of the sentence since the copula is a grammatical word and, unlike the semantically full lexical items, does not contribute to the semantic interpretation of the sentence it appears in.

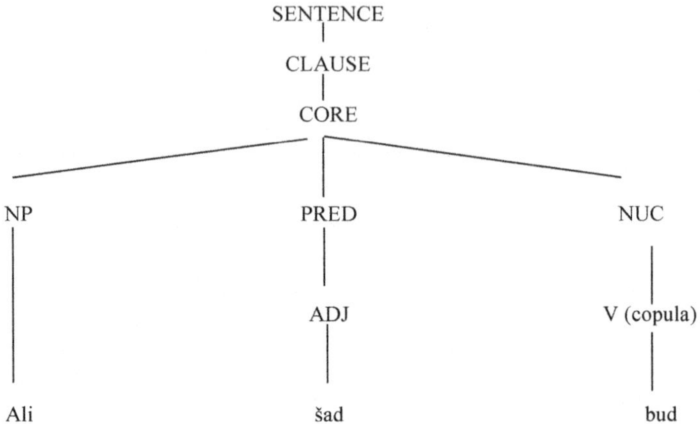

Figure 4.2 LSC of the adjective/copula combination in Persian.

RRG, too, postulates that in adjective/copula combinations the predicating role is fulfilled by the adjective and not the adjective/copula combination. Therefore, in RRG this construction is not viewed as a nuclear juncture, since the adjective in these forms is the only predicating element. In other words, the copula appears in the construction for the nucleus (NUC) formation without performing a predicating function (Van Valin, personal contact). That is, the NUC node in the layered structure of the clause is not followed by the PRED node; rather, the adjective is the element identified by the PRED node, as presented below (the example in (7) is repeated here as (10)).

(10)   Ali   šad   bud.
       Ali   glad   be-Past.3rd.Sg.
       'Ali was glad.'

As shown in Figure 4.2, in the layered structure of the clause for sentence (10), the predicative adjective *šad* 'glad' is dominated by the PRED node and the copula *bud* 'was' is not identified with PRED, to indicate that it does not have a predicating role and is instead functioning as a grammatical nucleus (NUC). The logical structure of the sentence is **be'** (x, [**predicate**]) with the copula *bud* 'was' as **be'**, 'Ali' as the (x), and the adjective *šad* 'glad' as **predicate'**. The copula *bud* is a single-argument stative nucleus in the sentence where the S-intransitivity coincides with its M-intransitivity. Also, on the basis of the thematic relations argued in the previous chapter, it can be concluded that the only argument in the above sentence is the **patient** of the whole proposition.

In the following section, the two adjectival constructions as the main concern of this chapter are examined. They comprise the light verbal constructions with *šodæn* 'become' and *kærdæn* 'make' where these two LVs combine with adjectives. The combination of these elements forms two types of adjectival nuclear junctures, namely, inchoative (*šodæn* 'become') vs. causative (*kærdæn* 'make') light verbal-adjectival NJs. The example in (8) illustrates the former construction, where the predicative adjective *šad* 'glad' conjoins the inchoative light verb *šod* 'became' to form the adjectival nuclear juncture *šad šod* 'became glad.' While (9) represents the latter, where the causative light verb *kærdæn* 'make' combines with the same predicative adjective *šad* 'glad' to build another kind of adjectival LVCs (causative).

4.3 Persian adjectival light verbal constructions

Persian adjectival LVCs have not received much attention in the literature; most analyses have been confined to a very brief description of adjective/light verb combinations and providing a few examples of these structures (Rastorgueva, 1964; Tabaian, 1979; Lambton, 1984 [1953]; Ghomeshi and Massam, 1994; Dabir-Moghaddam, 1997). There are a number of questions that are fundamental to this study and need to be dealt with in a more comprehensive analysis of the adjectival LVCs in Persian. The questions include what kind of adjectives or light verbs occur in the adjectival NJs, what is the semantic status of the LV, what similarities or differences exist between these constructions and other LVC types, how the two constituents contribute to argument and event structures, and how they are formed.

These questions can basically be categorized into two lines of enquiry. The first is descriptive and consists of two parts: first, investigating the nature and type of LVs capable of combining with adjectives, asking what kinds of light verbs fit into these constructions. Secondly, the study seeks to investigate the nature and type of the adjectives that can form these structures with light verbs. The second line of enquiry is analytical and theoretical. Here, the study asked how the two elements in the adjectival LVC fuse together and considered how to represent the analysis within the RRG framework.

4.3.1 *Light verbs in adjectival NJs: nature and type*

To answer the first question (from the first line of enquiry mentioned above), i.e. what kinds of light verbs can combine with non-verbal elements and form nuclear junctures, there is a need to establish a list of the light verbs in Persian. This study addresses the same list of light verbs provided by Karimi-Doostan (1997) presented in (46) in Section 2.3.2 of Chapter 2. These light verbs are, in fact, the commonest LVs used in Persian contexts. Out of the LVs in this list, there are, as mentioned before, basically two that can combine with adjectives, namely, the inchoative unaccusative *šodæn* 'become' and the causative *kærdæn* 'do/make' and their stylistic variant forms: *gæštæn/ gærdidæn* 'become/turn' for *šodæn* 'become' and *saxtæn* 'construct/make', *nemudæn* 'perform/do', *færmudæn* 'perform/do' for *kærdæn* 'do/make'. The above stylistic variant forms, although different in form, are essentially the same in terms of meaning, i.e. the variant forms of *gæštæn/gærdidæn* have the same meaning as *šodæn* and they all mean 'become/turn;' the variant forms of *nemudæn/færmudæn* are similar to *kærdæn* in meaning, i.e. they all mean 'make'. The only difference is in the level of their formality/informality. As an example, a more formal form for the sentence in (8) (*Ali šad šod* 'Ali glad became') is *Ali šad gærdid* 'Ali glad became'.

The light verbs, in general, and in the constructions presented in Section 4.2, as in (8) and (9), in particular, are not as full as heavy/full verbs in terms of semantic content. It will be argued in more detail later in this study that the light verb is not semantically completely empty or bleached, as some Persian analysts such as Vahedi-Langrudi (1996) have claimed. The following figures (illustrating the layered structure of the clause, semantic representation and their linking algorithm from semantics to syntax) for the two examples mentioned before (8, 9) are the way these light verbal/adjectival NJs are analyzed and schematized in RRG. The analysis is specifically based on Van Valin (2005) as the newest version of this theory, where PSA stands for the Privileged Syntactic Argument (subject) regardless of the active or passive status of the predicate of the sentence, NOM for the nominative form of the PSA, ACC (for accusative constructions), which refers to the highest direct core argument according to the privileged syntactic argument principles (given in (12), Section 3.4.4 of Chapter 3), and the numbers are related to the number of steps in the linking procedure of semantics to syntax (Chapter 3, Section 3.4.4). As Van Valin and LaPolla (1997) and Van Valin (2005) point out, both the adjective and the verb in these constructions (as presented in Figures 4.3 and 4.4) act as the nucleus or predicate (as the term 'nuclear

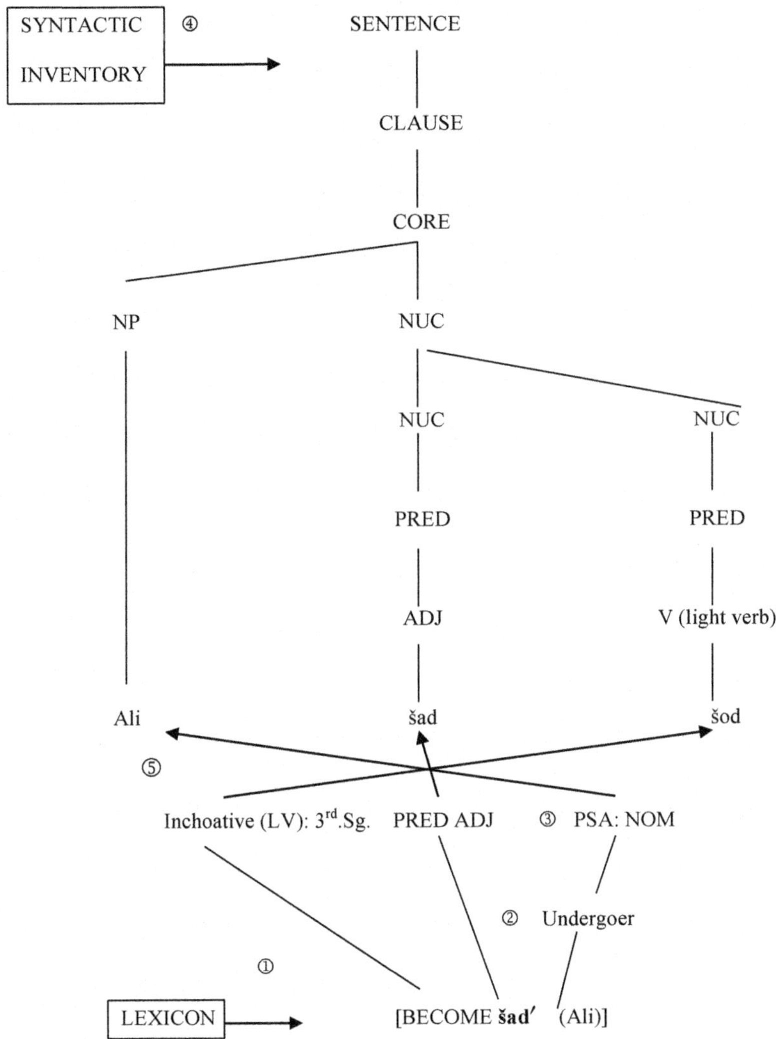

Figure 4.3 LSC for the adjectival/light verbal (inchoative) nuclear juncture and the linking from semantics to syntax.

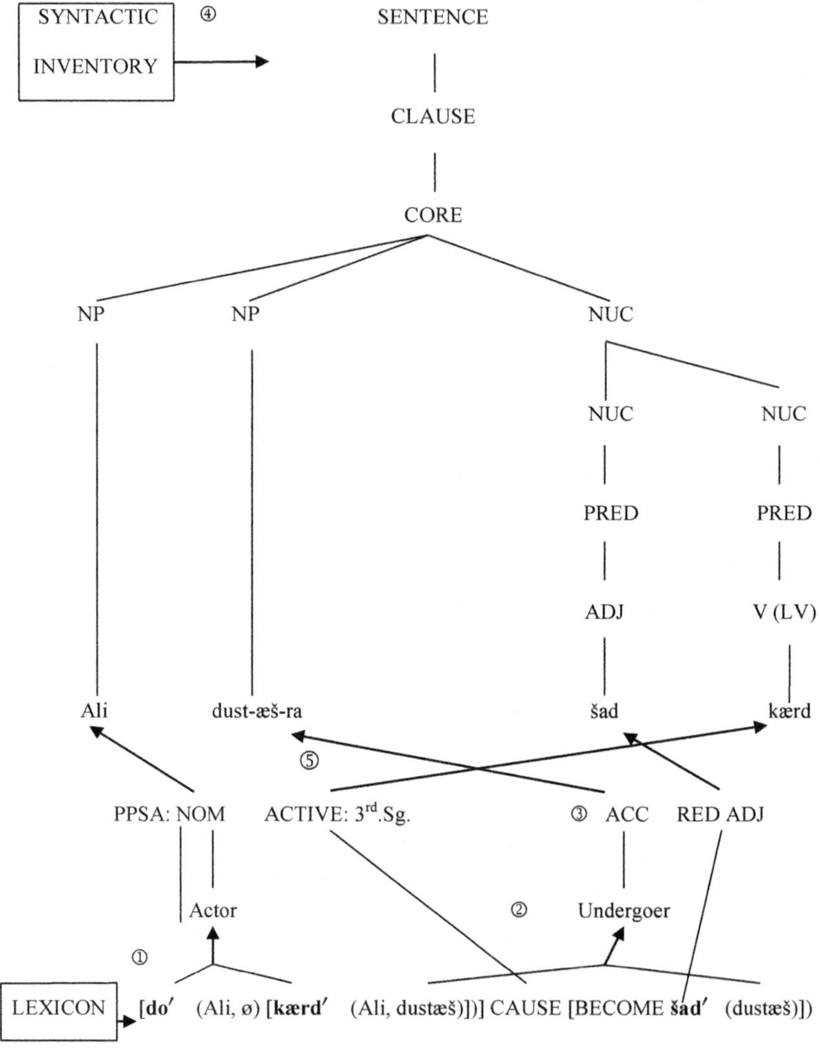

Figure 4.4 LSC for the adjectival/light verbal (causative) nuclear juncture and the linking algorithm from semantics to syntax.

juncture' implies). That is, in the case of the examples in (8) and (9) the adjective *šad* 'glad' along with the light verbal elements *šod* 'became' (in 8) and *kærd* 'made' (in 9) predicates the whole sentence. The point worth paying attention to here is that by replacing the LV *šod* 'became' in (8) by the LV *kærd* 'made' in (9), the logical structure of the whole (nuclear) juncture changes completely. That is, in (8) (with *šod* 'became') there is one argument or macrorole ('Ali'), which is the undergoer. The sentence in (9) with *kærd* 'made', on the other hand, has two macroroles, i.e. an actor (Ali) and an undergoer (*dust-æš*), and there is a causative relationship between the two arguments and both sentences have equal number of S-transitivity and M-transitivity arguments.

Consider the example in (11) (and Figure 4.5) for causative LV *kærd* 'made' in combination with the predicative adjective *narahæt* 'annoyed/ made annoyed' along with the following diagram, which represents the Layered Structure of the Clause (LSC) (in RRG terms) of this construction.

(11)   ali   dust-æš-ra   narahæt   kærd.
       Ali   friend-his-DOM   annoyed.Adj   make-Past-3rd.Sg.
       'Ali made his friend annoyed.'

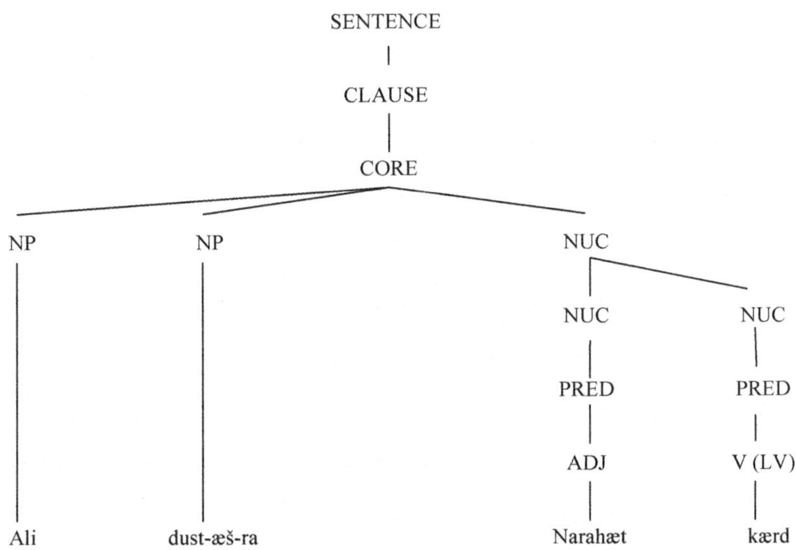

Figure 4.5 LSC for the adjectival/light verbal (causative) nuclear juncture.

The example in (11) is another example of nuclear juncture in which the first nucleus or predicate is an adjective followed by a light verbal element. The whole NJ *narahæt kærd* 'annoyed or made annoyed' bears telic aspectual information, i.e. the LV *kærd* 'made' (using *dær yek sacet* 'in an hour' expression) has a bounded reading. This is clear from the grammaticality of (11a) below, where the predicate occurs with the point adverbial phrase *dær yek sacet* 'in an hour', compared to the ill-formed and unacceptable (11b), where it occurs with a durative adverbial phrase *bæraye yek sacet* 'for an hour'. It can be shown that by replacing the preverbal element *-narahæt* 'annoyed'- with another adjective *-negæran* 'worried'-, which is represented in (11c), the sentence can be interpreted as atelic or unbounded.

(11) a. ali   dust-æš-ra   dær yek sacet narahæt
          kærd.
          Ali   friend-his-DOM   in   an   hour   annoyed.Adj
          make-Past-3rd.Sg.
          'Ali made his friend annoyed in an hour.'

      b. *ali   dust-æš-ra   bæraye yek sacet narahæt
          kærd.
          Ali   friend-his-DOM   for   an   hour   annoyed.Adj.
          make-Past-3rd.Sg.
          'Ali made his friend annoyed for an hour.'

      c. ali   dust-æš-ra   bæraye yek sacet negæran
          kærd.
          Ali   friend-his-DOM   for   an   hour   worried.Adj.
          make-Past-3rd.Sg.
          'Ali made his friend worried for an hour.'

(Note: The asterisk before the example sentence in (11b) denotes its ungrammaticality.)

A fundamental characteristic of these LVCs with light verbs is that part of the semantic load of the predicate is carried by the preverbal adjective, for example, *narahæt* 'annoyed' in (11a) and (11b). In order to determine the role of the light verb in the above nuclear junctures, the verbal element *kærd* 'did/made' may be replaced with the inchoative counterpart *šod* 'became', as shown in (11d) below. The expression *dær yek sacet* 'in an hour' can also be added to test whether there would be a change in the transition telicity of the nuclear juncture of (11a); that is, whether the change of the verbal element from *kærd* 'did/made' in (11a) to *šod* 'became' in (11d) has any effect on the bounded/unbounded reading of the construction.

> (11) d. dust-e   ali dær yek sæt narahæt šod.
>   friend-Ez Ali in   an   hour annoyed   become-Past.3rd.Sg.
>   'Ali's friend became annoyed in an hour.'

As is clear from (11d) above, there is no change in the telicity interpretation of the nuclear juncture; that is, the sentence in (11d) is quite well-formed and grammatical with the expression *dær yek sæt* 'in an hour'. Contrary to Megerdoomian's (2001b) claim, it is not always the light verb which contributes the aspectual information to the LVC, and as is observed in the NJs in (11a) and (11d) the LVC *narahæt šod* 'became annoyed' in (11d) has a telic interpretation like the construction in (11a), which implies that the change of the light verb had no effect on the transition/initiatory reading of the junctures. It can be noted, though, that the change in the light verbal element from *kærd* 'made' to *šod* 'became' does affect the argument structure of the LVC. The nuclear junctures in (11a) are a transitive/causative construction, while (11d) has an unaccusative/inchoative predicate status. This supports the idea that the LV in the adjectival NJs denotes its valency in these constructions.

Another important point regarding the adjectival LVCs is the fact that there is no agreement on adjectives. The following examples (11e)–(11g), which are different forms of the same sentence in (11), illustrate this characteristic of adjectives in Persian.

> (11) e. ali   dust-an-æš-ra   narahæt   kærd.
>   Ali   friends-Pl-his-DOM   annoyed.Adj.   make-Past.3rd.Sg.
>   'Ali made his friends annoyed.'
> (11) f. ali   bæradær-æš-ra   narahæt   kærd.
>   Ali   brother-his-DOM   annoyed.Adj   make-Past.3rd.Sg.
>   'Ali made his brother annoyed.'
> (11) g. ali   xahær-æš-ra   narahæt   kærd.
>   Ali   sister-his-DOM   annoyed.Adj.   make-Past.3rd.Sg.
>   'Ali made his sister annoyed.'

In (11e), the word *dust* 'friend' has been replaced with the plural form *dustan* 'friends', in order to determine if there is any type of agreement in number between the adjective *narahæt* 'annoyed' and the noun *dust* 'friend' in (11). To investigate the gender agreement this nominal element, i.e. *dust* 'friend', has been replaced with *bæradær* 'brother' in (11f) and *xahær* 'sister' in (11g). Again, no gender agreement is observed between the nominal and adjectival elements; that is, for both male *bæradær* 'brother' in (11f) and female *xahær* 'sister' in (11g) words, the adjective *narahæt* 'annoyed' is the same.

Like *šodæn* 'become', the causative LV *kærdæn* 'do/make', where combined with an adjective, cannot be an auxiliary. In (12) below, *kærdæn* 'do/ make' assigns an external argument role to 'Ali', meaning that 'Ali' is the subject or the privileged syntactic argument (in RRG's term) of the NJ *æsæbani kærd* 'made angry', while (contrary to Dabir-Moghaddam (1997), who refers to *kærdæn* 'make' combined with adjectives as an auxiliary verb), auxiliaries are not capable of this operation, i.e. *kærdæn* cannot be an auxiliary.

(12)   ali   dust-æš-ra   æsæbani   kærd.
       Ali   friend-his-DOM   angry   make-Past.3rd.Sg.
       'Ali made his friend angry.'

As is clear from the sentence in (12), *kærd* 'made' is a causative verb. This light verb, as mentioned earlier, is capable of assigning an external argument role to 'Ali', highlighting him as the privileged syntactic argument of the whole sentence. It should be noted that in Persian the use of LVs is one of a number of strategies for forming causative constructions. Dabir-Moghaddam (1982) divides these constructions into two major groups, Periphrastic and Lexical, each of which was further subdivided into a number of other categories. The causatives formed with *kærdæn* 'make' are classified under the lexical causative constructions. In his analysis, Dabir-Moghaddam (1997) refers to *kærdæn* as a causative auxiliary, since it combines with other elements to form causative constructions. In fact, *kærdæn* 'do/make' can be used in both transitive causative (as in (12), where *kærdæn* means 'make') and intransitive forms (as in (13) below, where *kærdæn* means 'do'). The following illustrates the latter form of *kærdæn* 'do' in Persian.

(13)   pærænde   pærvaz   kærd.
       bird   flying   do-Past.3rd.Sg.
       'The bird flew.'

The example in (13) represents the intransitive usage of the verb *kærdæn* with the meaning of 'do', i.e. 'the bird does the flying'. But the important point to mention here is that the preverbal constituent in (13) is not an adjective, but a noun. In order to examine whether adjectives, too, can be used with the intransitive usage of the LV *kærdæn* 'do', the Persian data were investigated. As a result of this examination, it became clear that only one of the eight groups of adjectives mentioned earlier, the **value** adjectives, can be used with the intransitive form of the verb *kærdæn* with the meaning 'do'. The following example (14) shows the intransitive usage of this verb with the 'value' adjective 'bad'.

> (14) Ali be dust-æš   bæd kærd.
> Ali to friend-his bad do-Past.3rd.Sg.
> 'Ali did bad to his friend.'

Unlike (12), in which *kærd* has the meaning of 'made' and acts as a transitive/causative verb, in (14), the LV *kærd* means 'did' and is an unaccusative intransitive verb, the noun *dust* 'friend' is an oblique argument, and '*Ali*' is the subject or the privileged syntactic argument of the sentence. The value adjective 'bad', along with the LV *kærd* in (14), make an adjectival nuclear juncture which is not a causative construction, i.e. *kærd* means 'did' (and not 'made'), operating as an intransitive verb rather than a transitive one.

4.3.2 Adjectives in adjectival NJs: nature and type

At the beginning of Section 4.3, two questions (based on the first line of enquiry related to the descriptive aspect of this study) regarding the adjectival LVCs were posed. Section 4.3.1 aimed at providing an answer to the first question on the nature and type of the light verbs which are capable of combining with adjective. The focus of the present section is on answering the second question regarding the nature and type of the adjectives that fit into the adjectival nuclear junctures. Vahedi-Langrudi (1996), citing Milsark (1977), points out that individual level adjectives do not enter the realm of complex predicate constructions with causative light verbal elements because changing an individual's permanent trait is not possible under normal circumstances (Vahedi-Langrudi, 1996, p. 9). However, this study agrees with Vahedi-Langrudi, who remarks that such individual level adjectives as *aqel* 'wise' can be acceptable in Persian when combined with the unaccusative LV *šodæn* 'become/turn' as shown in (15) below, while not acceptable with the causative LV *kærdæn* 'make/do' as in (16).

(15)   aqel   šodæn
       wise   become
       'become wise'

(16)   *aqel   kærdæn
        wise   make
        'make wise'

(Vahedi-Langrudi, 1996, p. 10)

In general, adjectives are of three major types, i.e. in terms of the number of elements involved in adjectival forms they include three groups: simple, compound and participle adjectives. Examples from each of these groups are presented below.

(17)   ræftar-e   an   bačče   madær-æš-ra   negæran   kærd.
       behaviour-Ez   that child   mother-his/her-DOM   worried   made
       'That child's behaviour made his/her mother worried.'

(18)   ræftar-e   an   bæčče   madær-æš-ra   del-negæran
       kærd.
       behaviour-Ez   that child   mother-his/her-DOM   heart-worried
       made
       'That child's behaviour made his/her mother worried.'

(19)   ræftar-e   an   bæčče   madær-æš-ra   ašofte   kærd.
       behaviour-Ez   that child   mother-his/her-DOM   agitated made
       'That child's behaviour made his/her mother agitated.'

In (17) above, the adjective *negæran* 'worried' is a plain adjective that is not derived from other classes of words and is a one-word adjective. In (18), on the other hand, the adjective *del-negæran* (Lit.: 'heart-worried') is a compound adjective comprising two words *del* 'heart' and *negæran* 'worried'. Unlike the adjectives in (17) and (18), the adjective *ašofte* 'agitated' in (19) is derived from another word, i.e. the verb *ašoftæn* 'make agitated/upset' in Persian. As a matter of fact, the deverbal adjective *ašofte* 'agitated' is the past participle of the verb *ašoftæn* 'upset/make upset or agitated'. All the sentences in (17), (18) and (19), as is clear from *kærd* 'made', are causative/ transitive constructions in which all the adjectives are predicate adjectives denoting an event or action.

The simple, compound and past participle or derived adjective can also combine with the inchoative/unaccusative LV *šodæn* 'become' to form adjectival nuclear junctures. The inchoative/intransitive forms of the examples in (17)–(19) can be illustrated as (17′)–(19′) below.

(17′) madær negæran šod.
mother worried become-Past.3rd.Sg.
'The mother became worried.'

(18′) madær del-negæran šod.
mother heart-worried become-Past.3rd.Sg.
'The mother became worried.'

(19′) madær ašofte šod.
mother agitated become.Past.3rd.Sg.
'The mother became agitated/upset.'

In the above sentences (17–19, 17′–19′) the LVs *kærdæn* 'make/do' and *šodæn* 'become/turn' represent their capability to make nuclear junctures with all types of adjectives mentioned above, namely, simple, compound and past participle forms. The important point to be taken into consideration here regarding the compound adjectives exemplified in (18) is that the element with which adjectives are combined can precede (like *del-negæran*, Lit.: 'heart-worried' in (18, 18′), where the noun *del* 'heart' precedes the adjective *negæran*) or follow it, as in *ašofte-xater* 'disturb-minded' given in (20) below, where the noun *xater* 'mind' is attached to the end of the adjective *ašofte* 'disturbed'.

(20) ræftar-e an bæčče madær-æš-ra
ašofte-xater kærd.
behaviour-Ez that child mother-his/her-DOM
disturb-minded made.
'That child's behaviour made his mother disturb-minded/agitated.'

In terms of the adjective type of the preverbal element in the adjectival nuclear junctures and, as mentioned before, this study has adopted Payne's (1997, p. 63) categorization, where adjectives are divided into eight major categories: **age, dimension, value, colour, physical characteristics, shape, human property** and **speed**. In fact, the three types of adjectives (discussed above), namely, simple, compound and even participle adjectives, can be classified under one of these eight groups on the basis of their internal semantic load (e.g. *ašoft-e kærdæn* 'make agitated' in (19) above can be placed under the category of 'human property' adjective), and that is why Payne's categories have been considered as the core concern of this section. In Persian, almost all the adjectives of these eight categories can combine with both *kærdæn* 'make/do' and *šodæn* 'become/turn'. The following examples (*kærdæn*: 21–28, *šodæn*: 21′–28′) illustrate the adjectival categories of age, dimension, value, colour, physical characteristics, shape, human property and speed:

Age adjective

> (21)   an   hadese   u-ra   pir   kærd.
> that accident him/her old make-Past.3ʳᵈ.Sg
> 'That accident made him/her old.'

> (21′)   u   be xatere   an   hadese   pir   šod.
> He/She to because that accident old become-Past.3rd.Sg.
> 'He became old because of that accident.'

Dimension adjective

> (22)   Mina   qesse-æš-ra   kutah   kærd.
> Mina story-her-DOM short make-Past.3ʳᵈ.Sg.
> 'Mina made her story short/shortened her story.'

> (22′)   qesse-ye Mina kutah šod.
> story-Ez Mina short become-Past.3rd.Sg.
> 'Mina's story became short.'

Value adjective

> (23)   Ali be xod-æš bæd kærd.
> Ali to self-his bad do-Past.3ʳᵈ.Sg.
> 'Ali did wrong/bad (things) to himself.'

> (23′)   nætije-ye   kar-e   Ali bæd šod.
> result-Ez (of) action-Ez Ali bad became-Past.3ʳᵈ.Sg.
> 'The result of Ali's action became bad.'

Colour adjective

(24) an-ha   xane-ešan-ra   abi   kærd-ænd.
that-Pl. house-their-DOM   blue   make.Past.3rd.-Pl.
'They made their house blue.'

(24´) xane   an-ha   abi   šod.
house   that-Pl.   blue   become-Past.3rd.Sg.
'Their house became blue.'

Physical characteristics adjective

(25) lebas-ha   čæmedan-ra   sængin   kærd.
clothes-Pl.   suitcase-DOM   heavy   make-Past.3rd.Pl.
'The clothes made the suitcase heavy.'

(25´) čæmedan   sængin   šod.
suitcase   heavy   become-Past.3rd.Sg.
'The suitcase became heavy.'

Shape adjective

(26) an-ha   mæsir-e   mosabeqe-ye   do-ra   gerd
kærd-ænd.
that-Pl.   route-Ez   race-Ez   running-DOM   round
make-Past.3rd.-Pl.
'They made the route of the running race round.'

(26´) mæsir-e   mosabeqe-ye   do   gerd   šod.
route-Ez   race-Ez   running   round   become-Past.3rd.Pl.
'The route of the running race became round.'

Human property adjective

(27) nomre-ye   xub-æš   dær   emtehan   u-ra   xošhal
kærd.
mark-Ez   good-his/her   in   exam   him/her   happy
make-Past.3rd.Sg.
'His/Her good mark in the exam made him/her happy.'

(27′) u   xošhal šod.
      He/She   happy   become-Past.3rd.Sg.
      'He/She became happy.'

Speed adjective

(28)   dočærxe sævar soræt-æš-ra   tond
       kærd.
       bicycle   rider   speed-his/her-DOM   quick/fast
       make-Past.3rd.Sg.
       'The cyclist made his speed fast/accelerated.'

(28′) soræt-e   dočærxe sævar tond   šod.
       speed-Ez bicycle   rider   quick/fast become-Past.3rd.Sg.
       'The speed of the cyclist became fast.'

As is clear from the examples, all the sentences with the LV *kærdæn* 'make/ do' in (21)–(28) do have equivalent forms with the LV *šodæn* 'become/turn' in (21′)–(28′); that is, all the causative/transitive sentences with *kærdæn* 'make/do' have inchoative/unaccusative/intransitive forms with *šodæn* 'become/turn'. In the meantime, all the adjectives in the eight mentioned categories can combine with the two LVs (*kærdæn* and *šodæn*) to form LVCs. The LV *kærdæn*, as mentioned before, has two meanings: 'make' and 'do'. The point worth mentioning here is that the only group of adjectives in which this LV (*kærdæn*) can appear with the second meaning, i.e. 'do', as mentioned before, is the **value** adjectives. The LV *kærdæn* has only the meaning of 'make' when accompanied by the other seven adjectival forms.

Along with the forms and types of the adjectives discussed above, the amount of the semantic load contributed by the adjectival elements is of crucial importance. Although, as mentioned before, the LVs are not semantically completely bleached elements and contribute to the argument structure, transitivity and aspectual information, the main semantic load is carried by the adjective. Consider the following examples.

(29)   pedær-æš xæste šod.
       father-his tired   become-Past.3rd.Sg.
       'His father became tired.'

(30) kar-e   ziyad   pedær-æš-ra   xæste   kærd.
      work-Ez   much   father-his-DOM   tired   make-Past.3rd.Sg.
      'Overwork made his father tired.'

The matrix semantic load of the two nuclear junctures, *xæste šod* 'became tired' in (29) and *xæste kærd* 'made tired' in (30), which is indeed 'the tiredness of the father' is the same even though the light verbs (*šod* 'became' and *kærd* 'made') used in the sentences are different.

In fact, the claim made in this section is contrary to what a number of Persian analysts have postulated. Tabaian (1979) claims that in Persian there are four auxiliaries, *kærdæn* 'do/make', *šodæn* 'become', *budæn* 'be' and *daštæn* 'to have', capable of combining with adjectives, nouns and adverbs. Dabir-Moghaddam (1997) adds to these two verbs *kærdæn* and *šodæn*, which he refers to as auxiliaries, and the verb *budæn* 'be', which, he claims, can also be used with adjectives to form complex predicates. According to Dabir-Moghaddam (1997), there are three auxiliary verbs that can combine with adjectives, namely, *budæn, šodæn* and *kærdæn*. Ghomeshi and Massam (1994), on the other hand, refer to the verbal elements combined with adjectives (including the participle adjectives such as *pærakænde* 'scattered') as light verbs. Also, Karimi-Doostan (1997) claims that the verbal elements *kærdæn* 'do/make' and *šodæn* 'become' are light verbs, while the verb *daštæn* 'have' (discussed in Chapter 4) is an auxiliary in Persian. Unlike Karimi-Doostan (1997), Mahootian (1997, p. 262) believes that the verbal elements *budæn* 'be' and *šodæn* 'become', when used with the predicative adjectives such as *æsæbani* 'angry' are, in fact, both copulas. In this study, i.e. Section 2.3.2 of Chapter 2, however, it was proposed that *budæn* 'be' should be considered as a copula, and the LV *šodæn* 'become' as an inchoative light verb, while *kærdæn* 'make' is a causative light verbal element (both are used in the adjectival nuclear junctures).

In sum, an attempt has been made to answer the two questions posed at the beginning of this chapter regarding the type and nature of the light verbs and adjectives in the adjectival LVCs. In the following part of the present chapter (Section 4.4) the focus is on the second line of the enquiry (posed in Section 4.3 above): how to characterize the fusing of the two elements and to determine the role of each of these elements in formulating the aspect type of the predicates in these constructions, since this is a fundamental step in RRG towards establishing the logical structure of predicates.

4.4 Aspectual/Aktionsart type of adjectival NJs

In this section, the aspectual properties of the adjectival LVCs are explored in order to characterize the two elements' fusion and to determine the role each element can play in the argument structure of the whole proposition, which are the issues related to the second line of enquiry mentioned at the beginning of Section 4.3 of the present chapter. The same diagnostic tests (introduced in Section 3.4.1 of Chapter 3) are applied to the adjectival nuclear junctures. Each test is separately applied to the sentences given in Section 4.3 for different adjectival categories of **age, dimension, value, colour, physical characteristics, shape, human property** and **speed**. The tests are given in Appendix A and the sentences used in this appendix are the same as those in Section 4.3.2, with the exception that they are marked as (a)–(e) related to the five tests (i.e. all the examples related to the first test, which is used to distinguish state verbs from other verb classes (activity, achievement, accomplishment), are marked as (a), the second test used for identifying activity verbs as (b), the third test applied to identifying achievement verb class as (c), the fourth test as (d), and the fifth test as (e); the fourth and the fifth tests are used to distinguish achievement and accomplishment from state and activity verbs). In fact, in Section 4.3.2 the examples in (21)–(30) are devoted to the LV *kærdæn* 'make/do' and the sentences in (21′)–(30)′ to the LV *šodæn* 'become', which indicates that in Appendix A, too, those numbers without the (′) sign are related to *kærdæn* 'make/do' and those with (′) correspond to *šodæn*. The tests (along with the adjective type) are mentioned briefly in each part. The results of the application of the five diagnostic tests to the mentioned sentences are presented in Tables 4.1–4.5.

The findings of applying test 1 to the adjectival LVCs, presented in Table 4.1, indicate that their behaviour is not consistent using the progressive expression *dær hal-e* 'in process of'. The two LVs *kærdæn* 'make' and *šodæn* 'become' cause the sentences in (23a) and (23′a) with the value adjective, in (25a) and (25′a) with the physical characteristics adjective, and in (27a) and (27′a) with the human property adjective to be ungrammatical and ill-formed. On the contrary, the combination of these two LVs (*kærdæn* and *šodæn*) with the age adjective in (21a) and (21′a), with the dimension adjective in (22a) and (22′a), the colour adjective in (24a) and (24′a), the speed adjective in (28a) and (28′a), and finally with the shape adjective in (26a) and (26′a) has made well-*formed* and acceptable sentences. The result of the second test application is shown in Table 4.2.

Table 4.1 Result of the application of the first Aktionsart test to the Persian adjectival NJs with the light verbs *kærdæn* 'make/do' and *šodæn* 'become' and the eight adjective types

Adjective type	Test 1		Adjective type	Test 1	
Age	kærdæn:	Yes	Physical	kærdæn:	No
	šodæn:	Yes	characteristics	šodæn:	No
Dimension	kærdæn:	Yes	Shape	kærdæn:	Yes
	šodæn:	Yes		šodæn:	Yes
Value	kærdæn:	No	Human property	kærdæn:	No
	šodæn:	No		šodæn:	No
Colour	kærdæn:	Yes	Speed	kærdæn:	Yes
	šodæn:	Yes		šodæn:	Yes

Table 4.2 Result of the application of the second Aktionsart test to the Persian adjectival NJs with the light verbs *kærdæn* 'make/do' and *šodæn* 'become' and the eight adjective types

Adjective type	Test 2		Adjective type	Test 2	
Age	kærdæn:	No	Physical	kærdæn:	No
	šodæn:	No	characteristics	šodæn:	No
Dimension	kærdæn:	No	Shape	kærdæn:	No
	šodæn:	No		šodæn:	No
Value	kærdæn:	No	Human property	kærdæn:	No
	šodæn:	No		šodæn:	No
Colour	kærdæn:	No	Speed	kærdæn:	Yes
	šodæn:	No		šodæn:	Yes

Interestingly, as shown in Table 4.2, almost all the adjectival LVCs behave consistently with regard to the second test, i.e. the use of the adverb *fæalane* 'actively'. In other words, with the exception of the speed adjective/*kærdæn* combination in (28b), where the sentence is acceptable using *fæalane,* the rest of the adjective types do not behave grammatically in combination with the two LVs (*kærdæn* and *šodæn*) along with the mentioned adverb. That is, they are ill-formed. The findings of the third diagnostic test are summarized in Table 4.3.

In the process of applying the third test (the use of the adverb 'slowly' (*aheste*)), the result of which is presented in Table 4.3, it became clear that the two LVs (*kærdæn* and *šodæn*) yield compatible results with regard to all adjective types; that is, wherever the LV *kærdæn* 'make' in combination with a particular adjective is well-formed, the LV *šodæn* 'become' is grammatical, too. In sum, these two LVs in (21c) and (21´c) with the age adjective, in (22c) and (22´c) with the dimension adjective, in (24c) and (24´c) with the colour adjective, in (25c) and (25´c) with the shape adjective, and last in (28c) and (28´c) with the speed adjective form grammatical and acceptable sentences. On the contrary, the nuclear junctures with these LVs make ill-formed sentences with the value adjectives in (23c) and (23´c), with the physical characteristics adjectives in (25c) and (25´c), and finally with the human property adjectives in (27c) and (27´c). The result of the fourth test application procedure is presented in Table 4.4.

With regard to the result of the fourth test (the use of the expression *bæraye yek saæt* 'for an hour'), shown in Table 4.4, the behaviour of all the LVCs formed with the adjectival preverbal elements and the LV *kærdæn* 'make/do' is compatible with that of the LV *šodæn* 'become'. Out of the eight pairs of the adjectival LVCs, only one pair forms grammatical and acceptable sentences with the expression *baraye yek saæt* 'for an hour', i.e. the sentences with the speed adjective in (28d) with *kærdæn* and in (28´d) with *šodæn*. The other seven pairs with other adjective types are ill-formed using the same expression. The result of the final test is schematized in Table 4.5.

The findings of the application of test 5 (the use of the expression *dær yek saæt* 'in an hour') to the various adjectival nuclear junctures, as presented in Table 4.5, indicate that the sentences in (21e) and (21´e) with the age adjective, in (22e) and (22´e) with the dimension adjective, in (24e) and (24´e) with the colour adjective, and finally in (26e) and (26´e) with the shape adjective are quite acceptable in Persian. Unlike these sentences, the examples with the value adjective in (23e) and (23´e), with the physical characteristics adjective in (25e) and (25´e), with the human property adjective in (27e) and (27´e), and with the speed adjective in (28e) and (28´e) form ill-formed sentences.

The crucial point worth noticing here is that the result of applying the tests to all the sentences with the LV *kærdæn* 'make/do' is the same as those with the LV *šodæn* 'become'. In other words, whenever a sentence with the combination of an adjective and the light verb *kærdæn* 'make/do' is ill-formed, the sentence with the nuclear juncture of that adjective and the light verb *šodæn* 'become' is ill-formed and yields the same result. And whenever a test causes the sentence with *kærdæn* to be acceptable, the same story takes place with the combination of the same adjective and *šodæn*. This indicates that the change in the light verbal element has no major role in characterizing the aspect type of the whole nuclear juncture. On the contrary, the adjectival nuclear junctures that have the same adjective type yield the same verb class even though they may have different LVs.

Table 4.3 Result of the application of the third Aktionsart test to the Persian adjectival NJs with the light verbs *kærdæn* 'make/do' and *šodæn* 'become' and the eight adjective types

Adjective type	Test 3		Adjective type	Test 3	
Age	kærdæn:	Yes	Physical	kærdæn:	No
	šodæn:	Yes	characteristics	šodæn:	No
Dimension	kærdæn:	Yes	Shape	kærdæn:	Yes
	šodæn:	Yes		šodæn:	Yes
Value	kærdæn:	No	Human property	kærdæn:	No
	šodæn:	No		šodæn:	No
Colour	kærdæn:	Yes	Speed	kærdæn:	Yes
	šodæn:	Yes		šodæn:	Yes

Table 4.4 Result of the application of the fourth Aktionsart test to the Persian adjectival NJs with the light verbs *kærdæn* 'make/do' and *šodæn* 'become' and the eight adjective types

Adjective type	Test 4		Adjective type	Test 4	
Age	kærdæn:	No	Physical	kærdæn:	No
	šodæn:	No	characteristics	šodæn:	No
Dimension	kærdæn:	No	Shape	kærdæn:	No
	šodæn:	No		šodæn:	No
Value	kærdæn:	No	Human property	kærdæn:	No
	šodæn:	No		šodæn:	No
Colour	kærdæn:	No	Speed	kærdæn:	Yes
	šodæn:	No		šodæn:	Yes

Table 4.5 Result of the application of the fifth Aktionsart test to the Persian adjectival NJs with the light verbs *kærdæn* 'make/do' and *šodæn* 'become' and the eight adjective types

Adjective type	Test 5		Adjective type	Test 5	
Age	kærdæn:	Yes	Physical	kærdæn:	No
	šodæn:	Yes	characteristics	šodæn:	No
Dimension	kærdæn:	Yes	Shape	kærdæn:	Yes
	šodæn:	Yes		šodæn:	Yes
Value	kærdæn:	No	Human property	kærdæn:	No
	šodæn:	No		šodæn:	No
Colour	kærdæn:	Yes	Speed	kærdæn:	No
	šodæn:	Yes		šodæn:	No

Table 4.6 Tests for determining Aktionsart type of Persian adjectival NJ

Adjective type	NJ	Test 1	Test 2	Test 3	Test 4	Test 5
Age	pir kærd 'made old'	Yes	No	Yes	No	Yes
	pir šod 'became old'	Yes	No	Yes	No	Yes
Dimension	kutah kærd 'made short'	Yes	No	Yes	No	Yes
	kutah šod 'became short'	Yes	No	Yes	No	Yes
Value	bæd kærd 'did wrong/bad'	No	No	No	No	No
	bæd šod 'became bad'	No	No	No	No	No
Colour	abi kærd 'made blue'	Yes	No	Yes	No	Yes
	abi šod 'became blue'	Yes	No	Yes	No	Yes
Physical characteristics	sængin kærd 'made heavy'	No	N	No	No	No
	sængin šod 'became heavy'	No	No	No	No	No
Shape	gerd kærd 'round made'	Yes	No	Yes	No	Yes
	gerd šod 'became round'	Yes	No	Yes	No	Yes
Human property	xošhal kærd 'made happy'	No	No	No	No	No
	xošhal šod 'became happy'	No	No	No	No	No
Speed	tond kærd 'made quick'	Yes	Yes	Yes	Yes	No
	tond šod 'became quick'	Yes	Yes	Yes	Yes	No

The summary of the findings for the five Aktionsart tests for the Persian adjectival LVCs or nuclear junctures (NJs) with different adjective types (given in Appendix A) are presented in Table 4.6. As is clear from this table, the test application has yielded some interesting results, i.e. all the adjectival nuclear junctures are divided into three groups. The first group comprises the four adjectival LVCs with the age, dimension, colour and shape adjectives. For these constructions, there are three 'yes' results for the first, third and fifth tests and two 'no' results for the second and fourth tests, which indicates that these constructions belong to the accomplishment verb class. On the contrary, for the second group, which consists of the three adjectival LVCs with the value, physical characteristics and human property adjectives (which appear in bold form in the table), the result for all tests is 'no', indicating that they belong to the achievement class. Finally, the result of the third group, which embodies the nuclear juncture with the speed adjective, is 'yes' for all the tests except the fifth test with the 'no' result, where it belongs to the activity aspect type. In other words, the difference in the adjective types of these three groups has caused them to behave differently with regard to the test application. This interesting finding will be dealt with in more detail in Sections 4.5 and 4.5.1.

On the basis of the outcome of the diagnostic tests applied to the adjectival LVCs with different adjective types, the verb classes of these Persian nuclear junctures are determined and then summarized in Table 4.7, Section 4.5 below. In fact, by applying these diagnostic tests the semantic classification is established and the basis for the semantic representation of the predicate and the logical structure of the constructions is provided.

4.5 Discussion

As mentioned above, the findings of the adjectival NJs examination are presented in Table 4.7. In this table, the aspect types of all the adjectival/light verbal nuclear junctures along with their logical structures are presented. The basic verb classes of these NJs have been divided into activity, achievement and accomplishment, and the adjective type of each class of predicates is highlighted. As is clear from Table 4.7, no stative adjectival LVCs have been found in the Persian examples, i.e. there is no state verb in the collected data that combines with the adjective (of any type) to form an adjectival LVC. This may be in part due to the fact that among all the Persian light verbs only two, i.e. *kærdæn* 'make/do' and *šodæn* 'become', can combine with the adjectives and in part due to the inherent nature of the combination of these light verbs and the predicative adjectives, which may not correspond to the state of affairs. With regard to other types of the basic three aspect types, i.e. activity, achievement and accomplishment, it is observed that the majority of the adjectival nuclear junctures in Persian are of the accomplishment class, and the achievement and activity predicates are placed in second and third place, respectively. In addition, the change in the light verbal element of the adjectival NJs (from *kærdæn* 'make/do' to *šodæn* 'become') makes no difference to the aspect type of the whole juncture; that is, the aspectual properties of the whole juncture are not predictable from those of the verbal element.

The important point that arises from Table 4.7 is that even though the behaviour of the LV *kærdæn* 'make/do' is compatible with that of *šodæn* 'become' (i.e. whatever the verb class of the former, the same is true for the latter), they are different in terms of the number of their arguments. Unlike *kærdæn* (which takes two arguments), the LV *šodæn* is univalent in all the adjectival nuclear junctures taking one argument (x) and they are all intransitive. This will be discussed in more detail later in Section 4.5.2. With regard to the contribution of the preverbal/verbal elements in determining the aspectual properties of the whole juncture, it should be noted that even though the LV *kærdæn* 'make' is an activity predicate when used as a full/heavy

Table 4.7 Summary of LS and Aktionsart type of the Persian adjectival/light verbal predicates

Verb class	Adjective type	Adjectival NJ	Logical structure (LS)
Activity	Speed	-tond <u>kærd</u> 'made quick'	[**do′** (x, Ø)] CAUSE [BECOME **tond′** (x, y)])
		-tond <u>šod</u> 'became quick'	**do′** (x, [**tond šodæn′** (x)])
Achievement	Value	-bæd <u>kærd</u> 'did wrong/bad things'	[INGR **predicate′** (x)] CAUSE [INGR **bæd′** (x, y)]
		-bæd <u>šod</u> 'became bad'	INGR **bæd šodæn′** (x)
	Physical characteristics	-sængin <u>kærd</u> 'made heavy'	[INGR **predicate′** (x)] CAUSE [INGR **sængin′** (x, y)]
		-sængin <u>šod</u> 'became heavy'	INGR **sængin šodæn′** (x)
	Human property	-xošhal <u>kærd</u> 'made happy'	[INGR **predicate′** (x)] CAUSE [INGR **xošhal′** (x, y)]
		-xošhal <u>šod</u> 'became happy'	INGR **xošhal šodæn′** (x)
Accomplishment	Age	-pir <u>kærd</u> 'made old'	[BECOME **predicate′** (x)] CAUSE [BECOME **pir′** (x, y)]
		-pir <u>šod</u> 'became old'	BECOME **pir šodæn′** (x)
	Dimension	-kutah <u>kærd</u> 'shortened'	[BECOME **predicate′** (x)] CAUSE [BECOME **kutah′** (x, y)]
		-kutah <u>šod</u> 'became short'	BECOME **kutah šodæn′** (x)
	Colour	-abi <u>kærd</u> 'painted/made blue'	[BECOME **predicate′** (x)] CAUSE [BECOME **abi′** (x, y)]
		-abi <u>šod</u> 'became blue'	BECOME **abi šodæn′** (x)
	Shape	-gerd <u>kærd</u> 'made round'	[BECOME **predicate′** (x)] CAUSE [BECOME **gerd′** (x, y)]
		-gerd <u>šod</u> 'became round'	BECOME **gerd šodæn′** (x)

verb, only one LVC (*tond kærd* 'made quick') belongs to the activity aspect type, and the other seven LVCs (out of the eight adjectival NJs with *kærdæn*) belong to either achievement or accomplishment. That is, the aspect type of these LVCs is not predictable from that of the verbal element with the exception of one case. In terms of the other eight LVCs which are formed with the LV *šodæn* 'become', it should be pointed out that this verbal element has no independent aspect type since, as mentioned in Section 2.3.2 of Chapter 2, it has no full/heavy verb form and, therefore, the aspect type of the whole NJ from that of the verbal element cannot be predicted. In the following section, the event structure of the adjectival LVCs and the contribution of the two constituents are scrutinized.

4.5.1   Event structure of adjectival NJs

From the analysis of the adjectival nuclear junctures it was found that only two light verbs have the capability of combining with adjectives to form nuclear junctures. The interesting finding of the study is that both these light verbs belong to the phase class of verbs. The notion of phase verbs, 'originally developed by Coseriu (1976)' (Coseriu and Geckeler, 1981), refers to verbs that make reference to a particular phase of an event (e.g. start, continue, finish, stop). As proposed by Saeedi (2009a), the light verbs in the Persian LVCs correspond to a particular phase of an event. With regard to the adjectival NJs, it was found that the two light verbs used in these constructions act as two phase verbs; that is, *kærdæn* 'make/do' refers to the process and *šodæn* 'become' denotes the result or endpoint of an event. This is presented in Table 4.8, where the LV *kærdæn* means 'make/do' in adjectival NJs, unlike the nominal LVCs where this verb means 'do' (Saeedi, 2009a).

To use Engerer's (2007) terminology the two phase verbs (*kærdæn* 'make/ do' and *šodæn* 'become') refer to the continuative and result (resultative) phases, respectively, shown in Figure 4.6.

The combination of the continuative phase verb *kærdæn* 'make/do' (both meanings of this verb show the process of the 'doing' or 'making' event) and the result phase verb *šodæn* 'become' with different adjective types, as

Table 4.8 Features of LVs as phase verbs in Persian adjectival NJs

Light verb	LVs' phase features
šodæn 'become'	Result
kærdæn 'make/do'	Process

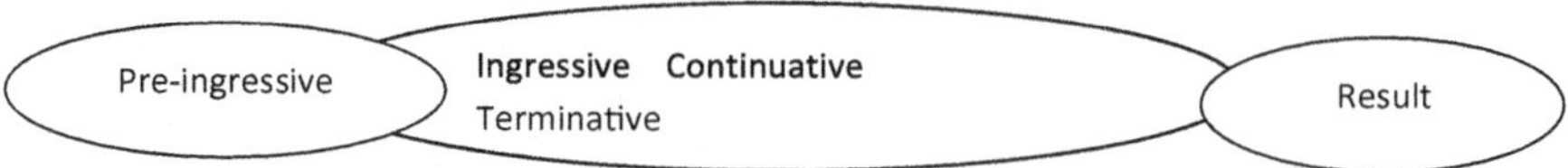

Figure 4.6 Phases of an event.

demonstrated in Table 4.9, yields interesting results. As is clear from Table 4.9, the adjectival NJs are of two types: resultative and non-resultative. That is, the adjectival LVCs formed with the two phase verbs, i.e. *kærdæn* 'make/ do' and *šodæn* 'become', with the adjective types of age, dimension, colour, shape and speed belong to the resultative constructions, while fusion of the same phase verbs with the value, physical characteristics and human property adjectives (which appear in bold type in Table 4.9) yield non-resultative constructions. In other words, even though the phase verbs in both groups are the same, the use of different adjective types has yielded different results. That is, in the resultative constructions the age, dimension, colour, shape and speed adjectives belong to the **scalar** adjective types involving a process. As Saeed (2003) points out, resultative constructions involve the process whose final point of completion is indeed the focus of attention. On the contrary, in the non-resultative adjectival LVCs the value, physical characteristics, and human property adjectives are of **state/attribute** type; that is, these adjectives do not involve a process of event and, therefore, cannot be resultative by nature. As is clear from Table 4.9, this is also applicable to the adjectival NJ with the value adjective, although in this construction the meaning of the verbal element *kærdæn*, unlike other LVCs with other adjective types, is 'do', which supports the important role of the adjective type in this respect. That is, the inherent nature of these two adjective types as scalar and state/ attribute has caused these adjectival nuclear junctures to behave differently and belong to either resultative or non-resultative event types.

As a matter of fact, Tables 4.6 and 4.7 are further evidence for this phenomenon and are consistent with what was demonstrated in Table 4.9. The findings of the application of the five diagnostic tests in Table 4.6 show that the three NJs with the value, physical characteristics and human property adjective types are the only ill-formed constructions with the first test (the use of the progressive expression 'in process of'), the third (the use of the adverbs 'quickly', or 'slowly') and the fifth test (the use of the expression 'in an hour'). That is, unlike other LVCs presented in this table, the result of these three tests is 'no'. This indicates that these three constructions do not involve a process of event and consequently cannot be resultative. As mentioned

Table 4.9 Event type of the adjectival NJs in Persian

Adjective type	NJ	Event type		
Age	pir kærd 'made old'	Age adj. + 'make'	→	Resultative
	pir šod 'became old'	Age adj. + 'become'	→	Resultative
Dimension	kutah kærd 'made short'	Dim. adj. + 'make'	→	Resultative
	kutah šod 'became short'	Dim. adj. + 'become'	→	Resultative
Value	bæd kærd 'did wrong/bad'	Val. adj. + 'do'	→	**Non-resultative**
	bæd šod 'became bad'	Val. adj. + 'become'	→	**Non-resultative**
Colour	abi kærd 'made blue'	Col. adj. + 'make'	→	Resultative
	abi šod 'became blue'	Col. adj. + 'become'	→	Resultative
Physical characteristics	sængin kærd 'made heavy'	Ph./ch. adj. + 'make'	→	**Non-resultative**
	sængin šod 'became heavy'	Ph./ch. adj. + 'become'	→	**Non-resultative**
Shape	gerd kærd 'round made'	Sh. adj. + 'make'	→	Resultative
	gerd šod 'became round'	Sh. adj. + 'become'	→	Resultative
Human property	xošhal kærd 'made happy'	Hu./Pr. adj. + 'make'	→	**Non-resultative**
	xošhal šod 'became happy'	Hu./Pr. adj. + 'become'	→	**Non-resultative**
Speed	tond kærd 'made quick'	Sp. adj. + 'make'	→	Resultative
	tond šod 'became quick'	Sp. adj. + 'become'	→	Resultative

above, this can also be observed in Table 4.7, where these constructions are the only adjectival NJs that belong to the achievement verb class with the logical structure [INGR **predicate′** (x)] CAUSE [INGR **predicative adjective** (x, y)]. That is, achievement constructions are instantaneous, do not take place in a time span, and do not belong to the resultative event type; that is, they have the feature of [+punctual], indicating that they lack internal duration. The [+punctual] feature of achievement LVCs distinguishes them from the other adjectival nuclear junctures with activity and accomplishment aspect types, which have the [–punctual] feature and involve temporal duration and therefore are of resultative event type. Consider, for instance, *pir kærd* 'make old' in (21) repeated here as (31) with the age adjective *pir* 'old' and *bæd kærd* 'did wrong/bad (things)' in (22) repeated here as (32) with the value adjective *bæd* 'bad'.

(31) an   hadese   u-ra   pir kærd.
      that accident him/her   old make-Past.3ʳᵈ.Sg.
      'That accident made him/her old.'

(32) Ali be xod-æš   bæd kærd.
      Ali to self-his   bad do-Past.3ʳᵈ.Sg.
      'Ali did wrong/bad (things) to himself.'

The adjectival NJ *pir kærd* 'made old' in (31) with the age adjective *pir* 'old' is an accomplishment construction with the [–punctual] feature where the event 'making old' has internal duration, i.e. it takes place over a period of time (in real situations nobody gets old all of a sudden), bearing a resultative event type. On the contrary, the adjectival NJ *bæd kærd* 'did bad/wrong (things)' in (32) with the value adjective *bæd* 'bad' is an achievement construction with the [+punctual] feature where the event 'doing bad' is instantaneous and does not happen over a time span, i.e. somebody does something wrong at a particular point of time.

The discussion in this section indicates that the adjectival element in the adjectival nuclear junctures contributes to the result event type or attribute and makes these constructions behave as resultative. In addition, the inchoative and causative light verbs in these constructions belong to the phase class of verbs. The change in the LV has no effect on the event type of the adjectival LVCs. In other words, the light verbs are bleached with regard to event type demonstrated in Figure 4.6 in this section. This is consistent with their behaviour in the nominal NJs, where the major role in providing the event type is played by the preverbal element and LVs contribute to the phase of event carrying tense, aspect and mood (TAM) and operator features (as shown in Section 4.7). Having examined the event structure of the adjectival LVCs in this section, the author now moves on to explore the capability of these elements in assigning argument structure in more detail.

4.5.2 Argument structure

The discussion has been categorized into two parts: the first part (4.5.2.1) analyzes the syntactic valency or transitivity of the adjectival NJs, and the second (4.5.2.2) focuses on their semantic valency or thematic roles.

4.5.2.1 Syntactic valency

As the logical structures of the two LVs (*kærdæn* 'make/do' and *šodæn* 'become') presented in Table 4.7 indicate, in all verb classes and all adjective types the light verb *kærdæn* 'make/do' is used transitively, having (y) features. In fact, the transitivity status of the whole adjectival nuclear juncture (with *kærdæn* 'make/do') is matched with that of the full/heavy form of the verbal element. For the inchoative light verb *šodæn* 'become' one argument or macrorole feature has been presented as (x), showing the intransitive reading of this predicate. As schematized in the logical structures of the adjectival NJs with the light verb *kærdæn* 'make/do', all of the examples with this verbal element are provided with causative features; that is, the logical structures of activity, achievement and accomplishment predicates with this light verb are all presented as […] CAUSE [do …], [INGR …], or [BECOME …]. In other words, regardless of the aspect type of the predicates, all the adjectival LVCs examined in this chapter belong to the causative class presenting the causative nature of the light verb *kærdæn* 'make/do' in the adjectival NJs. This indicates that the verbal element (either *kærdæn* 'make/do' or *šodæn* 'become') in these constructions plays a more important role in determining the transitivity/causativity status of the whole juncture, and the adjective's role is not as influential as that of the light verb. This is contrary to what is claimed by Karimi-Doostan (1997, 2005), who maintains that light verbs are not capable of determining the number of arguments in light verbal constructions. In fact, the problem with the previous studies of the Persian LVCs, including Karimi-Doostan's analysis, is that there has been no categorization of these constructions based on the specific type of the preverbal element, while in this study it has been shown that the degree of the contribution of the two elements to the argument structure corresponds to the type of the preverbal element used in these nuclear junctures. As discussed above, in the adjectival NJs, for instance, the role of the light verb outweighs that of the non-verbal (adjectival) element with regard to the argument structure, while the majority of the examples used by Karimi-Doostan belong to the nominal LVCs, where the noun in these constructions plays a more important role in the argument structure. This has caused the above-mentioned analyses to make such a claim regarding the complete bleachness of the light verbs. In order to examine the impact of the adjectival/light verbal elements in characterizing the semantic valency or thematic roles of the whole construction, this issue is explored in the following section.

4.5.2.2   Semantic valency or thematic roles

As discussed above, in adjectival LVCs the syntactic valency or the transitivity status of the whole construction is in direct correspondence with the (in)transitivity reading of light verbs. To determine the amount of the LV contribution to the semantic valency of these constructions, consider the adjectival LVCs *kutah kærdæn* 'make short' and *kutah šodæn* 'become short' with the dimension adjective *kutah* 'short' used in examples (22) and (22′) and repeated here as (33) and (33′), respectively.

> (33)   Mina   qesse-æš-ra   kutah   kærd.
> Mina   story-her-DOM   short   make-Past.3rd.Sg.
> 'Mina made her story short/shortened her story.'

> (34′)   qesse-ye   Mina   kutah   šod.
> story-Ez   Mina   short   become-Past.3rd.Sg.
> 'Mina's story became short.'

As is clear from the above sentences, the privileged syntactic argument *Mina* is the agent and *qesse* 'story' is the patient of the sentence in (33) with two macroroles or arguments (x, y), as the logical structure of [BECOME **kutah kærd′** (x)] CAUSE [BECOME **kutah′** (x, y)] presents. On the contrary, the replacement of the LV *kærd* 'made' in (33) with the inchoative LV *šod* 'became' (the infinitive form is *šodæn* 'become') makes the sentence in (33′) monovalent with *qesse* 'story' as the patient of the sentence. The behaviour of *kærdæn* 'make' with the dimension adjective *kutah* 'short' in (33) above is consistent in all the adjectival NJs, where this light verb has been used with different adjective types (age, dimension, value, colour, physical characteristics, shape, human property and speed). That is, in all the adjectival

LVCs explored in this study *kærdæn* is capable of assigning the same types of thematic roles to the sentence arguments with the privileged syntactic argument as the agent and the second argument or the direct core argument as the patient. The important point is that this is consistent with the heavy form of *kærdæn* 'make', where it assigns the same thematic roles to its (x) and (y) arguments. The same compatibility is observed between the above example in (33′) with the logical structure BECOME ***kutah šodæn'*** (x) and all the sentences with the LV *šodæn* 'become' and different types of adjective mentioned earlier. In other words, in all the adjectival NJs analyzed in this study *šodæn* is used with one patient macrorole or argument as the only thematic role assigned by this light verb. In the next section, a schematic representation of the features of the adjectival nuclear junctures examined in this chapter will be demonstrated.

4.5.3   Adjectival NJs' lexical-syntactic features

4.5.3.1   Lexical features of adjectival NJs

The adjectival LVCs show some lexical characteristics, indicating that the two elements or nuclei act as a single unit. Following the discussions in Section 2.3.1 of Chapter 2, the lexical features of the adjectival NJs provide the ground for the main objective in Chapter 6: to formulate an account for the predicate formation of these constructions. The major lexical characteristics discussed in Chapter 2 are as follows.

1. Even though the first lexical feature, i.e. 'having the same argument structure as the heavy single verb', is not applicable to the adjectival LVCs and they do not have a full/heavy verb form unlike the nominal NJs (Saeedi, 2009a), it is mentioned here to compare different types of nuclear junctures with regard to this lexical feature.
2. The adjectival NJs can be used to form gerundive and agentive nominals as in (34) and (35) below, respectively.

(34)   kutah   kærd-æn-e   an   tænab   mohem   æst.
       short   make-Suf.-Ez   that   rope   important   is
       'Making that rope short/shortening that rope is important.'

(35)   kutah   kærdæn   ⟶   kutah-kon-ænde
       short   make.Inf.   short-present stem-Suf.
       'make short'   'person who makes (sth.)'

3.   The adjectival LVCs can be used to form adjective-*i* and participle adjective as in (36) and (37) below, respectively.

(36)   in   tænab   kutah   šodæn-i   n-ist.
       this   rope   short   become.Inf.-Suf.   Neg.-is
       'This rope is not to be shortened.'

(37)   kutah   šodæn   tænab-e   ⟶   kutah-šod-e
       short   become   rope-Ez short-became-PPART.
       'become short'   'the shortened rope'

4.   The formation of manner adverbial from the adjectival NJs is not possible, which can be due to the inherent nature of adjectives not corresponding to manner adverbials.
5.   Finally, the stress in these constructions falls on the adjectival element, treating them as a whole unified element. As demonstrated above, the applicable lexical features to the adjectival LVCs indicate that the two elements in the nuclear junctures act as a single unit.

4.5.3.2   Syntactic features of adjectival NJs

Like the nominal LVCs (Saeedi, 2009a), the adjectival nuclear junctures show some syntactic properties, which are presented as follows.

Intervening elements

a. The negative prefix ne-/næ-

A negative prefix is possible for all kinds of adjectival NJ mentioned in this study, for example, the accomplishment adjectival NJ with dimension adjective type *kutah kærdæn* 'make short/shorten', which is the same adjectival NJ used in the discussion of the lexical properties.

(38)   dust-æm   tænab-ra   kutah   næ-kærd.
       friend-my   rope-DOM   short   Neg.-made
       'My friend did not make the rope short.'

b. The progressive/durative mi-

This feature is applicable to all types of adjectival LVCs.

    (39) dust-æm   tænab-ra   kutah mi-kon-æd.
           friend-my rope-DOM short DUR-make-3rd.Sg.
           'My friend makes the rope short.'

c. The imperative form (present stem of verb + *(*be-*))*

This feature is applicable to all types of adjectival NJs.

    (40) tænab-ra   kutah (be)-kon.
           rope-DOM short (IMP)-make
           'Make the rope short.'

Note that the imperative prefix (*be-*) as in the above example, or for some verbs (*bo-*), is sometimes optional; that is, the imperative form of the verb is made with the present stem of the verb without the necessary use of the prefix, as is the case for some examples in the following section.

*d. The imperative negative (*næ-* + present stem of verb)*

This feature is applicable to all types of adjectival NJs.

    (41) tænab-ra   kutah næ-kon.
           rope-DOM short Neg.-IMP-make
           'Do not make the rope short.'

e. The future auxiliary xah *'want'*

This feature is applicable to all types of adjectival NJs.

    (42) dust-æm   tænab-ra   kutah xah-æd-kærd.
           friend-my rope-DOM short want-3rd.Sg.-made
           'My friend will make the rope short.'

f. Adjective intervention

This feature is applicable to colour adjectives.

    (43) u   divar-ra   abi-ye rošæn kærd.
           he/she wall-DOM blue-Ez light make.Past.3rd.Sg.
           'He/She makes the wall light blue.'

Note that since it is not possible to apply 'adjective intervention' to the example used in this section for adjectival NJs, i.e. *kutah kærdæn* 'make short', it has been replaced with another sentence from the adjectival LVCs, i.e. *abi kærdæn* 'make blue' with the colour adjective *abi* 'blue' in the above example.

g. DOM and 'this' intervention

This feature is not applicable to adjectival NJs.

Relativization

The relative pronoun *ke* 'that' interrupts the two preverbal/verbal elements. This feature is not applicable to adjectival LVCs.

Focused by WH-question word

For example, *č* 'what'. This feature is not applicable to adjectival NJs.

Coordination

The preverbal element can coordinate with another element by coordination conjunctions (e.g. *væ* 'and'). This feature is applicable to all types of adjectival LVCs.

> (44) dust-æm   tænab-ra   kutah væ   monæzzæm kærd.
>   friend-my   rope-DOM   short and tidy   made
>   'My friend will make the rope short and tidy.'

Of all the syntactic properties presented above, only three features are not applicable to the adjectival nuclear junctures. As mentioned earlier, how RRG accounts for these features of the Persian LVCs will be discussed in Chapter 6. The section below will try to determine the nexus-juncture linkage and schematize the constructional schema for the adjectival nuclear junctures.

4.6 Constructional schemas of adjectival NJs

In order to determine the nexus-juncture type of the adjectival NJs and compatible with the procedure in RRG, in this section the negation nuclear operator has been used as the sharing operator between the two structurally independent elements in these constructions. To illustrate this phenomenon, consider example (22) in Section 4.3.2 with the dimension adjective *kutah* 'short' repeated here as (38) with the Persian nuclear negation operator *næ-*.

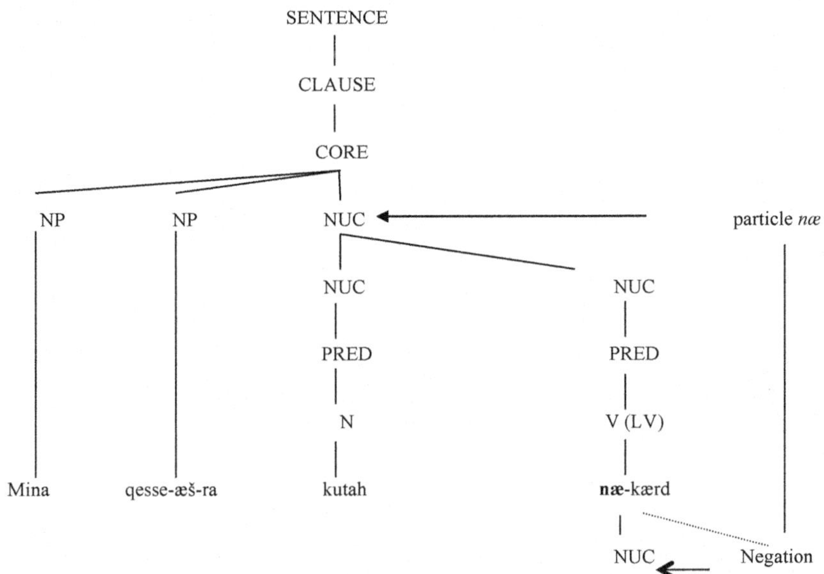

Figure 4.7 Operator sharing in Persian adjectival NJs.

Figure 4.7 schematizes the structural independence of the two PRED nodes that share this operator; that is, the negation operator has scope over both elements. It should be noted here that the same phenomenon regarding the nuclear negation operator sharing between the two constituents takes place in all the adjectival LVCs with different adjective types and the two causative (*kærdæn* 'make') and inchoative (*šodæn* 'become') light verbs. That is, both construction types belong to the nuclear cosubordination linkage form.

> (38)   Mina   qesse-æš-ra   kutah   næ-kærd.
>   Mina   story-her-DOM   short   Neg.Op.-make-Past.3rd.Sg.
>   'Mina did not make her story short/shortened her story.'

To summarize the representation of the syntactic, morphological, semantic and pragmatic features along with the nexus-juncture linkage type of these constructions, a constructional schema is presented in Tables 4.10 and 4.11 below for each of the two groups of Persian adjectival nuclear junctures (following the discussion and principles in Section 3.4.4 of Chapter 3).

Table 4.10 Constructional schema for Persian adjectival NJs with the causative light verb *kærdæn* 'make/do' (first group)

Construction: Persian adjectival nuclear juncture

SYNTAX:

    Juncture: nuclear

    Nexus: cosubordination

    Construction type: light verbal (adjective + light verb)

    $[_{CL} [_{CORE}$ NP $[_{NUC} [_{NUC}$ ... ADJ] $[_{NUC}$ ... V(LV)]] NP ...] ...]

    Unit template(s): (3.6) (see Section 3.4.4.1 in Chapter 3)

    PSA: none

    Linking: default

MORPHOLOGY:

    $PRED_{NUC1}$: one of the adjective types

    $PRED_{NUC2}$: phase verbs: the causative light verb *kærdæn* 'make/do':

    [predicate′ (x, Ø)] CAUSE [BECOME **predicative adj′** (x, y)])

    [INGR **predicate′** (x)] CAUSE [INGR **predicative adj′** (x, y)]

    [BECOME **predicate′** (x)] CAUSE [BECOME **predicative adj′** (x, y)]

SEMANTICS: $[PRED_{NUC1}]$ CAUSE $[PRED_{NUC2}]$, $PRED_{NUC2}$ [+static]

PRAGMATICS:

    Illocutionary force: unspecified

    Focus structure: unspecified

Table 4.11 Constructional schema for Persian adjectival NJs with the inchoative light verb *šodæn* 'become' (second group)

Construction: Persian adjectival nuclear juncture

SYNTAX:

    Juncture: nuclear

    Nexus: cosubordination

    Construction type: light verbal (adjective + light verb)

    $[_{CL} [_{CORE}$ NP $[_{NUC} [_{NUC}$ ...] $[_{NUC}$ ...]]

    Unit template(s): (3.6) (see Section 3.4.4.1 in Chapter 3)

    PSA: none

    Linking: default

MORPHOLOGY:

    $PRED_{NUC1}$: one of the adjective types

    $PRED_{NUC2}$: Phase verbs: the inchoative light verb *šodæn* 'become'

    do′ (x, **[predicate′** (x)])

    INGR **predicate′** (x)

    BECOME **predicate′** (x)

SEMANTICS: $[PRED_{NUC1}]$ CAUSE $[PRED_{NUC2}]$, $PRED_{NUC2}$ [−static]

PRAGMATICS:

    Illocutionary force: unspecified

    Focus structure: unspecified

4.7 Summary

This chapter has been devoted to the analysis of Persian adjectival light verb constructions, or in RRG's terms, nuclear junctures. In fact, the analysis of the nominal LVCs (Saeedi, 2009a) can be extended to these lexical inchoative (*šodæn* 'become') and causative (*kærdæn* 'make') elements and adjectives. In this chapter, the four propositions (mentioned in Chapter 1) were investigated; that is, the first and second propositions were examined by analyzing the argument structure, the aspect type or verb class, and the event structure of the adjectival LVCs, and the third and fourth propositions were investigated by analyzing the lexical-semantic features of these constructions. The investigation shows that they are nuclear junctures based on the RRG framework. To fulfil the objective and to provide the ground for the main analysis, in Sections 4.1 and 4.2 adjective types were explored in terms of two major parameters, namely, modification and predication. Then, on the basis of these two adjective classes the architecture of the Persian adjective system was described. Section 4.3 discussed the types of light verbs and adjectives that combine to form adjectival LVCs and presented the Layered Structure of the Clause for these nuclear junctures. The section explored the argument structure and event structure of these constructions. Section 4.4 characterized the fusing of the two preverbal/light verbal elements, examining the aspect types of the adjectival nuclear junctures, and the findings of this analysis were discussed syntactically and semantically. Section 4.5 summarized the findings of the adjectival nuclear junctures examination, presenting their logical structure. Sections 4.5.1 and 4.5.2 explored the contribution of the two preverbal/light verbal elements to the event and argument structures, including the syntactic (transitivity) and semantic (thematic roles) valency of the LVCs. The lexical and syntactic features of the adjectival NJs were discussed in Section 4.5.3. Finally, in Section 4.6, the nexus-juncture linkage type and the constructional schemas for the two major types of adjectival LVCs were presented, formalizing the syntactic, morphological, semantic and pragmatic features of these constructions and highlighting their differences with regard to syntactic and semantic characteristics.

In this chapter, the aim has been to provide a comprehensive analysis of the adjectival nuclear junctures, which have not received much attention in the literature. Unlike such studies of light verbal constructions as Karimi-Doostan (1997), the present investigation of adjectival LVCs provides a detailed examination of the type and nature of the two constituents and their contribution to the event and argument structure and the aspect type of the whole juncture. The findings of the present chapter have revealed that only the causative and the inchoative light verbs (*kærdæn* 'make/do' and *šodæn* 'become', respectively) can fuse with adjectives to form nuclear junctures which act as a single unit. Like the nominal LVCs (Saeedi, 2009a), the light verbs in these constructions belong to the phase class of verbs referring to a particular phase of an event and are bleached with regard to the event type or attributes. In fact, the preverbal or adjectival elements which can be of age, dimension, colour, shape and speed contribute to the event structure and cause these constructions to be resultative, i.e. they belong to the result phase of an event. The only adjectival NJs that are not resultative are those formed with the value, physical characteristics and human property adjective types, which is due to the inherent nature of these adjectives, that do not involve a process and cannot be resultative. The causative and inchoative adjectival LVCs can be of activity, achievement and accomplishment verb class, where the two nuclei in these constructions act as a unified element. In sum, the behaviour of these constructions is similar to that of the nominal NJs (examined in Saeedi, 2009a) with the same nexus-juncture linkage, i.e. nuclear cosubordination. In addition, in both constructions the preverbal element has the leading role in the aspect type of the whole nuclear juncture and the verb class of the LVC is predictable from that of the verb in just a few cases and in the majority of the constructions it is the preverbal element which is more important. The difference between the adjectival LVCs and the nominal ones that were investigated by Saeedi (2009a) is that in the former the transitivity of all the adjectival NJs is predictable from that of the verbal element, while in the latter the nominal element is also a determining constituent in the argument structure (transitivity) of the whole construction.

Notes

1. Particles such as the direct object marker *ra-*.
2. Except for superlative adjectives which precede nouns and in some literary styles where attributive adjectives may precede nouns, as in *šad pesæri didæm* 'happy boy I saw'.
3. Note that in the Persian orthography initials and proper nouns (unlike English, for instance) are not capitalized. In fact, there is no capitalization procedure, but in the Persian examples used in this study proper nouns are mostly capitalized to differentiate them from other word classes.

5

Prepositional Predicates

5.0 Introduction

In this chapter, a distinction is made between adverb-light verb and preposition-light verb combinations, and it is pointed out that in the latter type, prepositional nuclear junctures, it is a prepositional phrase rather than a simple preposition that fuses with the light verb. This follows from the categorical distinction between adverbs and prepositions: prepositions require another element to form a Nuclear Juncture (NJ) with a light verb while adverbs do not. That is, a preposition, unlike other word classes, needs a complement, which can be a noun, a preposition or another class of word. Consequently, in the prepositional light verbal constructions (LVCs) the preposition does not stand alone, but needs another element or complement, which is typically either a noun or another preposition. This chapter aims to investigate these prepositional constructions, which in Role and Reference Grammar (RRG) terms are adpositional NJs, where the verbal or light verbal elements join with a prepositional phrase. Since in Persian there is no class of postposition, wherever adposition is mentioned, it refers to prepositions. Also, in RRG adpositions are one of the two categories of adjuncts or non-arguments (the other being adverbials) having the features of [−V, −N], and like adjectives are not universal valid categories. That is, in some languages such as Dyirbal, for instance, there is no category of adposition (Van Valin and LaPolla, 1997).

To begin the main account of this study, in Section 5.1 different types of Persian prepositions and prepositional phrases are described. Then a distinction is made between predicative and non-predicative prepositions; some examples are provided in which the layered structure of the clause is schematized. In Sections 5.2–5.7 the main five diagnostic tests are applied to a wide range of examples from our Persian data to determine the verb class of the prepositional (P) LVCs and the amount of contribution of each of the preverbal/verbal elements in the transitivity status and the aspectual properties of the whole NJ. Due to the large number of examples in these sections (5.2–5.7) and for reasons of space all the tables of the test applications have been moved to Appendix B. Section 5.8 analyzes and discusses the findings of the present chapter (in more detail), focusing on any probable pattern of regularities. Section 5.9 investigates the event structure, i.e. event attributes and types of prepositional nuclear junctures. In Section 5.10 the argument structure of the prepositional NJs, including the syntactic and semantic valency, are scrutinized. In order to present the linking algorithm of the constructions under question, Section 5.11 examines this linking procedure from semantics to syntax and provides the layered structure of the related examples. The lexical and syntactic features of the prepositional NJs are examined in Section 5.12. The constructional schema of the adpositional NJs is demonstrated in Section 5.13, depicting a clearer image of the morphological, syntactic, semantic and pragmatic parameters. The distinction between the prepositional LVCs and phrasal verbs is dealt with in Section 5.14. Finally, Section 5.15 summarizes the findings of the present chapter. Consistent with the procedure adopted in the previous analytical chapter (4), this chapter aims at investigating the four propositions (mentioned in Chapter 1), i.e. the first and second propositions are investigated by scrutinizing the event structure, the verb class and the argument structure, and the third and fourth propositions are dealt with by examining the lexical-semantic and syntactic features of the prepositional LVCs in this chapter and how RRG accounts for these syntactic characteristics in the final chapter (6).

5.1 Types of preposition

In Modern Persian or Farsi, there are generally two types of prepositions: simple/bare as in (1a–b) and compound as in (1c) below. Simple or bare prepositions include such prepositions as:

(1) a. *ændær* 'in', *æz* 'from', *ba* 'with', *bær* 'on', *bæraye* 'for', *bæhr* 'for', *be* 'to', *beyn* 'between', *bi* 'without',
     joz 'except', *næzd* 'with, by', *miyan* 'among', *piš* 'front', *pey* 'after', *ta* 'up to' and *dær* 'in'.

Some of the simple prepositions in Persian, as Mahootian (1997) also notes, take *ezafe* (the suffix *-e* or sometimes *-ye* is called *ezafe* in Persian and is the same as 'of' in English), and include:

(1) b. *bedun-e* 'without', *birun-e* 'outside', *jelow-ye* 'in front of',
     næzdik-e 'near', *miyan-e*, or as pronounced in
     spoken Persian *miyun-e*, 'between', *pæhlu-ye* 'by', *pošt-e* 'behind',
     ru-ye 'on', *tu-ye* 'in' and *zir-e* 'under'.

As noted by Shamisa (2001, p. 214), compound prepositions may be formed
by combining prepositions, for example:

(1) c. *æz bæraye* 'because of' (Lit.: 'from for'), *æz bæhre* 'for' (Lit.:
     'from for'; *bæhre* is more formal than
     bæraye), *æz ruye* 'out of' (Lit.: 'from on'), *dær bareye* 'about'
     (Lit.: 'in about') and *dær næzde* 'front, with' (Lit.: 'in with/by').

Prepositions can also refer to: (a) the place or location (e.g. *dær xiyaban* 'in
street'); (b) the direction (e.g. *betæraf-e mædrese* 'towards school'); and (c)
the time (e.g. *qæbl æz mædrese* 'before school', Lit.: 'before from school').
In Persian prepositional phrases (PPs), the preposition takes a noun phrase as
its argument and heads the PP; its canonical position is before the verb and
after the direct object (Mahootian, 1997), as in (2) below.

(2) Ali ketab-ra   æz   dust-æš   gereft.
    Ali book-DOM   from   friend-his   take.Past.3rd.Sg.
    'Ali took the book from his friend.'

In (2) above, the preposition *æz* 'from' takes the noun *dust* 'friend' as its
argument and the whole prepositional phrase *æz dust-æš* 'from his friend'
follows the direct object *ketab* 'book' preceding the verb of the sentence
(*gereft* 'took'). The prepositional phrases can appear in other positions, i.e.
they can sometimes be moved to the right of the predicate of the sentence
(especially for some prepositions such as the simple preposition *be* 'to', or
the compound prepositions *tu-ye* 'in-Ezafe', *ru-ye* 'on-Ezafe'). Consider the
sentence in (3) below.

(3) Ali ræft   be   mædrese.
    Ali went   to   school
    'Ali went to school.'

As is clear from (3) above, the prepositional phrase *be mædrese* 'to school' appears to the right of the verb (*ræft* 'went'), and *mædrese* 'school' is in fact the noun taken by the preposition as its argument.

As mentioned before, in RRG it is maintained that the predicative role of sentences is not always played by the verbal elements; rather, sometimes the noun, adjective, adverb or preposition predicates the ideas expressed in the statements. Thus, prepositions or prepositional phrases can be of a predicative type, like other classes of words. That is, prepositions or prepositional phrases can be of two types, i.e. predicative or non-predicative. In RRG, those adpositions in the periphery of the clause are of the former type (predicative) and those marking oblique core arguments belong to the latter class (non-predicative) (Van Valin and LaPolla, 1997, p. 52; Van Valin, 2005, p. 21). According to RRG, whether a preposition is predicative or non-predicative basically depends on which verb it appears with, i.e. the English preposition 'from', for instance, is non-predicative when it appears with the verb 'take', licensing a source argument (for example, 'Sally took the book from the boy'), while it is predicative with a verb like 'die' (for example, 'she died from malaria') and its semantic argument is treated as a core argument structurally with the nucleus (NUC) and predicate (PRED) nodes dominating the preposition (Van Valin and LaPolla, 1997; Van Valin, 2005).

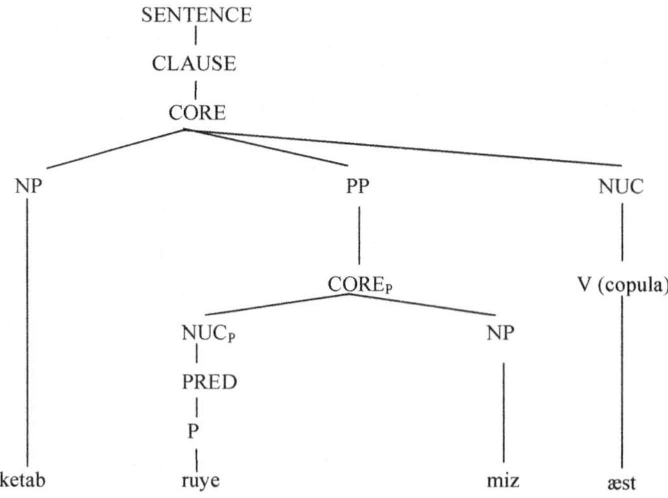

Figure 5.1 LSC of a copula/prepositional predicate in a Persian sentence.

Another form of predicative prepositional phrase is where a copula accompanies this class of words, as in 'the book is on the table', i.e. in RRG it is postulated that in these constructions the copula is a grammatical word dominated with the NUC node and the prepositional phrase bears the predicative function (presented with the PRED node) of the whole sentence. In (4) and Figure 5.1 the logical structure and the Layered Structure of the Clause (LSC) of a similar example in Persian are presented. As is clear from this figure, the main **core** of the sentence is followed by the noun phrase (NP), the prepositional phrase (PP) and the nucleus (NUC) which, according to RRG, is the copula or the grammatical nucleus/verb of the sentence and, in fact, does not have a predicating role (i.e. it is not followed by the PRED node). The PP node is in turn followed by $CORE_p$ (the subscripted $_p$ before this node or other nodes in this figure indicates that this core belongs to the prepositional phrase and is not the main core of the sentence), which dominates the NP (*miz* 'table') and the preposition *ruye* 'on' as the predicate of the whole proposition. The $CORE_p$ node is followed by NUC_p and the NP. In fact, the preposition *ruye* 'on' along with the NP *miz* 'table' predicate the whole sentence, and the copula *ast* 'is', as pointed out before, is just a grammatical word. As mentioned in the previous chapter on the nominal NJ, in the languages where a copula is not used in the examples like the sentence in (4) this predicative role of the preposition is even more pronounced. As shown in Figure 5.1, in Persian the use of a copula with the predicative prepositions is similar to English, i.e. the copula *æst* 'is' is a grammatical word (NUC) without being followed by a PRED node. In other words, the main predicative function of the sentence is borne by the prepositional phrase or, indeed, the preposition (P).

(4) ketab ruye miz æst.
    book on   table is
    'The book is on the table.'

In RRG, three types of prepositions (prepositional phrases) are analyzed following Jolly (1991, 1993) (Van Valin and LaPolla, 1997). The first type of prepositions is adjunct-marking non-predicative prepositions, as in 'Mary gave the book to John', where 'to John' is an argument (ARG) of the sentence followed by the preposition 'to' and the NP 'John', which have no predicating function. The second type is adjunct predicative prepositions, as in 'Mary saw John after school', where the prepositional 'after school' is the PERIPHERY node of the sentence followed by CORE, which in turn is followed by the NUC (PRED) node for the preposition 'after' and the ARG (NP) node for 'school'. That is, the preposition 'after' is indeed part of the predicate structure of the whole proposition. Finally, the third type is argument-adjunct predicative prepositions, as in 'Yulanda put the book in the box' (cf. Van Valin and LaPolla, 1997, p. 162), where 'in the box' is an AAJ (argument adjunct) followed by PP and CORE nodes, respectively. This CORE node in turn is followed by the NUC (PRED) node for the preposition 'in' and ARG (NP) for 'the box'. In this latter type of prepositions, the predicative function and the semantic structure of the verb 'put' is fulfilled with the preposition 'in', which is a predicative adjunct. That is, if the preposition 'in' is omitted, as 'Yulanda put the book ... the box', the semantic architecture of the sentence (for the intended meaning) is damaged. In other words, in this type of preposition (argument-adjunct predicative preposition), unlike the second type (adjunct predicative preposition), the prepositional phrase is not the periphery; rather, it is an adjunct argument of the main core, and the meaning of the sentence is not complete without the prepositional phrase (Van Valin and LaPolla, 1997).

Persian prepositional LVCs where a light verbal element combines with a prepositional phrase to form nuclear junctures are similar to the third type of prepositions focused on in RRG analysis, i.e. argument-adjunct predicative prepositions. In fact, in the prepositional LVCs in Persian the meaning of the verb and the sentence is not complete without the prepositional phrase. The important point to bear in mind here is that in Persian LVCs the two predicative parts (the verbal element and the predicative prepositional phrase) form a nuclear juncture (NJ); that is, the NUC node is followed by two NUC nodes, being also followed by two PRED nodes, one of which is the light verbal element and the other one is the prepositional phrase. That is, in Persian sentences like (5) below the predicative role of the sentence is played with the combination of the preverbal (prepositional phrase) and the verbal elements,

(5) Ali　æz　　donya　ræft.
　　 Ali　from　world　go.Past.3ʳᵈ.Sg.
　　 'Ali passed away.'

As shown above, in (5) *æz donya ræft* 'passed away' (Lit.: 'from world went') is the prepositional NJ, i.e. *ræft* 'went' is the light verb (as mentioned before, it is called a light verb since the semantic load of the sentence is not complete with the verbal element alone, i.e. it has a light predicating role)

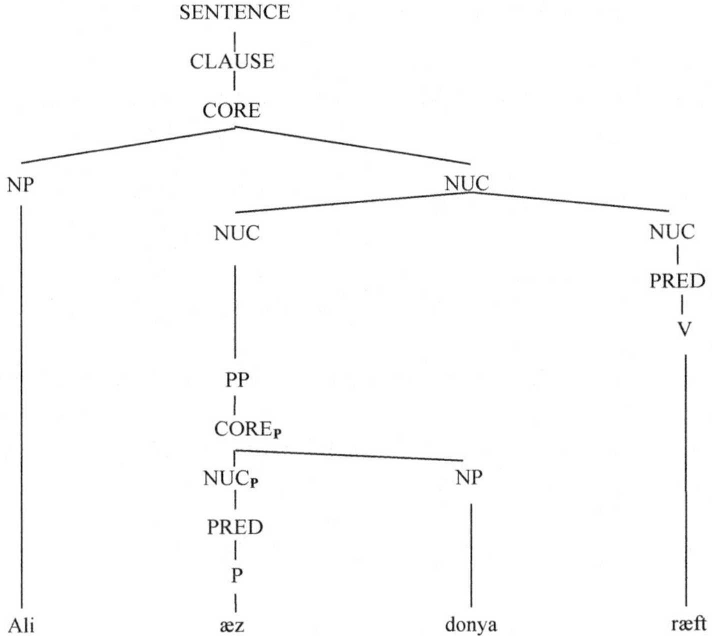

Figure 5.2 LSC for a prepositional/light verbal nuclear juncture in Persian.

and *æz donya* 'from world' is the prepositional phrase, with *æz* 'from' as the preposition and *donya* 'world' as the argument (NP) of the prepositional phrase. In fact, the combination of the two verbal and non-verbal elements predicates the whole sentence and the omission of the preposition from the sentence (*Ali … donya ræft* 'Ali … world went') damages the semantic parameter of the sentence. The layered structure of the clause of the example in (5) is presented in Figure 5.2. (Note that in the older version of RRG, i.e. Van Valin and LaPolla, 1997, all the NPs are preceded by the ARG node and all the predicative prepositional phrases are preceded by the AAJ (argument adjunct), which are eliminated in Van Valin, 2005.)

From the collected data it emerges that out of all the prepositions listed in (1a–c) at the beginning of this section, only some of them can combine with light verbs to make prepositional LVCs. Additionally, of all the light verbs listed in (46), Section 2.3.2 of Chapter 2, which are the commonest verbs in our collected examples and are considered as the basis for our analysis, only some can join the prepositional phrases to form prepositional NJs.

5.2 Preposition *æz* 'from'

One of the most productive prepositions in Persian is *æz* 'from', which can combine with a light verb along with either another preposition (Prep.) or an NP (concrete or abstract) to build a prepositional LVC. As mentioned earlier, the distinction between a preposition and an adverb in these constructions is that the preposition is accompanied by another element, which is typically either another preposition or a noun (complement). That is, there are usually three positions or elements in these constructions: the first position is filled by a preposition, the second by either another preposition or a noun (an NP complement), and the third by a light verb. In Section 5.2.1 below, the combination of two prepositions (one of which is *æz* 'from') and the light verb is examined, and in Section 5.2.2 the combination of the preposition (*æz* 'from') and an NP along with the light verb is analyzed. The point to consider here is that this preposition can fuse with both noun types, i.e. concrete or abstract, and in these constructions NP or N is part of the LVC and not its argument.

5.2.1 ([æz 'from' + Prep.] LV)

The present section, as mentioned before, aims at examining the first group of Persian prepositional LVCs, where the preposition *æz* 'from' and another preposition fuse with the light verb to make NJs. The most common light verbs in the data having the capability of joining the combination of *æz* 'from' and another preposition to construct prepositional NJs are *šodæn* 'become', *daštæn* 'have', *kærdæn* 'make/do', *bordæn* 'take/carry' and *ræftæn* 'go'. And the most common prepositions that can appear in combination with *æz* 'from' and the light verb are *bær* 'on/over', *beyn* 'between', *piš* 'before' and *miyan* 'among'. In the following section, each of the prepositional constructions made of *æz* 'from', prepositions and light verbs (mentioned above), i.e. ([*æz* 'from' + Prep.] LV], is explored separately.

5.2.1.1 ([æz 'from' + bær 'on/over'] LV)

The first common preposition capable of joining *æz* 'from' and LV to form a prepositional LVC is *bær* 'on/over'. Examples of prepositional NJs made with the combination of these two prepositions and LV are: *æz bær šodæn* 'memorize' (Lit.: 'from on/over become'), *æz bær kærdæn* 'memorize' (Lit.: 'from on/over make'), *æz bær daštæn* 'know by heart/have memorized' (Lit.: 'from on/over have'), which are exemplified and discussed below.[1]

As mentioned before, the diagnostic tests and the results tables are given in Appendix B.

æz bær šodæn *'memorize' (Lit.: 'from on/over become')*

    (6) danešamuz-an hæme-ye sorud-ra æz bær šod-ænd.
         student-Pl. all-Ez song-DOM from on/over become.Past.-3rd.Pl.
         'The students memorized the whole song.'

æz bær kærdæn *'memorize' (Lit.: 'from on/over make')*

    (7) danešamuz-an hæme-ye sorud-ra æz bær kærd-ænd.
         student-Pl. all-Ez song-DOM from on/over make.Past.-3rd.Pl.
         'The students memorized the whole song.'

æz bær daštæn *'know by heart/have memorized' (Lit.: 'from on/over have')*

    (8) danešamuz-an hæme-ye sorud-ra æz bær dašt-ænd.
         student-Pl. all-Ez song-DOM from on/over have.Past.-3rd.Pl.
         'The students memorized the whole song.'

As Table 1 in Appendix B shows, the first two LVCs in (6) and (7) are accomplishments, while the third prepositional NJ in (8) belongs to the achievement verb class. Note that there is a mismatch between the aspectual class of these LVCs and that of the corresponding full/heavy verbs; that is, the full form of *daštæn* 'have' is stative and *kærdæn* 'make/do' is an activity verb. The verb *šodæn* 'become' is an inchoative LV in Persian which actually does not have a full form; that is, it is not used as a full predicate and mostly acts as a light verb (for example, it is used as an LV in adjectival, nominal or prepositional NJs) or as an auxiliary (as explained in Chapter 2, Section 2.3.2). In terms of transitivity it should be noted that while out of the three verbs (*šodæn* 'become', *kærdæn* 'make/do', *daštæn* 'have') one is intransitive, namely, the inchoative light verb *šodæn* 'become', and the other two are transitive (i.e. the causative verb *kærdæn* 'make/do' and the stative verb *daštæn* 'have'), all three prepositional NJs are transitive where used in combination with the prepositions *æz* 'from' and *bær* 'on/over'. In fact, even the intransitive inchoative light verb *šodæn* 'become' turns into a transitive form when it fuses with the compound prepositions *æz bær* 'from on/over'.

5.2.1.2   ([*æz* 'from' + *beyn* 'between'] LV)

The next preposition (after *bær* 'on/over' examined above) having the capability of joining *æz* 'from' to form a light verbal/prepositional NJ is *beyn* 'between', and the most common LVs used in combination with these two prepositions are *ræftæn* 'go' and *bordæn* 'take/carry', where *æz beyn ræftæn* means 'be wiped out' (Lit.: 'from between go') and *æz beyn bordæn* has the meaning of 'wipe out' (Lit.: 'from between take/carry'). These two prepositional LVCs are investigated applying the five diagnostic tests (given in Table 2 of Appendix B), and since *æz beyn bordæn* is the causative transitive form of *æz beyn ræftæn*, the same sentence is used to have a better ground for comparing the two prepositional constructions with different light verbs.

æz beyn ræftæn *'be wiped out' (Lit.: 'from between go')*

> (9) tæmam-e   šæhr   æz   beyn   ræft.
> all-ez   city   from   between   go.Past.3rd.Sg.
> 'The whole city was wiped out.'

æz beyn bordæn *'wipe out' (Lit.: 'from between take/carry')*

> (10)   seyl   tæmam-e šæhr-ra   æz   beyn   bord.
> flood all-Ez   city-DOM   from   between   take/carry.Past.3rd.Sg.
> 'The flood wiped out the whole city.'

As Table 2 in Appendix B shows, both of the LVCs in (9) and (10) belong to the accomplishment group, as do the corresponding full/heavy verbs. Similarly, the valency patterns of these LVCs and their corresponding heavy verbs match: *ræftæn* 'go' is intransitive, as is *æz beyn ræftæn* 'be wiped out' (Lit.: 'from between go'), while *bordæn* 'take/carry' is transitive, as is *æz beyn bordæn* 'wipe out' (Lit.: 'from between take/carry'), as shown by the Direct Object Marker (DOM) *-ra* attached to the object *šæhr* 'city' in the examples (10a)–(10e) in Table 2, Appendix B.

5.2.1.3   ([*æz* 'from' + *piš* 'before/front'] LV)

Another preposition able to join *æz* 'from' to form prepositional nuclear junctures is *piš* 'before/front', and the LV used with these two prepositions is *bordæn* 'take/carry'. The prepositional nuclear juncture *æz piš bordæn* 'accomplish/manage' (Lit.: 'from before/front take/carry') is analyzed using the five diagnostic tests (given in Table 3 of Appendix B).

æz piš bordæn *'manage' (Lit.: 'from before/front take/carry')*

> (11) an   vækil   kar-ha -ra   ba-deqqæt æz   piš
> bord.
> that barrister work-Pl.-DOM with-care   from   before/front
> took
> 'That barrister managed all the work carefully.'

In Table 3 in Appendix B, it is shown that the prepositional NJ *æz piš bordæn* 'manage' (Lit.: 'from before/front take') is an achievement LVC, while the full form of the verb *bordæn* 'take' is indeed accomplishment. On the contrary, the transitive status of the verb *bordæn* (when used as a full/heavy predicate) has a more important role in the transitive status of the whole NJ.

5.2.1.4   ([æz 'from' + *miyan* 'among'] *bordæn* 'take/carry')

Another preposition able to fuse with *æz* 'from' and the light verb *bordæn* 'take/carry' is *miyan* 'among'. Since the prepositional NJ *æz miyan bordæn* 'wipe out' (Lit.: 'from among take/carry') has the same semantic load as *æz beyn bordæn* 'wipe out' (Lit.: 'from between take/carry'), the same example in (10) is repeated here as (12) for the prepositional LVC with *miyan* 'among', in order to determine the amount of the contribution of the preverbal element.

> (12) seyl   tæmam-e šæhr-ra   æz   miyan bord.
> flood all-Ez   city-DOM from   among take/carry.Past.3rd.Sg.
> 'The flood wiped out the whole city.'

Comparing the results of Table 4 in Appendix B for the prepositional light verbal construction (PLVC) *æz miyan bordæn* 'wipe out' (Lit.: 'from among take/carry') and Table 5.2 for *æz beyn bordæn* 'wipe out' (Lit.: 'from between take/carry') and *æz beyn ræftæn* 'be wiped out', it is found that there is no difference in terms of the verb class of the three NJs (i.e. all of them are accomplishment (BECOME **predicate'** (x) or (x, y)), which is the same as the full form of the verb *bordæn* 'take/carry'), even though these constructions have different LVs and the second preposition in one is *miyan* 'among' and in the other two is *beyn* 'between'. In fact, the only similarity in these constructions is that the first preposition in all of them is *æz* 'from'. Also, the transitivity reading of *æz miyan bordæn* 'wipe out' (presented in

Table 4 in Appendix B) is the same as the other two LVCs with *bordæn*, i.e. it is of transitive type. Analyzing the first group of the prepositional NJs, i.e. the combination of *æz* 'from' and another preposition (*bær* 'on/over', *beyn* 'between', *piš* 'before/front', *miyan* 'among') with a light verb (for example, *daštæn* 'have', *šodæn* 'become', *kærdæn* 'make/do', *ræftæn* 'go' and *bordæn* 'take/carry'), the author now moves on to examine the second group of these constructions. That is, in Section 5.2.2 below those prepositional light verb constructions are investigated that are made from the preposition *æz* 'from', an NP and a light verb.

5.2.2 ([$_{pp}$ *æz* 'from' + NP] LV)

As mentioned before, in this group of prepositional NJs the preposition *æz* 'from' fuses with a noun and an LV to form an LVC. Examining the data of the present study, it became clear that the most common LVs used in this group are *ræftæn* 'go', *bordæn* 'take/carry' and *gereftæn* 'take/catch', respectively. The nouns used in these constructions are generally of two major types, namely, concrete and abstract nouns. These prepositional/light verbal structures are investigated on the basis of the light verbs division (the results of the tests are presented in Appendix B).

5.2.2.1 ([$_{pp}$ *æz* 'from' + NP] *ræftæn* 'go')

Since *ræftæn* 'go' is one of the most common LVs used in the prepositional constructions with *æz* 'from' and an NP, there are a lot of concrete and abstract nouns that are capable of fusing with this LV and the preposition *æz* to form LVCs. In the following sections, two NJs are used with the light verb *ræftæn* 'go' and the preposition *æz* 'from', i.e. one with the concrete noun *dæst* 'hand' (*æz dæst ræftæn* 'be lost', Lit.: 'from hand go') and another with the abstract noun *huš* 'consciousness' (*æz huš ræftæn* 'lose consciousness/faint', Lit.: 'from consciousness go').

æz dæst ræftæn *'be lost' (Lit.: 'from hand go')*

> (13) forsæt-e   tælayee-e   mæn   æz   dæst   ræft.
> opportunity-Ez golden-Ez me/I /my from hand go.Past.3rd.Sg.
> 'My golden opportunity was lost.'

æz huš ræftæn *'lose consciousness' (Lit.: 'from consciousness go')*

> (14) u   dær xiyaban æz   huš   ræft.

he/she   in   street   from   consciousness   go.Past.3rd.Sg.
'He/She lost his/her consciousness/fainted in the street.'

As presented in Table 5 in Appendix B, the verb class of the two prepositional constructions *æz dæst ræftæn* 'be lost' (Lit.: 'from hand go') and *æz huš ræftæn* 'lose consciousness' (Lit.: 'from consciousness go') is achievement, which is not compatible with the verb class of the full/heavy form of the verb *ræftæn* (as an accomplishment predicate). But the intransitivity status of this verbal element has had a direct influence on the intransitive reading of the whole NJs. Also, the type of NP that is concrete vs. abstract nouns has not changed the verb class architecture of the NJs.

5.2.2.2   ([$_{pp}$ *æz* 'from' + NP] *bordæn* 'take/carry')

The next light verb used in the prepositional constructions with *æz* 'from' and an NP is *bordæn* 'take/carry', which is examined below (in the NJ *æz yad bordæn* 'forget', Lit.: 'from remembrance take/carry', with the abstract noun *yad* 'remembrance'), applying the five diagnostic tests (given in Appendix B).

æz yad bordæn *'forget' (Lit.: 'from remembrance take/carry')*

>   (15)   pedær-æm   xatere-ye   an   hadese-ra   æz
>   yad   bord.
>   father-my   memory-Ez   that   accident-DOM   from
>   remembrance   took.3rd.Sg.
>   'My father forgot the memory of that accident.'

The NJ *æz yad bordæn* 'forget' in (15) is an achievement LVC, unlike that of the full form of the verb (as an accomplishment predicate). On the contrary, the transitive reading of this verb has a strong influence on the transitive structure of the whole NJ (as a transitive construction).

5.2.2.3   ([$_{pp}$ *æz* 'from' + NP] *gereftæn* 'take/catch')

The last prepositional nuclear juncture with *æz* 'from' examined in the section below is *æz sær gereftæn* 'do all over again' (Lit.: 'from head take/catch') with the light verb *gereftæn* 'take/catch' and the concrete noun *sær* 'head'.

æz sær gereftæn *'do all over again' (Lit.: 'from head take/catch')*

>   (16)   kudæk   gerye-ra   æz   sær   gereft.

child   crying-DOM   from   head   take.Past.3rd.Sg.
'The child started crying all over again.'

Unlike the other prepositional constructions with *æz* 'from', an NP and the light verbs *ræftæn* 'go' and *bordæn* 'take/carry' (as presented in Tables 5–6 in Appendix B), the achievement verb class of the full form of the verb *gereftæn* 'take/catch' has a direct impact on the NJ *æz sær gereftæn* 'do all over again' (Lit.: 'from head take/catch'). Furthermore, the whole LVC is transitive, following the transitivity status of the heavy/full form of the verbal element *gereftæn*. In the following section (5.3), the second preposition occurring in the prepositional NJs is examined, namely, *ba* 'with'.

5.3 *ba* 'with'

In Persian, the preposition *ba* 'with' is not as productive as *æz* 'from' (examined in Sections 5.2, 5.2.1 and 5.2.2 above). That is, unlike *æz,* the preposition *ba* 'with' is not capable of fusing with both an NP and another preposition to form LVCs. In other words, it can combine with an NP to make a prepositional LVC, but in the data of this study no NJs were found that were made from the combination of this preposition (*ba* 'with') with another preposition and light verb in Persian. Also, the number of LVs and NPs capable of fusing with this preposition is limited. In fact, in the collected examples the most common light verbs appearing in these constructions are *šodæn* 'become' and *kærdæn* 'make/do', and the most frequent nouns capable of fusing with these constructions are abstract ones. In the following section, two prepositional NJs (*ba xæbær šodæn* 'become informed' (Lit.: 'with news become')) and *ba xæbær kærdæn* 'inform' (Lit.: 'with news make/do')) made with *ba* 'with', the NP 'news', and the mentioned light verbs (*šodæn* 'become' and *kærdæn* 'make/do') are analyzed, applying the diagnostic tests (given in Appendix B). And in order to determine the amount of the contribution of each of these light verbs, the same sentence is used for both of the constructions.

5.3.1 *([$_{PP}$ ba 'with' + NP] šodæn 'become')*

(17) pedær-æm   æz   hadese   ba   xæbær   šod.
father-my   from   accident   with   news   become.Past.3rd.Sg.
'My father became informed of the accident.'

5.3.2   *([$_{PP}$ ba 'with' + NP] kærdæn 'make/do')*

    (18) Hamid pedær-æm-ra   æz   hadese   ba   xæbær kærd.
           Hamid father-my-DOM from accident with news
           make.Past.3rd.Sg.
           'Hamid informed my father of the accident.'

As presented in Table 8 in Appendix B, both of the prepositional NJs with *ba* 'with' belong to the achievement verb class, even though in both the same NP and LVs have been used. On the contrary, the intransitive status of the light verb *šodæn* 'become' and the transitive reading of *kærdæn* 'make/do' have had a direct influence on the (in)transitivity interpretation of the whole NJs. The important point regarding the above two NJs is that the combination of the preposition *ba* 'with' and NPs (as in the case of our example *ba xæbær* 'informed', Lit.: 'with news') is sometimes considered as an adjective, i.e. the whole juncture is regarded as an adjectival LVC and not a prepositional NJ, since some adjectives are made by joining a preposition and an NP.

5.4   *bær* 'on/over'

The next preposition used in the prepositional NJs is *bær* 'on/over' which, like *ba* 'with' examined above, fuses with an NP and a light verb to make LVCs, i.e. in the data any other prepositions that have the capability of combining with *bær* 'on/over' and LVs to form a nuclear juncture were not found, and most of the nouns found in this group were of a concrete type (as the examples used in this section present). Also, the most frequent light verbs used in the prepositional constructions (with *bær* 'on/over' and an NP) are *ræftæn* 'go' and *dadæn* 'give', as in *bær bad ræftæn* 'be squandered' (Lit.: 'on/over wind go') and *bær bad dadæn* 'squander' (Lit.: 'on/over wind give') with the NP *bad* 'wind', which are examined below using the same examples.

5.4.1   *([$_{PP}$ bær bad] ræftæn) 'be squandered' (Lit.: 'on/over wind go')*

    (19) hæme-ye pul-ha-yæš   bær   bad   ræft.
           all-Ez   money-Pl-his/her on/over wind go.Past.3rd.Sg.
           'All his/her money was squandered.'

5.4.2 *([$_{PP}$ bær bad] dadæn) 'squander' (Lit.: 'on/over wind give')*

(20) u   hæme-ye pul-ha-yæš-ra   bær   bad
      dad.
      he/she all-Ez   money-Pl.-his/her-DOM   on/over wind
      give.Past.3rd.Sg.
      'He/She squandered all his/her money.'

As mentioned before, the preposition *bær* 'on/over' is capable of joining an NP (as in the case of our example *bad* 'wind' in (19)–(20)) and an LV to form a prepositional LVC. The two NJs *bær bad ræftæn* 'be squandered' (Lit.: 'on/over wind go') and *bær bad dadæn* 'squander' (Lit.: 'on/over wind give') are two instances of these LVCs where the intransitive/accomplishment light verb *ræftæn* 'go' and the transitive/achievement light verb *dadæn* 'give' mix with the nominal element *bad* 'wind' and *bær* 'on/over' to make prepositional LVCs. Both of these NJs, however, belong to the accomplishment verb class with the features of [–static], [+telic], [–punctual]. With regard to (in)transitivity structure, it should be mentioned that both NJs follow the (in) transitivity status of the verbal elements in the junctures, i.e. the construction with *ræftæn* 'go' (as an intransitive verb) is intransitive and the one with *dadæn* 'give' is transitive, following the intransitive reading of this predicate. So far, three prepositions (*æz* 'from', *ba* 'with' and *bær* 'on/over'), which are used to make prepositional/light verbal constructions, have been examined. Now, the next preposition, namely, *be* 'to', which is one of the most productive prepositions in Persian, is to be analyzed in the following section (5.5).

5.5 *be* 'to'

As mentioned above, the preposition *be* 'to' is very productive; it is, indeed, capable of combining with both an NP and another preposition to form LVCs along with light verbs. In other words, there are two groups of prepositional constructions with *be* 'to', i.e. one group embodying *be* 'to' + Preposition + LV and the other *be* 'to' + NP + LV, which are investigated in Sections 5.5.1 and 5.5.2, respectively.

5.5.1 *([be 'to' + Prep.] LV)*

The first group of LVCs where two prepositions fuse with a light verb is not as productive as the second group (combination of *be* 'to', an NP and an LV). In the data of the present study, there is a preposition capable of combining with *be* 'to' and light verbs to make NJs, namely, *miyan* 'among'. Furthermore, there are not so many light verbs which are able to join the constructions, and *aværdæn* 'bring', for instance, is the only light verb found which can join the prepositional phrase *be miyan* 'to among' to form a prepositional NJ.

be miyan aværdæn *'broach/bring up' (Lit.: 'to among bring')*

> (21) modir   mozu-e   pul-ra   be   miyan aværd.
>   manager subject-Ez   money-DOM   to   among bring.Past.3rd.Sg.
>   'The manager broached/brought up the subject of money.'

Unlike the first group of NJs made with *be* 'to', where this preposition combined with another NP and LV, in the NJ examined above (Table 10 in Appendix B) *be* 'to' fuses with another preposition (in the case of our example, *miyan* 'among') and an LV (*aværdæn* 'bring') to form a prepositional LVC. Even though the full form of this LVC is accomplishment, its nuclear juncture form with the prepositional phrase *be miyan* 'to among' belongs to the achievement verb class. Compatible with other NJs examined, *be miyan aværdæn* 'broach/bring up' is transitive, following the transitive reading of the full form of the verb. In Section 5.5.1, the prepositional NJs with *be* 'to' and another preposition fusing with the light verb were discussed. In the following section, the second group of constructions with the preposition *be* 'to', NP and LV is examined.

5.5.2   ([$_{pp}$ be 'to' + NP] LV)

The second group of prepositional NJs with *be* 'to' comprises those with the combination of this preposition, an NP (either concrete or abstract) and verbal elements. Also, the most common LVs appearing in these constructions include *amædæn* 'come', *aværdæn* 'bring', *gereftæn* 'take/catch', *daštæn* 'have', *kærdæn* 'make/do', *zædæn* 'hit/strike', *xordæn* 'eat', *kešidæn* 'pull' and *bordæn* 'take/carry', which can be used with both concrete and abstract nouns. In the following section, some prepositional constructions made with these light verbs, NPs and *be* 'to' are investigated.

be dæst amædæn *'be obtained' (Lit.: 'to hand come')*

> (22) pul-e   ziyad-i   dær in   moamele be dæst
> amæd.
> money many-Ind.A. in this deal   to hand
> come.Past.3rd.Sg.
> 'A lot of money was obtained in the deal.'

be huš amædæn *'gain consciousness' (Lit.: 'to consciousness come')*

> (23) saeed be huš   amæd.
> Saeed to consciousness come.Past.3rd.Sg.
> 'Saeed gained his consciousness.'

As is clear from Table 11 in Appendix B, the LVCs *be dæst amædæn* 'be obtained' in (22) and *be huš amædæn* 'gain consciousness' in (23) have the same verb class, namely, achievement, even though the full form of the verb is accomplishment and the two constructions are different in terms of noun types, i.e. the former has a concrete noun (*dæst* 'hand') and the latter an abstract noun (*huš* 'consciousness'). Following the intransitive status of the full form of *amædæn* 'come', the whole nuclear juncture has an intransitive interpretation.

be yad aværdæn *'remember' (Lit.: 'to remembrance bring')*

> (24) mæn esm-æš-ra   be yad   aværd-æm.
> I   name-his/her-DOM   to remembrance bring.Past-1st.Sg.
> 'I remembered his/her name.'

be yad daštæn *'remember' (Lit.: 'to remembrance have')*

> (25) mæn esm-æš-ra   be yad   dar-æm.
> I   name-his/her-DOM   to remembrance have-1st.Sg.
> 'I remember his/her name.'

The two NJs *be yad aværdæn* 'remember' in (24) and *be yad daštæn* 'remember' in (25) (as shown in Table 12 in Appendix B) are achievement predicates, having the same prepositions (*be* 'to') and noun (*yad* 'remembrance') but different light verbs (*aværdæn* 'bring' vs. *daštæn* 'have'). In fact, the difference in the verbal elements of the two LVCs does not have a direct impact on their verb class, even though the same sentence has been used for both constructions. Furthermore, the transitive status of *daštæn* 'have' (as a stative verb) and *aværdæn* 'bring' (as an accomplishment predicate) influences the two junctures, making them transitive constructions.

be kar bordæn *'use' (Lit.: 'to work take/carry')*

>   (26)   an-ha   æslæhe-ye   jædid-ra   dær   jæng   be   kar
>   bord-ænd.
>   that-Pl.   weapon-Ez   new-DOM   in   war   to   work
>   take/carry.Past-3rd.Pl.
>   'They used the new weapon in the war.'

be kar gereftæn *'use' (Lit: 'to work take/catch')*

>   (27)   an-ha   æslahe-ye   jædid-ra   dær   jæng   be   kar
>   gereft-ænd.
>   that-Pl.   weapon-Ez   new-DOM   in   war   to   work
>   take/catch.Past-1st.Sg.
>   'They used the new weapon in the war.'

As presented in Table 13 in Appendix B, the two adpositional (prepositional) constructions *be kar bordæn* 'use' in (26) and *be kar gereftæn* 'use' in (27) belong to the accomplishment class, i.e. the verb class of the verbal elements is not the only determining factor in this regard. Compatible with the results of other constructions examined in this section, the transitivity feature of the verbal elements (when used as heavy/full forms) has affected the transitive interpretation of the adpositional LVCs.

be pa kærdæn *'put on/wear (on the foot)' (Lit.: 'to foot make/do')*

>   (28)   an   bačče   xod-æš   kæfš-ra   be   pa   kærd.
>   that   child   self-his/her   shoe-DOM   to   foot   make.Past.3rd.Sg.
>   'That child put on the shoes on his/her own.'

Another light verb used in the adpositional (prepositional) constructions with the preposition *be* 'to' and an NP is *kærdæn* 'make/do'. Applying the five diagnostic tests to the LVC *be pa kærd* in (28) with this LV, it became clear that even though the verb class of the full form of the verbal element (*kærdæn* 'make/do') is activity, the whole adpositional NJ is an accomplishment. Also, the transitive reading of the verb (when used as a heavy predicate) has caused this LVC to be a transitive construction.

be dærd xordæn *'be useful' (Lit.: 'to pain eat')*

> (29) an   ačar-e   kohne be dærd xord.
>   that spanner-Ez old   to pain eat.Past.3rd.Sg.
>   'That old spanner was useful.'

be jib zædæn *'pocket' (Lit.: 'to pocket hit/strike')*

> (30) agha-ye Tæmæddon sæhm-e šoræka-ye xod-ra   hæm
>   be jib   zæd
>   Mr.-Ez Tæmæddon share-Ez partner-Ez self-DOM too
>   to pocket   hit/struck
>   'Mr. Tæmæddon pocketed his own partners' shares too.'

As is clear in Table 15 in Appendix B, the NJ *be dærd xordæn* 'be useful' in (29) is an achievement, while the full form of the verbal element is an activity verb. On the contrary, there is no difference between the transitivity status of their full/independent form and the LVC, i.e. both are transitive. Like the NJ *be dærd xordæn* 'be useful', *be jib zædæn* 'pocket' in (30) belongs to the achievement verb class (INGR **predicate'** (x, y)), while the verbal element (*zædæn* 'hit/strike') is an activity verb when used in the full form. Also, following the transitive reading of the full form of the verb in the construction, the whole juncture has a transitive interpretation.

be xun kešidæn *'kill' (Lit.: 'to blood pull')*

In the above construction (*be xun kešidæn*) with the light verb *kešidæn* 'pull', usually the noun *xun* 'blood' appears with the noun *xak* meaning 'soil'; that is, the combination of two nouns (*xun* 'blood' and *xak* 'soil'), which are connected with *væ* 'and', join with the preposition *be* 'to' and *kešidæn* 'pull' to form an NJ. Therefore, in the following example from the data, along with the noun *xun* 'blood', the noun *xak* 'soil' occurs in the construction as an instance of the prepositional phrases where the preposition fuses with a compound noun and the verbal element.

> (31) eskændær mærdom-e ziyad-i-ra   be xak væ xun
>   kešid.
>   Alexander people-Ez many-Ind.A to soil and blood
>   pull.Past.3rd.Sg.
>   'Alexander killed many people.'

The LVC in (31) is, indeed, an accomplishment, while the full/heavy form of the verbal element is an activity, but the whole NJ is transitive following the full form of the verb. In the following section, the combination of light verbs and another preposition, i.e. *bi* 'without', is examined.

5.6 *bi* 'without'

In Persian *bi* 'without' is one of the productive prepositions combined with another noun and an LV to make an NJ. As mentioned in Section 5.3 on the preposition *ba* 'with', the constructions made with *bi* 'without', NP and LV (along with the constructions made of *ba* 'with', NP and LV) are sometimes considered as adjectival NJs, since the combination of *bi* 'without' (or *ba* 'with', which has the opposite meaning to *bi* 'without', as in *ba deqqæt* 'careful/with care' and *bi deqqæt* 'careless/without care') and the NP (mostly of abstract type) acts as a compound adjective. The most frequent light verbs used in the prepositional constructions with *bi* 'without' are *šodæn* 'become' and *kærdæn* 'make'. As mentioned above, this preposition is productive, since it can combine with a large number of nouns and the light verbs *šodæn* 'become' and *kærdæn* 'make'. In the collected examples of this study, no combination of this preposition with another preposition was found to make nuclear juncture. That is, all the constructions used with *bi* 'without' are formed with the combination of *bi* 'without' and an NP, as in *bi hes šodæn* 'become numb/anaesthetized' (Lit.: 'without feeling become') and *bi hes kærdæn* 'make numb/anaesthetize' (Lit.: 'without feeling make'), which are discussed below.

bi hes šodæn *'become numb/anaesthetized' (Lit.: 'without feeling become')*

    (32)   dæst-æm bi   hes   šod.
            hand-my without feeling become.Past.3rd.Sg.
            'My hand became numb/anaesthetized.

bi hes kærdæn *'make numb/anaesthetize' (Lit.: 'without feeling make')*

    (33)   doktor dæst-æm-ra   bi   hes   kærd.
            doctor hand-my-DOM without feeling make.Past.3rd.Sg.
            'The doctor numbed/anaesthetized my hand.'

As presented in Table 18 in Appendix B, the two prepositional NJs with *bi* 'without', the abstract noun *hes* 'feeling', and the light verbs *šodæn* 'become' and *kærdæn* 'make' belong to the achievement verb class. Consider, for instance, the light verb *kærdæn* 'make/do' (in the above NJ *kærdæn* has the meaning of 'make' rather than 'do') is an activity predicate as a full form. The same story, however, does not hold true with regard to transitivity; that is, the (in)transitivity status of the two prepositional NJs (*bi hes šodæn* 'become numb/anaesthetized' (intransitive) and *bi hes kærdæn* 'make numb/ anaesthetize' (transitive)) is the same as the full form of the verbs in the constructions. So far, five of the most common prepositions (*æz* 'from', *ba* 'with', *bær* 'on/over', *be* 'to', *bi* 'without') that are capable of making a prepositional LVC through fusing with either another preposition or an NP and LVs have been examined. In the following section, the last frequent and productive preposition used in the prepositional phrase of the light verbal constructions, i.e. the preposition *dær* 'in', is discussed.

5.7 *dær* 'in'

As mentioned before, a prepositional LVC in Persian can form in two ways, i.e. it can be a combination of two prepositions or a preposition and an NP with an LV. The preposition or adposition (in RRG terms) *dær* 'in' in Persian has both of these capabilities. In other words, it can combine with either another preposition or an NP along with an LV to make adpositional NJs. The former group is examined in Section 5.7.1 and the latter in Section 5.7.2 below. Furthermore, the most common light verbs that can combine with this preposition are *daštæn* 'have' and *gereftæn* 'take', which form the prepositional NJs in both of the above groups.

5.7.1   *([dær 'in' + Prep.] LV)*

The adposition *dær* 'in' can fuse with such common prepositions as *miyan* 'among' or *bær* 'on/over' and the LVs *daštæn* 'have' and *gereftæn* 'take' to form a Prepositional Nuclear Juncture (PNJ). The examples used here are *dær bær daštæn* 'incur' and *dær bær gereftæn* 'surround' examined below.

5.7.1.1   *dær bær daštæn* 'incur' (Lit.: 'in on/over have')

(34) saxt-e   in   sæd hæzine-ha-ye   ziyadi dær bær
      dašt.
      building-Ez this dam expense-Pl.-Ez much   in   on/over
      have.Past.3rd.Sg.
      'The building of this dam incurred large expenses.'

As shown in Table 19 in Appendix B, the prepositional light verbal construction (PLVC) *dær bær daštæn* 'incur' in (34) is an achievement LVC, while the full form of the verbal element (*daštæn* 'have') belongs to the stative verb category. On the contrary, the transitive status of this verb has a direct influence on the transitive reading of the whole juncture. As mentioned before, the compound prepositions *dær bær* can also fuse with the light verb *gereftæn* 'take' to form an NJ (*dær bær gereftæn* 'surround', Lit.: 'in on/over take'), which is discussed below.

5.7.1.2   *dær bær gereftæn* 'surround' (Lit.: 'in on/over take')

(35) seyl   hæme-ye   šæhr-ra   dær   bær   gereft.
      flood   all/whole-Ez city-DOM   in   on/over take.Past.3ʳᵈ.Sg.
      'The flood surrounded the whole city.'

Like the LVC in (35), the aspectual properties of the full form of the verbal element of the NJ *dær bær gereftæn* 'surround' in (35) have had no impact on the verb class of the whole LVC. In other words, even though the verb *daštæn* 'have' is a stative predicate, the prepositional LVC with this verbal element is of accomplishment type. The transitivity reading of this verb (*daštæn* 'have'), however, has a direct influence on the transitive form of the prepositional construction (the compound preposition *dær bær* 'in on/over' and the light verb *daštæn* 'have'), i.e. they are both transitive.

In the above section (5.7.1), the first group of prepositional LVCs with the preposition *dær* 'in', i.e. the combination of two prepositions and light verbs, was discussed. Now there is a shift to analyzing the second group in the following section (5.7.2), which focuses on those prepositional nuclear junctures formed with the preposition *dær* 'in' and a noun fused with light verbs.

5.7.2   ([$_{pp}$ dær 'in' + NP] LV)

It was found that in the data of the present study the LVs *dæštæn* 'have' and *gereftæn* 'take' are the most common light verbs appearing in the second group of the prepositional LVCs with *dær* 'in'. That is, the combination of this preposition with an NP and LV. Also, skimming through the collected examples, it became clear that in this group, the preposition *dær* 'in' can fuse with both concrete and abstract nouns out of which one example with a concrete noun (*dæst* 'hand') and one with an abstract noun (*extiyar* 'authority') have been selected for examination in the present section. The sentence used for the diagnostic test application is the same for both prepositional phrases (*dær dæst*, Lit.: 'in hand' and *dær extiyar*, Lit.: 'in authority') and the light verbs *daštæn* 'have' and *gereftæn* 'take'. Therefore, the prepositional NJs under parallel examination in the section below are *dær dæst daštæn* 'have/exercise authority over' (Lit.: 'in hand have') with the concrete noun (*dæst* 'hand') versus *dær extiyar daštæn* 'have/exercise authority' (Lit.: 'in authority have') and *dær dæst gereftæn* 'take charge of' (Lit.: 'in hand take') versus *dær extiyar gereftæn* 'take charge of' (Lit.: 'in authority take') with the abstract noun (*extiyar* 'authority'). As is clear, the meaning of the two constructions in each pair is the same.

5.7.2.1 *dær dæst daštæn* vs. *dær extiyar daštæn* 'have/exercise authority over'

(36) u   edare-ye   šerkæt-ra   dær dæst dašt.
      he/she running-Ez company-DOM in   hand have.Past.3rd.Sg.
      'He/She had exercised authority over the company.'

(36′) u   edare-ye   šerkæt-ra   dær extiyar
       dašt.
       he/she running-Ez company-DOM in   authority
       have.Past.3rd.Sg.
       'He/She had exercised authority over the company.'

As schematized in Table 21 in Appendix B, the two prepositional LVCs belong to the same verb class, i.e. achievement, even though they have different nouns. They are both transitive following the transitivity status of the verbal element (*daštæn* 'have').

5.7.2.2 *dær dæst gereftæn* vs. *dær extiyar gereftæn* 'take charge of'

(37) u   edare-ye   šerkæt-ra   dær dæst gereft.
      he/she running-Ez company-DOM in   hand take.Past.3rd.Sg.
      'He/She took charge of the company.'

(37′) u   edare-ye   šerkæt-ra   dær extiyar
       gereft.
       he/she running-Ez company-DOM in   authority
       take.Past.3rd.Sg.
       'He/She took charge of the company.'

Both of the prepositional NJs presented in Table 22 in Appendix (B) are of the achievement transitive type, indicating that the verb class and the transitive reading of the verbal element (when used as a full form of the predicate) has had a direct impact on the whole NJ. The reason for this may be that even though the nouns in these NJs are different, they are basically the same in their semantic content, i.e. the prepositional phrase *dær dæst* 'in hand' in (37) has the same meaning as *dær extiyar* in (37´) when fused with *gereft* (or *dašt* 'had' in (36), (36´)); that is, they both mean 'take the control (of something) in one's hand or authority'. The only difference is that the latter (*dær extiyar*) is used in more formal situations.

In the above section, the prepositional NJs with *dær* 'in' were examined where this preposition can combine with a light verb and either another preposition or another NP to form an LVC. But there are some limited cases in Persian where a preposition can join with not one but two other prepositions to form a prepositional phrase that can fuse with a light verb to construct a prepositional nuclear juncture. The preposition *dær* 'in' has this capability, i.e. it can fuse, for instance, with the preposition *be* 'to' and another *dær* 'in' along with a light verb to form a prepositional LVC. The most common light verbs which appear in the construction *dær* 'in' + *be* 'to' + *dær* 'in' are *šodæn* 'become' and *kærdæn* 'make', as in *dær be dær šodæn* 'become homeless/wandering' (Lit.: 'in to in become') and *dær be dær kærdæn* 'make homeless/wandering' (Lit.: 'in to in make'). The point worth mentioning here is that although the combination of the three prepositions *dær be dær* (Lit.: 'in to in') is a compound preposition, it actually acts as an adjective meaning 'homeless/wandering', i.e. the whole NJ acts as an adjectival light verbal construction; therefore, this apparently prepositional LVC is not examined in the present section due to its adjectival function.

5.8 Discussion

As mentioned earlier (Section 5.2), there are usually three elements in the prepositional NJs, which fill the three positions in these constructions. The first (initial) position is filled by a preposition, the second (middle) by another preposition, or a noun as complement, and the third position by a light verb. Examining the data from the present study, it became clear that out of the list of the Persian prepositions presented at the beginning of this chapter, six prepositions can appear in the initial position, namely, *æz* 'from', *ba* 'with', *bær* 'on/over', *be* 'to', *bi* 'without' and *dær* 'in'. There is also a limited number of prepositions, such as *bær* 'on/over', *beyn* 'between', *piš* 'before' and *miyan* 'among', that appear in the second or middle position in the prepositional LVCs. In fact, not all the Persian prepositions have the capability of fusing with the light verbs to form prepositional nuclear junctures. Furthermore, the prepositions that appear in the initial position comprise basically two groups, i.e. the first group is those prepositions that can join either another preposition or a noun along with an LV to make a prepositional LVC, such as *æz* 'from', *be* 'to' and *dær* 'in'; the second group comprises those adpositions that can fuse with a noun (not another preposition) and an LV to construct a prepositional/light verbal construction, such as *ba* 'with', *bær* 'on/over' and *bi* 'without'.

It was found that all the prepositions in Persian nuclear junctures belong to the **locative** class of prepositions. Locative, also called spatial, prepositions refer to the location of an object, activity or event. Following Bjerre (2003), these prepositions have been categorized as directional and state, as schematized in Figure 5.3.

The investigation has revealed that the prepositions in the first group (mentioned above) capable of combining with either a noun or another preposition, namely, *æz* 'from', *be* 'to' and *dær* 'in', belong to either state or directional locative prepositions, where the former refers to the stative location of entities and the latter to the directional relation that exists between the source or beginning of an event, the path or process, and the goal or endpoint. In fact, the preposition *æz* 'from' denotes the source, *be* 'to' marks the goal, and *dær* 'in' shows the stative location. However, all the prepositions in the first group, i.e. *ba* 'with', *bær* 'on/over' and *bi* 'without', which can combine with or be followed by a noun (not a preposition) belong to the state locative prepositions denoting the stative location of entities. In the case of *bi* 'without', it should be noted that this preposition, unlike *ba* 'with', denotes the state where something is absent when it is combined with a noun in a prepositional phrase such as in *bi deqqæt* 'without care' or 'careless'. There is a need to recall that all the prepositions in the first group discussed above appear in the initial position in the prepositional phrase of the Persian NJs.

With regard to the prepositions that appear in the second or middle position in Persian prepositional NJs, namely, *bær* 'on/over', *piš* 'front/before',

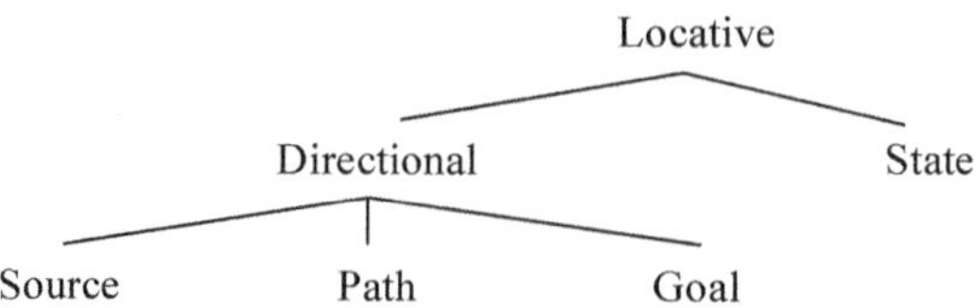

Figure 5.3 Types of prepositions.

Table 5.1 Locative preposition types in Persian prepositional NJs

A. Initial position preposition	Locative preposition type
1. Combined with either another preposition or a noun:	
a. æz **'from'**	**-Source** (directional)
b. be **'to'**	**-Goal** (directional)
c. dær **'in'**	**-Stative location** (state)
2. Combined with a noun (not another preposition):	
a. ba **'with'**	**-Stative location** (state)
b. bær **'on/over'**	**-Stative location** (state)
c. bi **'without'**	**-Stative location** (state)
B. Second or middle position preposition	
a. bær 'on/over'	**-Stative location** (state)
b. piš **'front/before'**	**-Stative location** (state)
c. beyn 'between'	**-Path** (directional)
d. miyan **'among'**	**-Path** (directional)

beyn 'between' and *miyan* 'among', it has emerged that the first two prepositions (*bær* and *piš*) belong to the state locative and the last two (*beyn* and *miyan*) to the path directional locative prepositions. The findings regarding the type of the prepositions in the prepositional phrase of the Persian LVCs are summarized in Table 5.1.

The effect of these locative/spatial prepositions in the prepositional light verb constructions will be discussed in more detail later in this chapter (Section 5.9).

In terms of the nominal element combined with different types of locative prepositions, it should be noted that abstract nouns are more common than concrete ones. In general, there were 34 adpositional LVCs analyzed in this chapter, among which the most productive prepositions are *æz* 'from' and *be* 'to', each with 11 occurrences or NJs, and the least productive ones are *ba* 'with', *bær* 'on/over' and *bi* 'without', each with two LVCs. And the preposition *dær* 'in' stands in the middle with six occurrences.

With regard to the light verbs capable of combining with adpositional phrases to form prepositional NJs, it should be mentioned that the most common light verbs showing this capability are *šodæn* 'become', *kærdæn* 'make', *daštæn* 'have', *ræftæn* 'go', *bordæn* 'take/carry', *gereftæn* 'take', *dadæn* 'give', *amædæn* 'come', *aværdæn* 'bring', *xordæn* 'eat', *zædæn* 'hit/strike' and *kešidæn* 'pull'. Among these light verbs, the most productive ones with respect to the number of occurrences in the data are *bordæn* 'take/carry', *daštæn* 'have' and *gereftæn* 'take', each with five NJs; the least productive ones are *dadæn* 'give', *xordæn* 'eat', *zædæn* 'hit/strike' and *kešidæn* 'pull', each with one construction.

The findings of the diagnostic tests applied to the prepositional NJs (numbered 1–34 in Table 5.2) examined in this chapter, including the verb class and the logical structure, are presented in Table 5.2.

In terms of aspectual properties, it should be stated that even though this study, as mentioned in previous chapters, is not based on corpus-oriented generalizations and it is not intended to provide any frequency references, sometimes the number of occurrences are referred to as an indicator of the commonality of some construction types. With regard to the prepositional LVCs analyzed in this chapter, it was observed that out of the 34 adpositional NJs examined 22 belong to the achievement verb class and 12 to the accomplishment type, i.e. the majority of the prepositional LVCs in the collected data are of achievement type, bearing such features as [–static], [+telic] and [+punctual] with the logical structure INGR **predicate'** (x) or (x, y). In fact, no NJs were found in the data with the state or activity verb class.

Also, by taking a careful look at Table 5.2 it becomes clear that the verb class of the prepositional light verbal constructions is not always dependent on the aspectual properties of the verbal elements. That is, as with other types of Persian LVCs discussed in the previous chapters, the verb is not the only determining factor in characterizing the verb class of the adpositional or prepositional constructions. In fact, out of the 34 NJs examined in this chapter, in 23 (numbered 2, 3, 6, 8, 9, 10, 13, 15, 16, 17, 18, 19, 21, 22, 23, 24, 25, 26, 28, 29, 30, 31, 32 in Table 5.2) the aspectual properties of the LVC are not predictable from the aspect type of the verbal element, as in the accomplishment LVC *æz bær kærdæn* 'memorize' (number 2 in Table 5.2) and the achievement NJ *ba xæbær kærdæn* 'inform' (number 13 in Table 5.2), while the verbal element *kærdæn* is activity. In eight constructions (numbered 4, 5, 7, 11, 14, 20, 33, 34 in Table 5.2) out of the 34 LVCs, the verb class has had a direct impact on the aspectual properties of the whole NJ, as in the NJs *æz beyn ræftæn* 'wipe out' and *bær bad ræftæn* 'be squandered' (numbers 4 and 14, respectively, in Table 5.2) with the verbal element *ræftæn* 'go', where the accomplishment class of the full form of this verb causes the whole nuclear junctures to be of accomplishment type. In the three remaining cases out of the 34 prepositional LVCs, the verbal element is *šodæn* 'become', which has no independent aspect type since this LV, as mentioned in previous chapters, has no full/heavy verbal form.

Table 5.2 Logical structure of the Persian prepositional/light verbal NJs

Preposition	Verb class	Prepositional NJ (infinitive form)	Logical structure (LS)
æz + Prep. + LV: æz bær + LV	Acc.	1. -æz bær šodæn (Lit.: 'from on/over become') 'memorize'	BECOME æz bær šodæn' (x)
		2. -æz bær kærdæn (Lit.: 'from on/over make') 'memorize'	BECOME æz bær kærdæn' (x, y)
		3. -æz bær daštæn (Lit.: 'from on/over have') 'know by heart'	INGR æz bær daštæn' (x, y)
æz beyn + LV	Ach.	4. -æz beyn ræftæn (Lit.: 'from between go') 'be wiped out'	BECOME æz beyn ræftæn' (x)
		5. -æz beyn bordæn (Lit.: 'from between take/carry') 'wipe out'	BECOME æz beyn bordæn' (x, y)
æz piš + LV	Acc.	6. -æz piš bordæn (Lit.: 'from front take/carry') 'manage'	INGR æz piš bordæn' (x, y)
æz miyan + LV	Ach.	7. -æz miyan bordæn (Lit.: 'from among take/carry') 'wipe out'	BECOME æz miyan bordæn' (x, y)
æz + NP + LV	Acc.	8. -æz dæst ræftæn (Lit.: 'from hand go') 'be lost'	INGR æz dæst ræftæn' (x)
		9. -æz huš ræftæn (Lit.: 'from consciousness go') 'lose consciousness'	INGR æz huš ræftæn' (x)
		10. -æz yad bordæn (Lit.: 'from remembrance take/carry') 'forget'	INGR æz yad bordæn' (x, y)
		11. -æz sær gereftæn (Lit.: 'from head take') 'do all over again'	INGR æz sær gereftæn' (x, y)
ba + NP + LV	Ach.	12. -ba xæbær šodæn (Lit.: 'with news become') 'become informed'	INGR ba xæbær šodæn' (x)
		13. -ba xæbær kærdæn (Lit.: 'with news make') 'inform'	INGR ba xæbær kærdæn' (x, y)

(cont.)

(cont.)

Preposition	Verb class	Prepositional NJ (infinitive form)	Logical structure (LS)
bær + NP + LV	Acc.	14. -bær bad ræftæn (Lit.: 'on/over wind go') 'be squandered'	BECOME bær bad ræftæn' (x)
bær + NP + LV	Acc.	15. -bær bad dadæn (Lit.: 'on/over wind give') 'squander'	BECOME bær bad dadæn' (x, y)
be + NP + LV	Ach.	16. -be dæst amædæn (Lit.: 'to hand come') 'be obtained'	INGR be dæst amædæn' (x)
		17. -be huš amædæn (Lit.: 'to consciousness come') 'gain consciousness'	INGR be huš amædæn' (x)
		18. -be yad aværdæn (Lit.: 'to remembrance bring') 'remember'	INGR be yad aværdæn' (x, y)
		19. -be yad daštæn (Lit.: 'to remembrance have') 'remember'	INGR be yad daštæn' (x, y)
	Acc.	20. -be kar bordæn (Lit.: 'to work take/carry') 'use'	BECOME be kar bordæn' (x, y)
		21. -be kar gereftæn (Lit.: 'to work take') 'use'	BECOME be kar gereftæn' (x, y)
		22. -be pa kærdæn (Lit.: 'to foot make') 'put on/wear (on the foot)'	BECOME be pa kærdæn' (x, y)
	Ach.	23. -be dærd xordæn (Lit.: 'to pain eat') 'be useful'	INGR be dærd xordæn' (x)
		24. -be jib zædæn (Lit.: 'to pocket hit/strike') 'pocket'	INGR be jib zædæn' (x, y)
	Acc.	25. -be (xak væ) xun kešidæn (Lit.: 'to (soil and) blood pull') 'kill'	BECOME be (xak væ) xun kešidæn' (x, y)
be + Prep. + LV	Ach.	26. -be miyan aværdæn (Lit.: 'to among bring') 'broach/bring up'	INGR be miyan aværdæn' (x, y)

(cont.)

(cont.)

Preposition	Verb class	Prepositional NJ (infinitive form)	Logical structure (LS)
bi + NP + LV	Ach.	27. -bi hes šodæn (Lit.: 'without feeling become') 'become numb/ anaesthetized'	INGR bi hes šodæn' (x)
		28. -bi hes kærdæn (Lit.: 'without feeling make') 'make numb/ anaesthetize'	INGR bi hes kærdæn' (x, y)
dær + Prep. +LV:	Ach.	29. -dær bær daštæn (Lit.: 'in on/over have') 'incur'	INGR dær bær daštæn' (x, y)
dær bær + LV	Acc.	30. -dær bær gereftæn (Lit.: 'in on/over take') 'surround' 'have/exercise authority over'	BECOME dær bær gereftæn' (x, y)
dær + NP + LV	Ach.	31. -dær dæst daštæn (Lit.: 'in hand have') 'have/exercise authority over'	INGR dær dæst daštæn' (x, y)
		32. -dær extiyar daštæn (Lit.: 'in authority have') 'have/exercise authority over'	INGR dær extiyar daštæn' (x, y)
		33. -dær dæst gereftæn (Lit.: 'in hand take') 'take charge of'	INGR dær dæst gereftæn' (x, y)
		34. -dær extiyar gereftæn (Lit.: 'in authority take') 'take charge of'	INGR dær extiyar gereftæn' (x, y)

Consequently, in the majority of the prepositional constructions (23 out of 34 constructions) there is a discrepancy between the verb class of the full/ heavy verb form and that of the whole prepositional nuclear juncture. As a matter of fact, this is not unexpected since the [OUTPUT] LV construction is viewed as a single predication composed of the [INPUT] LV constituent elements. That is, the single event is then passed to the RRG linking system from semantics to syntax to be discussed later in Section 5.10. Section 5.9 below aims at analyzing the event structure of the prepositional nuclear junctures.

5.9   Event structure of prepositional NJs

Consistent with the findings of the adjectival LVCs, the investigation of the prepositional LVCs has revealed that the light verbs fusing with the prepositional phrases belong to the 'phase' class of verbs, as shown in Table 5.3.

As is clear from Table 5.3, the light verbs occurring in the prepositional LVCs belong to the phase group of verbs. The only exception to the above list is the light verb *daštæn* 'have', which denotes state or attribute and is in fact a non-phase verb; that is, unlike the phase light verbs, it does not refer to particular phases of an event demonstrated in Figure 5.4.

The light verbs capable of fusing with the prepositional phrases in Persian refer to the continuative (process), terminative (endpoint) or result (resultative) phases of an event, as presented in Table 5.3. Interestingly, this parallels the findings with the adjectival NJs discussed in Chapter 4. The exception is the non-phase verb *daštæn* 'have'. The other non-phase verb, *didæn* 'see', found in the data does not seem to occur in prepositional NJs. In general, most of the verbs in Persian LVCs belong to the phase type, and there are only a few non-phase verbs in these constructions. The same phenomenon takes place in Toratani's (2002) study on Japanese compound (complex) verb constructions, where the majority of verbs occurring in these structures

Table 5.3 Features of LVs as 'phase' verbs in prepositional NJs

Light verb		LVs' phase features
šodæn	'become'	Result
kærdæn	'make'	Process
dadæn	'give'	Result: x, y ⟶ z: endpoint, RRG 3 place PRED analysis
zædæn	'hit/strike'	Continue, process/start, process
gereftæn	'take/catch'	Endpoint
kešidæn	'pull'	Process
xordæn	'eat'	Process
amædæn	'come'	Process ⟵
ræftæn	'go'	Process ⟶
aværdæn	'bring'	Process: 'Do' activity, RRG 3 place PRED analysis
bordæn	'take/carry'	Process
daštæn	'have'	Attribute/State: Non-phase

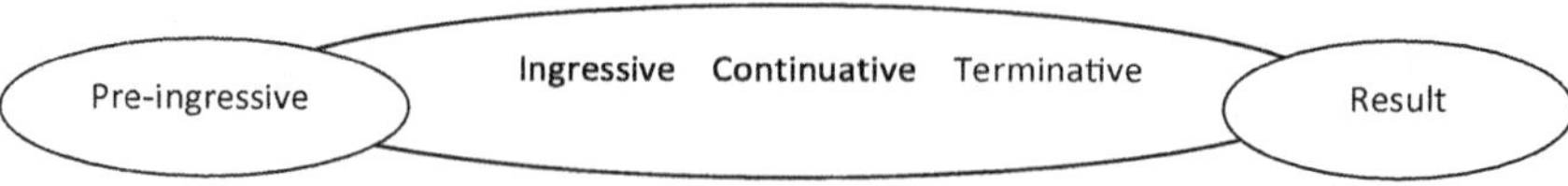

Figure 5.4 Phases of an event.

belong to phase verbs and there are just a few non-phase verbs. In Toratani's (2002) study, only such verbs as *sugi* 'exceed' and *kane* 'combine something with' belong to the non-phase verb class, while there are at least seven phase verbs appearing in compound verb constructions in Japanese.

As mentioned above, with the exception noted, the light verbs in the prepositional LVCs refer to a particular phase of an event. Consider the examples in Table 5.4, where the verbal element is the same in each pair

Table 5.4 LVs' phase features as process, endpoint and result in Persian prepositional NJs

Prepositional NJ	**LVs' phase feature**	**Logical structure**
(a) -æz bær šodæn (Lit.: 'from on/over become') **'memorize'**	Result	BECOME **æz bær šodæn′** (x)
(a′) -ba xæbær šodæn (Lit.: 'with news become') **'become informed'**		INGR **ba xæbær šodæn′** (x)
(b) -æz beyn ræftæn (Lit.: 'from between go') **'be wiped out'**	Process	BECOME **æz beyn ræftæn′** (x)
(b′) -bær bad ræftæn (Lit.: 'on/over wind go') **'be squandered'**		BECOME **bær bad ræftæn′** (x)
(c) -æz miyan bordæn (Lit.: 'from among take/carry') **'wipe out'**	Process	BECOME **æz miyan bordæn′** (x, y)
(c′) -æz yad bordæn (Lit.: 'from remembrance take/carry') **'forget'**		INGR **æz yad bordæn′** (x, y)
(d) -be miyan aværdæn (Lit.: 'to among bring') **'broach/bring up'**	Process	INGR **be miyan aværdæn′** (x, y)
(d′) -be yad aværdæn (Lit.: 'to remembrance bring') **'remember'**		INGR **be yad aværdæn′** (x, y)
(e) -dær bær gereftæn (Lit.: 'in on/over take') **'surround'**	Endpoint	BECOME **dær bær gereftæn′** (x, y)
(e′) -dær dæst gereftæn (Lit.: 'in hand take') **'take charge of'**		INGR **dær dæst gereftæn′** (x, y)

of the prepositional NJs and the first LVC in each pair is formed with the prepositional compound (two prepositions), while the second is made with a preposition and a noun. The light verb in the first (a, a′) pair, i.e. *šodæn* 'become', refers to the result (resultative) phase of the events, while the preposition-preposition combination (*æz bær* 'from on/over') in (a) with the source (directional) locative preposition *æz* 'from' and the state locative preposition *bær* 'on/over' implies the event type of 'memorizing'. That is, the combination of these two prepositions indicates that something has caused an entity (e.g. the thing is to be memorized) to move from a 'source' implied by *æz* 'from' as a locative source directional preposition and to be placed 'on' a location (e.g. one's memory) implied by *bær* 'on/over' as a locative stative location preposition. Additionally, the preposition-N combination (*ba xæbær* 'with news') in (a′) implies 'with information' or 'being informed'. In other words, the preposition *ba* 'with' shows that the 'state' of something exists and that 'something' is the noun following this preposition. It is a logical justification to claim that this is the reason why prepositions such as *ba* 'with' are followed by an N in the prepositional NJs and not another preposition, since semantically they need a noun whose stative location is characterized by such prepositions.

In the second (b, b′) (*ræftæn* 'go'), the third (c, c′) (*bordæn* 'take/carry') and the fourth (d, d′) (*aværdæn* 'bring') pairs, the light verbs refer to the continuative or process phase of events and the preverbal prepositional constructions provide the actual event type or attribute. In the second pair, for instance, the prepositional NJ in (b) with the locative source (directional) preposition *æz* 'from' and the locative path (directional) preposition *beyn* 'between' imply that something has been wiped from a source (denoted by the source preposition *æz* 'from') and the path *beyn* 'between'. In fact, the whole juncture *æz beyn ræftæn* (using the gloss) means 'something goes from between', which means 'something is wiped out'. As is clear here, the two prepositions provide the information regarding the event attribute and the LV refers to the process of the 'wiping out' event which takes place over a time span. As demonstrated in Table 5.4, the same story takes place in the examples in (b′), (c, c′) and (d, d′), where the LV refers to the process inherent nature of the event and the prepositional elements provide the event type or subtypes.

In the fifth pair, however, the LV refers to the endpoint or terminative phase of the event, but the role of the preverbal element is the same as the other four examples mentioned above. That is, the preposition-preposition combination *dær bær* 'in on/over' (in (e)) with the two state locative prepositions *dær* 'in' and *bær* 'on/over' implies the 'surrounding' event. In other words, it indicates that 'something takes in and over something else', which is the same meaning of 'surround'. In addition, the preposition-N combination *dær dæst* 'in hand' in (e′) with the same state locative preposition (*dær* 'in') and the concrete noun (*dæst* 'hand') implies 'having (the control of something) in one's hand', which shows the type of the main event of the whole prepositional LVC.

In conclusion, in all the examples presented in Table 5.4, the light verb provides the information regarding the phase of an event, while the preverbal-prepositional elements play the role of determining the event type of the whole construction. As mentioned above, the combination of the two locative prepositions *æz bær* 'from on/over' in (a), for instance, implies the 'memorizing' event type. By taking a careful look at the glossary of the prepositional LVCs in Table 5.2 in Section 5.7, it becomes clear that the same story is true for all the prepositional nuclear junctures; that is, the preverbal-prepositional constituents determine the event type or attribute and the light verbs refer to particular phases of events and are in fact bleached with regard to the event type. Even though in such prepositional NJs as *æz bær daštæn* 'know by heart' (Lit.: 'from on/over have', presented in Table 5.2) with the non-phase verb *daštæn* 'have' the light verb denotes state or attribute and does not refer to a particular phase of an event, the prepositional elements provide the event type and the light verb is bleached in this respect. As a matter of fact, the findings of this section are in close affinity with the result of Chapter 4, where the light verbs belong to the phase class of verbs and are bleached with regard to event attribute.

5.10 Argument structure (syntactic and semantic valency)

With regard to the argument structure and the amount of contribution the preverbal or the prepositional elements make in the NJs, the interesting point to be highlighted here is that in the majority of the 34 prepositional LVCs analyzed in the present chapter, the argument structure of the whole complex nucleus in each example is exactly the same as the full/heavy form of the verbal element. In other words, in these constructions if the verbal element takes one argument with the logical structure of ... **predicate′** (x) when used as a full/heavy form, the NJ made with this verb takes one argument, too. And the same story takes place when there are two (**predicate′** (x, y)) or more arguments involved having (x) as the Privileged Syntactic Argument (PSA) and (y) as the Direct Core Argument (DCA). There is only one exceptional case where there is a discrepancy between the number of the arguments the full form of the verbal element takes and that of the whole prepositional NJ. That is, in the LVC *be dærd xordæn* 'be useful' (Lit.: 'to pain eat') with the preposition *be* 'to' in (29) (Section 5.6.2) the argument structure of the full form of the verb and the prepositional LVC do not match. In other words, even though *xordæn* 'eat' in *be dærd xordæn* 'be useful' in (29) takes two arguments as a full predicate, it has one argument (x) as an adpositional LVC, as shown in Table 5.2.

Another parameter worth discussing here is the transitivity structure of the prepositional NJs and the role of the prepositional phrase and the verbal elements in this respect. Compatible with the above discussion regarding the argument structure of the prepositional LVCs, the transitivity status of all (with the exception of the LVC in (29) Section 5.6.2 discussed above) the adpositional constructions examined in this chapter is the same as the verbal element involved in the NJs. This indicates that in prepositional LVCs the role of the verbal element outweighs that of the preverbal-prepositional elements in determining the transitivity architecture of the NJs, which is compatible with the findings of the adjectival LVC type (examined so far), where in all the constructions analyzed the number of the syntactic arguments is matched with that of the verbal element.

In terms of the semantic valency or thematic roles assigned by the prepositional NJs, it should be pointed out that a clear consistency is observed between the type of semantic argument of the adpositional constructions and the full independent form of the verbal element. That is, whenever the full/heavy verb assigns the (x) argument an agentive thematic role, the prepositional NJ assigns the same agent role, and whenever the role is a patient the argument of the prepositional NJ is a patient, too. The same story takes place with the (y) argument and there is compatibility between the semantic role assigned by the full verb and the prepositional LVC. The only exception to this is the prepositional LVC *be dærd xordæn* 'be useful' (Lit.: 'to pain eat') in (29), where the full/heavy form of the verb *xordæn* 'eat' assigns an agentive role to the (x) argument (and a patient role to the (y) argument), while in the NJ *be dærd xordæn* 'be useful' (used in (29) and repeated here as (29′)) this construction assigns the (x) argument a patient role (having no (y) argument).

> (29′) an ačar-e   kohne be dærd xord.
>   that spanner-Ez old   to   pain eat.Past.3rd.Sg.
>   'That old spanner was useful.'

As presented in (29′) above, the prepositional LVC with the light verb *xordæn* 'eat' or *xord* 'ate' (as the inflected past tense form) takes one (x) argument and assigns it a patient thematic role, unlike its full/heavy form. As mentioned before, this NJ is the only case among the 34 prepositional constructions examined in this chapter where the semantic valency of the adpositional NJ is not compatible with that of the full/heavy form of the verbal element in the LVC. This further supports the idea that in the Persian prepositional NJs the impact of the verbal element is more significant in characterizing the semantic/thematic roles of the whole construction. The reason for this could be the subject of further investigations. In order to have a more detailed discussion of the prepositional NJs and their linking procedure from semantics to syntax, they are presented in Section 5.11 below.

5.11   Semantics to syntax of prepositional NJs

In order to illustrate the semantic to syntax algorithm and the Layered Structure of the Clause (LSC) for the Persian prepositional light verbal NJs, the prepositional nuclear juncture *æz beyn ræftæn* 'be wiped out' (Lit.: 'from between go') used in (11) (in Section 5.2.1), repeated here as (38), has been selected. The LSC and the semantics to syntax linking algorithm of this example is presented in Figure 5.5.

> (38)   tæmam-e   šæhr   æz   beyn   ræft.
>   all-ez   city   from   between   go.Past.3rd.Sg.
>   'The whole city was wiped out.'

As presented in Figure 5.5, *æz beyn ræft* 'be wiped out' (Lit.: 'from between go') is an accomplishment intransitive prepositional LVC with the logical structure BECOME **predicate′** (x). That is, it takes one argument or macrorole as the actor, which is in fact the Privileged Syntactic Argument (PSA) of the sentence, and the prepositional phrase combined with the light verb is made of two prepositions (not a preposition and an NP). As is clear from the LSC below and the semantics to syntax linking figure, the first nucleus (NUC) of the light verbal construction is a prepositional phrase (PP) followed by a CORE$_{p}$ node, which is further followed by two NUC$_{p}$ nodes, i.e. the two elements are prepositions. In some types of prepositional LVCs (discussed earlier in this chapter), however, the second element can be a noun, i.e. the second node following CORE$_{p}$ is indeed an NUC$_{N}$.

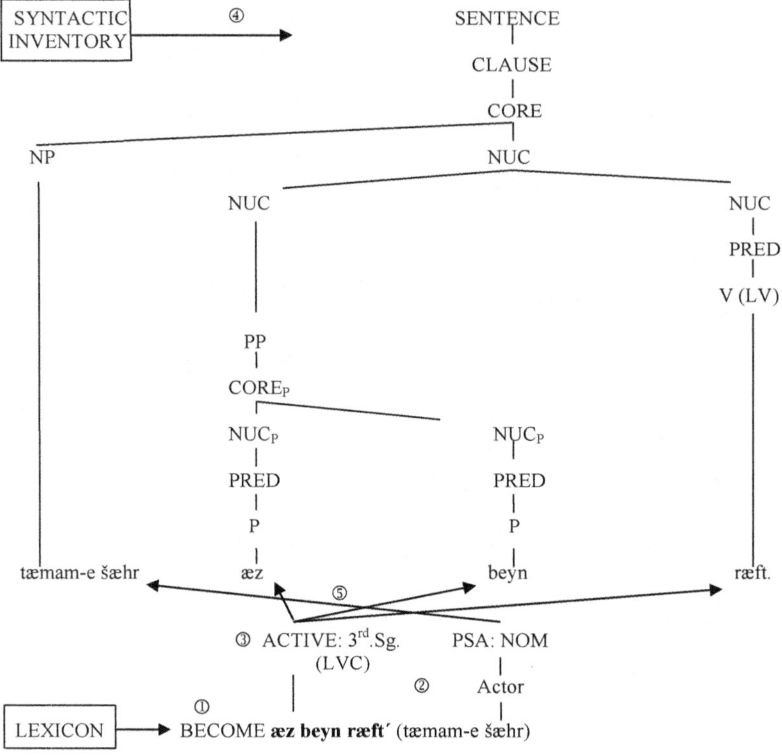

Figure 5.5 Semantics to syntax linking in the Persian accomplishment intransitive prepositional nuclear juncture (Prep. + Prep. + LV).

Analyzing the amount of contribution of the preverbal and verbal elements in characterizing the verb class, transitivity, event and argument structure of the adpositional/prepositional NJs in Sections 5.8–5.10 and their linking procedure from semantics to syntax in Section 5.11, there can now be a shift to examining the lexical-syntactic characteristics of these constructions in Section 5.12 below.

5.12   Prepositional NJs' lexical-syntactic features

5.12.1   *Lexical features of prepositional LVCs*

Following the discussion in Section 2.3.1 of Chapter 2, the lexical characteristics of the prepositional nuclear junctures are examined in this section
to pave the way for the main objective, i.e. to provide a unified account for
the formation of these LVCs within the RRG framework. Consistent with the
adjectival LVCs, examined before, the prepositional NJs exhibit some lexical
features which show that these constructions act as a single predicate. These
lexical features are as follows.

1. The prepositional NJs, consistent with the adjectival and adverbial
    LVCs, do not have a full/heavy verb form, and although this feature is
    not applicable to these constructions, it is mentioned here to compare
    different types of LVCs with respect to this lexical characteristic.
2. The prepositional LVCs can be used to form gerundive (39)–(40) and
    agentive nominals (41)–(44).
    Preposition + preposition + LV:

(39) a. æz   bær   kærd-æn-e   sorud   mohem   bud.
          from   on/over   make-Suf.-Ez   song   important   was
          'Memorizing the song was important.'

Preposition + NP + LV:

(40) b. bi   hes   kærd-æn-e   an   ozv   mohem
          bud.
          without   feeling   make.Past-Suf.-Ez   that   organ   important
          was
          'Making numb/Anaesthetizing that organ was important.'

Preposition + preposition + LV:

(41) a. æz   bær   kærdæn   ⟶   æz-bær-kon-ænde
          From   on/over   make.INF   from-on/over-make.Pr.-Suf.
          'memorize'   'person who memorizes'

Preposition + NP + LV:

(42) b. bi   hes   kærdæn ⟶ bi-hes-kon-ænde
     without feeling make.INF   without-feeling-make.
                                         Pr.-Suf.

     'make numb/anaesthetize'   'person/thing that makes
                                           numb'

3.   The prepositional NJs can be used to form adjective-*i* and participle adjectives, as in (43) and (44) below, respectively.

(43)   in   sorud   æz   bær   kærdæn-i   n-ist.
       this song   from on/over make.Inf.-Suf. Neg.-is
       'This song is not to be memorized.'

(44)   bi   hes   šodæn   ⟶ ozv-e   bi-hes-šod-e
       without feeling become.INF   organ-Ez without-feeling-
                                             became-PPART.

       'become numb/anaesthetized'   'the anaesthetized/numb
                                           organ'

(Note that for some participle adjectives of LVCs the past participle form of the verb *šodæn* 'become' can also accompany the construction and in the case of the example in (44) above the past participle of *šodæn* 'become', i.e. *šode* is optional.)

4.   The formation of the manner adverbial from the prepositional LVCs is not possible.

5.   The stress in these constructions falls on the first preverbal-prepositional element, treating the whole construction as a single word.

As presented above, the prepositional nuclear junctures in Persian have some lexical characteristics, indicating that these constructions behave as a unified element supporting the wordhood status of the two nuclei. Interestingly, the behaviour of these nuclear junctures is in close conjunction with that of the adjectival NJs, i.e. the two predicative elements fuse through the morphological derivation machinery in RRG, which will be demonstrated in detail in the final chapter of this study.

5.12.2   *Syntactic features of prepositional LVCs*

5.12.2.1   Intervening elements

The negative prefix *ne-/næ-*

For all the prepositional NJs in this research study a negative prefix is possible, e.g. the accomplishment prepositional NJ with the first group structure (Prep. + Prep. + LV) *dær bær gereftæn* 'surround'.

> (45) doktor an ozv-ra   bi   hes   næ-kærd.
> doctor that organ-DOM without feeling Neg.-make.Past.3ʳᵈ.Sg.
> 'The doctor did not anaesthetize/make numb that organ.'

The progressive/durative *mi-*

This feature is applicable to all types of prepositional LVCs.

> (46) doktor an ozv-ra   bi   hes   mi-kon-æd.
> doctor that organ-DOM without feeling DUR.-make-3ʳᵈ.Sg.
> 'The doctor makes numb/anaesthetizes that organ.'

The imperative form (present stem of verb + (*be-*))

Applicable to all types of prepositional NJs.

> (47) an ozv-ra   bi   hes   (be)-kon.
> that organ-DOM without feeling IMP.-make
> 'Make numb/anaesthetize that organ.'

The imperative negative (*næ-* + present stem of verb)

Applicable to all types of prepositional NJs.

> (48) an ozv-ra   bi   hes   næ-kon.
> that organ-DOM without feeling Neg.IMP.-make
> 'Do not make numb/anaesthetize that organ.'

The future auxiliary *xah* 'want'

Applicable to all types of prepositional NJs.

> (49) doktor an ozv-ra   bi   hes   xah-æd-kærd.
> doctor that organ-DOM without feeling want-3ʳᵈ.Sg.-make
> 'The doctor will make numb/anaesthetize that organ.'

Adjective intervention

Not applicable to prepositional NJs.

DOM and 'this' intervention

Not applicable to prepositional NJs.

5.12.2.2 Relativization

The relative pronoun *ke* 'that' interrupts the two preverbal/verbal elements. Not applicable to prepositional NJs.

5.12.2.3 Focused by WH-question word

For example, *č* 'what'. Not applicable to prepositional LVCs.

5.12.2.4 Coordination

The preverbal element can coordinate with another element by coordination conjunctions, e.g. *væ* 'and'. Applicable to all types of prepositional NJs.

> (50) doktor u-ra   bi   huš   væ   bi   hes
>   kærd.
>   doctor he/she without consciousness and without feeling
>   made
>   'The doctor made him unconscious and numb.'

So far, it has been shown that Persian nuclear junctures show some syntactic characteristics, which, as will be presented in Chapter 6, can be accounted for within the RRG architecture. In the following section, an attempt has been made to determine the nexus-juncture linkage type of the prepositional LVCs and present their morphological, semantic, syntactic and pragmatic features in a constructional template or schema.

5.13 Constructional schema of prepositional NJs

According to RRG, and as mentioned before, if two nuclei share the same nuclear operator and are structurally independent, the nexus-juncture linkage type of the construction is nuclear cosubordination. The prepositional LVCs in Persian, as presented in (45) and Figure 5.6, belong to this linkage type.

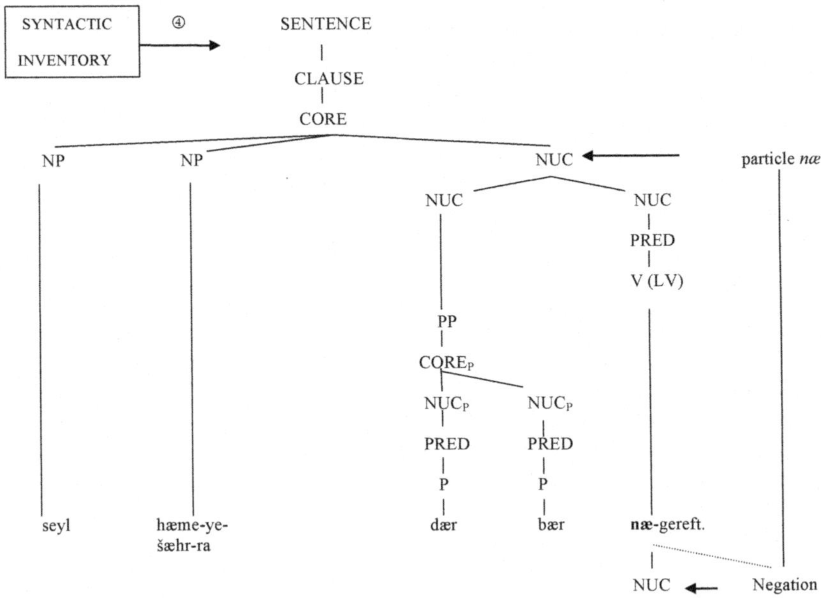

Figure 5.6 Operator sharing in Persian prepositional NJs.

(45) seyl   hæme-ye   šæhr-ra   dær   bær
      næ-gereft.
      flood   all/whole-Ez   city-DOM   in   on/over
      Neg.Op.-take.Past.3rd.Sg.
      'The flood did not surround the whole city.'

As demonstrated in Figure 5.6, the two NUC nodes are structurally independent, while sharing the negation nuclear operator *næ-*, which is attached to the verbal element in Persian. This indicates that the linkage type of the prepositional LVCs is nuclear cosubordination.

Now that the nexus-juncture linkage of these constructions, which is the same as that in the adjectival nuclear junctures, has been determined, the constructional schema of the prepositional nuclear junctures can be schematized (Table 5.5).

According to RRG, such constructional schemas as the one presented in Table 5.5 for Persian prepositional LVCs provide a detailed representation of the morphological, syntactic, semantic and pragmatic features.

Table 5.5 Constructional schema for Persian prepositional nuclear junctures

Construction: Persian prepositional nuclear juncture
SYNTAX:
Juncture: nuclear
Nexus: cosubordination
Construction type: light verbal (prepositional phrase + light verb)
$[_{CL} [_{CORE} NP [_{NUC} [_{NUC} … Prep. phrase] [_{NUC} … V(LV)]] NP …] …]$
Unit template(s): (3.6) (see Section 3.4.4.1 in Chapter 3)
PSA: none
Linking: default
MORPHOLOGY:
$PRED_{NUC1}$: prepositional elements: either (Prep. + Prep.) or (Prep. + NP)
$PRED_{NUC2}$: light verb: majority of phase verbs and one non-phase verb ('have')
[LV: [**predicate'** (x) or (x, y)] + ADV]
[LV: [**do'** (x, **predicate'** (x) or (x, y)] + ADV]
[LV: [INGR **predicate'** (x) or (x, y)] +PP]
[LV: [BECOME **predicate'** (x) or (x, y)] + PP]
SEMANTICS: $[PRED_{NUC1}]… + … [PRED_{NUC2}]$
PRAGMATICS:
Illocutionary force: unspecified
Focus structure: unspecified

5.14 Phrasal verbs and prepositional LVCs

As mentioned before, in Persian it is the prepositional phrases that combine
with the light verbs, not the preposition alone. That is, in prepositional LVCs,
unlike the adverbial ones discussed in Saeedi (2009a), the preposition takes
another complement, which can be a noun or another preposition. It is always
the whole phrase that plays the predicating role along with the verbal element
of the LVCs, i.e. they act as a single predicate. In fact, these phrases are of
two main types. In the first type, two (or in some rare situations more) prepositions combine with the light verb ([Prep. + Prep.] LV), and in the second
type a preposition and an NP (as in the example in (5), Section 5.1 above)
join the verbal element ($[_{PP}$ Prep. + NP] LV) to form nuclear junctures. The
structures of the two phrase types can be presented as follows:

Persian PLVCs: $[_{V2} PP [_{V1} V]$

The prepositional phrase (PP) in the above structure is the combination of
a preposition (filling the first position) and either another preposition $[_{PP} [P$
+ P]] or a noun $[_{PP} [P + NP]]$, which fill the second position. Rezai (2006),
working on particle (phrasal) verb and prepositional verb constructions in

English and Persian, points out that the prepositional verb constructions, like prepositional LVCs, can be distinguished from particle (phrasal) verb constructions by such properties as topicalization, where the prepositional phrase can be topicalized while the particle in phrasal verb constructions cannot. Consider the following two English examples (a, b) provided by Rezai (2006) and their topicalized forms in (a′, b′). Recall that the first sentence represents a prepositional phrase verb construction and the second a particle (phrasal) verb.

    a.   John ran up the road.
    b.   John tore up the card.
    a′. Up the road John ran.
    b′. *Up the card John tore.

(Note: The asterisk before the example sentence in (b′) denotes its ungrammaticality.)

As is clear from (b′), the particle in phrasal verb constructions cannot be topicalized, unlike the preposition in prepositional verb constructions. According to Rezai (2006), Persian has a few phrasal verbs that cannot be topicalized. The following example is provided by Rezai (2006) for particle (phrasal) verbs.

(46)   Reza tup-ra   birun ændaxt
       Reza ball-DOM   out   throw.Past.3rd.Sg.
       'Reza threw the ball out/threw out the ball.'

(46′) *Reza birun tup-ra   ændaxt
       Reza out   ball-DOM threw
       'Reza threw the ball out/threw out the ball.'

The topicalized form of the sentence in (46), provided in (46′), is not acceptable. This is contrary to such prepositional LVCs as *Ali æz donya ræft* 'Ali passed away' (Lit.: 'Ali from world went') in (5), Section 5.1 above. The prepositional phrase in this example can be topicalized as *æz donya Ali ræft* (Lit.: 'from world Ali went'). The important point here is that in topicalization of this sentence we cannot say **æz Ali donya ræft* (Lit.: 'from Ali world went'); that is, the preposition cannot be separated from its complement, which supports the constituency status of PP in the structure introduced above, namely, $[_{V2}$ PP $[_{V1}$ V]. The same story holds true for those prepositional LVCs where two prepositions form an NJ with a light verb. That is, in such sentences as *šæhr æz beyn ræft* 'the city was wiped out' (Lit.: 'city from between went') the two prepositions cannot be interrupted by another element, for example, **æz šæhr beyn ræft* 'from city between went'.

In this study, the phrasal verbs (as in (46) above) are distinguished from prepositional LVCs (as in (5), Section 5.1) by differentiating between the full and the light verbal forms of the verbal element. Consider the following three examples.

(47) u   bæčče-ra   birun   bord.
     he/she baby-DOM   out   take/carry.Pst.3rd.Sg.
     'He/She took the baby out.'

(48) u   tæmam-e kar-ha-ra   æz   piš
     bord.
     he/she all-Ez   work-Pl.-DOM   from   before/front
     take/carry.Past.3rd.Sg.
     'He/She managed all the work.'

(49) u   an   hadese-ra   æz   yad
     bord.
     he/she that accident-DOM   from   remembrance
     take/carry.Past.3rd.Sg.
     'He/She forgot that accident.'

The phrasal verb *birun bord* 'took/carried out' is used in (47), while two prepositional LVCs are used in the other two sentences; that is, in (48) two prepositions [PP] *æz piš* 'from before' and in (49) a preposition and a noun [P NP] *æz yad* (from remembrance) combine with the same verb (*bord* 'took/ carried') to form two types of prepositional LVCs ([PP + LV] and [P NP + LV]). Although the same verb has been used, this verb does not play the same semantic role in the two constructions, i.e. the phrasal verb in (47) and the prepositional LVCs in (48) and (49). As is clear, the meaning of the verb (*bord* 'took/carried') has not changed, even if it has been used along with the preverbal element *birun* 'out'. In other words, it is used as a full predicate with the meaning 'take/carry', while the same verb has been used as a light verb with the meaning, which is to some extent bleached, and the verb does not mean 'take or carry something'. That is, in the prepositional LVCs in (48) and (49) the verbal element cannot act as a full predicate whose meaning is more complete with a preposition; rather, the verb has a light role and the combination of the prepositional phrase and the LV act as a predicate, as the glossary of the constructions in (48) with the meaning 'managed' and in (49) with the meaning 'forgot' indicates. This means that the criterion for the distinction of the phrasal verb and the prepositional LVCs is in fact a semantic one on the part of the verbal element. On the part of the preverbal/prepositional element, it seems that the only preposition type that can occur in Persian phrasal verbs is the stative locative ones such as *birun* 'out', *tu* 'in' (as in *tu bordæn* 'take/carry in'), and none of the other preposition types of the prepositional LVCs (discussed in Section 5.8), i.e. directional (source, path and goal) prepositions, can partake in the phrasal verbs, as presented in the following sentences.

(50) *u   bæčče-ra   æz   bord.
      he/she   baby-DOM   from   take/carry.Pst.3ʳᵈ.Sg.
      'He/She took the baby from.'

(51) *u   bæčče-ra   beyn   bord.
      he/she   baby-DOM   between   take/carry.Pst.3ʳᵈ.Sg.
      'He/She took the baby between.'

(52) *u   bæčče-ra   be   bord.
      he/she   baby-DOM   to   take/carry.Past.3ʳᵈ.Sg.
      'He/She took the baby to.'

In (50) the source directional preposition *æz* 'from', in (51) the path directional preposition *beyn* 'between', and in (52) the goal directional preposition *be* 'to' have been used with the same verb (*bord* 'took/carried'), but none of these constructions is acceptable in Persian. That is, even though in both the phrasal verbs and the prepositional LVCs stative locative prepositions can be used, the directional prepositions can only occur in the prepositional light verbal constructions. As mentioned before, in the prepositional LVCs such prepositions as *æz* 'from', *be* 'to' and *dær* 'in' can join either another preposition or a noun, while *ba* 'with', *bær* 'on/over' and *bi* 'without' can join a noun (and not another preposition) to form a nuclear juncture with light verbs.

In those prepositional LVCs where the preposition takes a nominal element (₍ₚₚ [Prep. + NP] LV), the noun is not the complement of the verbal element. That is, unlike some nominal LVCs where the verb takes its complement and forms a nominal NJ through incorporation (e.g. *Ali qæza-ra xord*

'Ali ate the food', Lit.: 'Ali food-DOM ate', *Ali qæza-xord* 'Ali food-ate'), in these constructions the nominal element is not the verb's complement, as is the case in *Ali æz donya ræft* 'Ali passed away' (Lit.: 'Ali from world went') (given in (5), Section 5.1), where *donya* 'world' is in fact the preposition's complement and, as observed, it is not the complement of the verb, since the verbal element (*ræft* 'went') is in fact intransitive and cannot take a complement.

Another important issue to take into consideration is that the combinations of two prepositions in prepositional LVCs are different from those complex (compound) pronouns that exist in other contexts. In other words, none of the compound pronouns provided in (c), Section 5.1, appears in prepositional LVCs. That is, the first preposition in prepositional light verbal constructions forms a new PP, which is not the same as the (c) type of the compound prepositions discussed in Section 5.1. In other words, the LVC [P-P] combinations are distinct from other compound prepositions (as in (c)), which act like a P rather than a PP. In addition, the [P-P] in LVCs can be considered as a valid class, since these PPs can act as an adjective with a copula. Consider the prepositional LVC *æz bær kærdæn* 'memorize' (Lit.: 'from on/ over made') (in (7) above), where the PP *æz bær* 'from on/over' can be used in such copular sentences as *u dærs-ra æz bær æst* 'he/she remembers the lesson' (Lit.: 'he/she lesson-DOM from on/over is').

In general, in both phrasal verbs and prepositional LVCs a preverbal element joins a verb to form a new predicate, i.e. some overlapping is observed between the two constructions. This chapter draws heavily upon the analysis of the phrasal verb structures developed by Ackerman and Webelhuth (1998) who examined the phrasal predicates in Hungarian and German adopting a lexicalist approach for their analysis. In these languages a particle (a preverb) and a verbal element form a phrasal predicate where the elements are syntactically separable. As stated by Engerer (2007) in his book on phrasal verbs, Ackerman and Webelhuth's (1998) account of these constructions is a thorough and novel analysis of predicate structure. In their analysis, phrasal verbs and complex predicates are used interchangeably. Following Ackerman and Webelhuth, this study recognizes that Persian prepositional light verbs show similarities to phrasal verbs.

The phrasal verb constructions are referred to as complex predicates by Ackerman and Webelhuth (1998) since, as mentioned above, in both a preverbal and a verbal element combine to form a new predicate. In fact, complex predicates and phrasal verb constructions can be placed on a continuum and as maintained by Bolinger, 'being a phrasal verb is a matter of degree'

(Bolinger, 1971, p. 6). According to Keith Allen (2001), compounds, phrasal verbs and idioms should be listed in the lexicon, since in most cases the meanings of compounds, phrasal verbs and idioms cannot be correctly derived from the meanings of their constituents. Some scholars (e.g. O'Dowd, 1998; Televnaja, 2005) have divided verb phrases into the two groups of prepositional VPs and particle verbs. To illustrate the two constructions of phrasal verb which some, as mentioned before, prefer to refer to as 'particle verb' (e.g. Gries, 2000; Dehé, 2002; Jackendoff, 2002) and prepositional light verbal constructions, the following two sentences are provided from Russian (cf. Ackerman and Webelhuth, 1998) and Persian, respectively.

(53) guljajuschie pary obxodjat   ozero
      strolling   pairs around-go-3/pl lake-ACC
      'The strolling couples walk around the lake.'

(54) danešgah mærasem-e   bašokuhi   be   pa   dašt.
      university ceremony-Ez magnificent   to   foot have.Past.3rd.Sg.
      'The university arranged for a magnificent ceremony.'

In the Russian example in (53), the preverbal element *ob* 'around' forms a particle or phrasal verb with the verbal element *xodjat* 'go/walk', while in the Persian sentence in (54) a prepositional phrase *be pa* 'to foot' acts as the preverbal element which fuses with the light verbal constituent *dašt* 'had' to make a prepositional LVC. According to RRG, the preverbal/prepositional element which forms a complex nucleus (such as the English particle verbs *look at*, *decide on*, *rely on* and *listen to* or the prepositional phrases in the Persian LVCs) does not act as argument marker, but rather is part of the NUC. As claimed by Van Valin and LaPolla (1997, p. 653), the object or the direct core argument of these constructions is in fact the argument of the complex nucleus as a whole. In other words, in both sentences above, i.e. the preposition *ob* 'around' in (53) and the prepositional phrase *be pa* 'to foot' in (54), the preverbal elements play part of the predicating role of the whole Complex Predicate (CP) and appear under the PRED node. Consider the following Layered Structure of the Clause (LSC) of the phrasal verb *birun bord* 'took out' in (47).

As is clear from Figure 5.7, the construction *birun bord* 'took out' (Lit.: 'out took') is a phrasal verb and, like the prepositional LVCs, has more than one element to play the predicating role of the whole sentence. But unlike the prepositional light verbal constructions, in the Persian phrasal verbs the

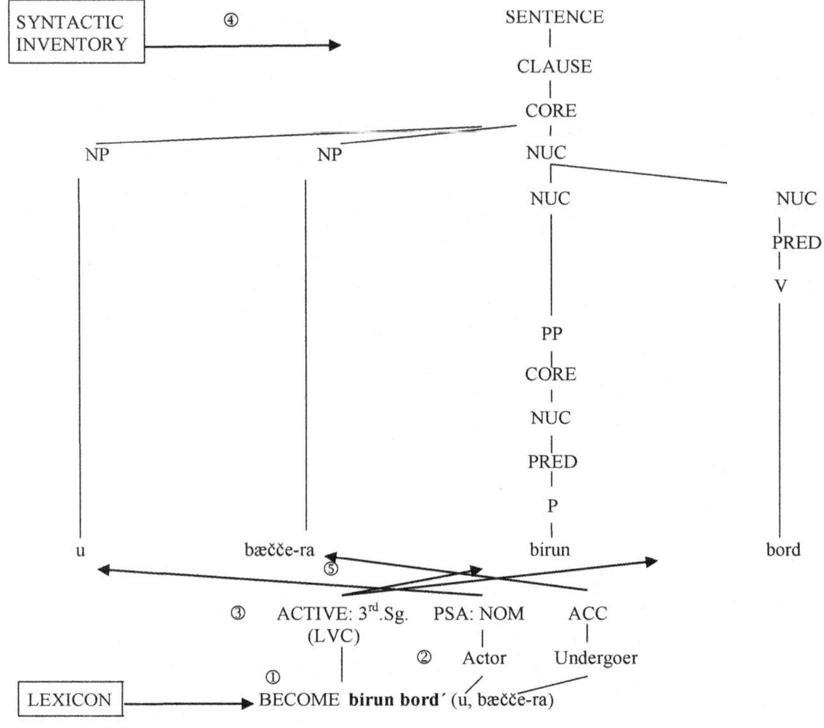

Figure 5.7 Semantics to syntax linking in the Persian phrasal verbs.

verbal element (*bord* 'took/carried') is a full/main predicate (V and not LV) with a full meaning which becomes more complete with the preverbal element. On the contrary, the verb in the prepositional LVCs is a light verb with a light meaning, and the full meaning of the whole construction may not be predictable from the meaning of the verbal element; rather, it is the combination of the meanings of the preverbal/prepositional constituents and the verbal element which acts as the predicate of the proposition.

5.15 Summary

The findings of the present chapter on prepositional LVCs have revealed that the preverbal-prepositional elements occurring in these constructions belong to the stative and directional (source, path and goal) locative prepositions and can be of two types, i.e. the combination of two prepositions or a preposition and a noun. It also emerged that, consistent with the adjectival NJs, the verbal elements in these LVCs belong to the 'phase' class of verbs referring to particular phases of events, and that the prepositional elements provide the information regarding the locative stative and directional event type or attribute. In other words, the light verbs are bleached with regard to the event type, i.e. they do not provide the information on what type of event the whole construction corresponds. One example of a non-phase verb, the state/attribute verb *dæštæn* 'have', which is capable of forming nuclear junctures with the prepositional elements, was also found in the data. This non-phase verb will be discussed in more detail in Chapter 6. Another interesting finding of the present chapter is that these constructions, too, exhibit some lexical properties supporting their wordhood status. Compatible with adjectival LVC types discussed in Chapter 4, the prepositional constructions have some syntactic characteristics which, as will be shown in the final chapter (6), can be accounted for by the RRG machinery. Consistent with adjectival LVCs, the prepositional NJs, as demonstrated in this chapter, correspond to the nuclear cosubordination linkage type. It was found that although the prepositional LVCs are similar to phrasal verbs in having both the preverbal and verbal elements, they are different with regard to full/light forms of the verbal element used in these constructions. That is, in phrasal verbs the full/heavy form of the verb is used, unlike the prepositional LVCs, where the light verb joins either two prepositions or a preposition and a noun to form a nuclear juncture and is to some extent bleached. Regarding the verb class and the argument structure of the prepositional NJs, a close compatibility is observed between these constructions and the adjectival LVCs examined in Chapter 4. That is, in the majority of the prepositional LVCs analyzed in this chapter the aspectual properties and the (in)transitivity status of the whole juncture is the same as that of the full form of the verbal elements. This means that in these two types of LVCs (adjectival and prepositional) the verbal element plays a stronger role in determining the argument structure and aspect type of the whole juncture.

Notes

1.   Note that in order to determine the light verb contribution to the verb class of the constructions, the sentence chosen from the Persian collected data is the same for all three prepositional LVCs mentioned above.

$$\boxed{6}$$

Conclusion

6.1 Propositions of the study

The purpose of this study has been to provide a comprehensive description of Persian light verbal constructions (LVCs) or nuclear junctures, which have been categorized into adjectival, nominal, adverbial and prepositional nuclear junctures (Saeedi, 2009a), adopting the Role and Reference Grammar (RRG) framework (Van Valin and LaPolla, 1997; Van Valin, 2005). The analysis is in fact the first RRG account of these constructions in Persian. The main concern of this study, which provides a detailed and comprehensive analysis of the full range of two major types of Persian LVCs (adjectival and prepositional), has been to investigate the morphosyntactic structure of these constructions, which have not received much attention in the literature, and to examine the role of each of the preverbal/verbal elements of the four types of complex predicates played on the argument structure, the aspectual properties, and the event structure of the construction. As a consequence, the present study has been able to characterize the degree of 'lightness' of the verbal component. To this end, four propositions have been formulated as follows.

1. Persian light verbs are not completely bleached elements in these constructions; they are semantically bleached with respect to event structure.
2. The preverbal constituents contribute differently, according to their grammatical category, to the semantic structure of the complex predicate.
3. These Persian LVCs can be given a unified account within RRG and do not display hybrid features or a 'dual nature' (Karimi-Doostan, 1997) that require special mechanisms in the grammar.
4. More generally, a characterization of the nuclear junctures is best provided in a functional account that facilitates explanation at the semantic-lexicon-morphosyntactic interface.

To investigate the four propositions, the two types of the adjectival and prepositional Nuclear Junctures (NJs) were examined in Chapters 4 and 5, respectively. In each chapter, a distinction was made between the predicative and non-predicative uses of the preverbal element and the five main diagnostic tests were applied to highlight the effect of each component on the aspectual properties of the light verbal constructions. Analyzing the findings of the test application procedure for each particular type of NJ, the writer explored the type of contribution of each element to the LVC event and argument structure, including the syntactic transitivity and semantic (thematic role) valency, in order to examine the first and second propositions. Finally, for each group of LVCs the Layered Structure of the Clause (LSC), the logical structure, the linking algorithm and the constructional schema were presented and discussed to investigate the fourth proposition and the appropriateness of the adopted framework for the present study. Since this study rejects the claim in proposition 3 that LVCs have a hybrid or dual nature and since it has become quite widespread in the literature, it will be dealt with in detail in Section 6.3.

6.2 Supporting propositions 1 and 2

In this study, the first proposition is supported by showing that light verbs (LVs) in Persian are not completely semantically bleached, as some scholars such as Vahedi-Langrudi (1996) and Karimi-Doostan (1997) have claimed. Following Grimshaw and Mester (1988), Mohammad and Karimi (1992) make the same claim and maintain that light verbs are bleached constituents and have no role in the argument structure of the whole construction. In Section 2.3.2 of Chapter 2 it was shown that the light verb is distinct from the other verbal subcategories of auxiliary, copula and heavy/full verb and should be specified as a distinct lexical category. The categorical distinctions between the light verb and other word classes had not been previously investigated in depth, and in some research studies (Dabir-Moghaddam, 1997) the terms light verb and auxiliary, for instance, have been used interchangeably. This study examined the differences between light verb and other verb classes, with the intention of clearing up some confusion, and examined the contribution of the light verb as a partially bleached element in combination with the two adjectival/prepositional preverbal elements in the two analytical chapters (4, 5). Adopting the Role and Reference Grammar theory, it was found that the predicating role of the whole LVC is played partially by the light verb and partially by the preverbal element and they both appear under the predicate (PRED) node in the LSC. That is, contrary to Karimi-Doostan (1997) who claims that the light verb is a completely bleached element, this study shows that these LVs contribute to such parameters as semantic content, argument structure (especially transitivity/causativity) and aspectual information. It has emerged from the findings that the type of this contribution depends on the specific category (noun, adjective, adverb, prepositional phrase) of the preverbal element. The contribution of the LV to the semantic content was discussed in Section 2.3.2 of Chapter 2, and the causativity was examined in Chapter 4 since it is not applicable to all types of LVCs.

This study has shown that the pre/non-verbal element is morphologically compounded with the LV to create a new verbal predicate available to the RRG linking system as a single predicate. In addition, the second proposition is supported by discovering compelling evidence that the type of contribution of the preverbal element differs based on its specific type. In fact, each of the preverbal element types contributes a different component to the new predication, such that:

- LV + N: N contributes the type of event (*run*, *walk*, *eat*, etc.) (Saeedi, 2009a);
- LV + Adj.: Adj. contributes the result state in a state of affairs (discussed in Chapter 4);
- LV + Adv.: Adv. contributes the location, direction or aspectual time of the unfolding of the event predication (Saeedi, 2009a);
- LV + PP: PP contributes to such event types as spatial/locative attributes which can be subdivided into state and directional prepositional phrases, where the latter can further be categorized into source, path and goal (discussed in Chapter 4).

With regard to the discussed LVCs, it is observed that there is a semantic relatedness between the meanings of the preverbal elements which derivationally compound with the LV to create the verbal predicate. This fact of the semantic relatedness of different preverbal elements in the analysis further reinforces the second proposition of this research.

In general, and as mentioned before, there is no specific perfect rule that can predict the argument structure and aspect type of the LVC from the preverbal/verbal elements. This is to be expected in the RRG machinery of the derivational morphology, since the [OUTPUT] LV construction is viewed as a single overall predication composed of the [INPUT] LV constituent elements. The single overall event is then passed to the RRG linking system (from semantics to syntax). The detailed procedure for the formation of the new predicate is discussed later in Section 6.4.

In terms of the event structure, the study has revealed that it is the preverbal constituent that provides the event information, since the event type of the LVC varies by changing the type of the non-verbal element within each word category, and all the light verbs in different types of Persian LVCs are bleached with regard to the event structure. This is contrary to the claim made by Folli, Harley and Karimi (2005), who maintain that if such light verbs as *šodæn* 'become', being inherently telic, combine with the non-verbal elements and form a complex predicate, it is the light verb which determines the event structure, and the preverbal constituents in these constructions have no role in this respect. That is, if an LVC is made with the LV *šodæn* 'become', the construction can either be achievement or accomplishment, following the telic inherent meaning of this LV. In this study, however, it is shown that in the adjectival LVCs, for instance, the complex predicate *tond šod* 'became quick' (Lit.: 'quick became') with the speed adjective (in Table 4.7 of Chapter 4) belong to the activity verb class with the atelic interpretation.

It has emerged from this study that the light verbs in the two examined types of nuclear junctures belong to the **phase** class of verbs and refer to a particular phase of an event, as presented in Figure 6.1, which is the same as Figure 4.6 in Section 4.5.1 of Chapter 4.

In Persian, the adjective and its associated noun need to co-occur within a certain word order discussed in Chapter 4 on adjectival LVCs. In order to have a deeper discussion of the syntactic features of Persian nuclear junctures, including the elements intervening in the preverbal and light verbal constituents, they are discussed in the following section. A general description of the same features in Section 2.3.1 of Chapter 2 is provided, and here an attempt has been made to give a more specific account of different types (adjectival and prepositional) of these constructions and compare them with regard to these features. In fact, the main purpose of the following section, as mentioned before, is to examine the third proposition; that is, the syntactic features of the Persian LVCs (in addition to their lexical ones) are not the manifestation of their dual (Megerdoomian, 2001b) nature.

Figure 6.1 Phases of an event.

6.3 Supporting proposition 3

6.3.1 Intervening elements

According to RRG, sometimes in some languages some elements may intervene between the two components of the NJs; in English, for instance, a noun phrase (NP) may appear between the two elements, as in *John forced the door open* (Van Valin and LaPolla, 1997, pp. 443–5); in some other languages adverbs may intervene between the two nuclei of the complex predicate. In Persian, the two types of adjectival and prepositional LVCs, as presented in each related chapter, allow most of the intervening elements (mentioned in Section 2.3.1 of Chapter 2) to occur within the complex. According to RRG, such intervening elements as the negation operators, including the negative prefixes *ne-* and *mæ-*, are considered as nuclear negation (Van Valin and LaPolla, 1997, p. 49) and are presented at the bottom part of the operators projection figure (3.5) introduced in Chapter 3 and repeated here as Figure 6.2. In RRG, the nuclear negation is known as narrow scope or internal negation, in comparison with the wide scope of the core negation. As presented in this section, the nuclear negation is placed in the top box of Figure 6.2 and is related to the operators projection part of this figure. In addition, other intervening elements of the Persian nuclear junctures such as progressive/durative *mi-*, the imperative form *be-*, and the imperative negative *næ-* are considered as 'aspect nuclear operators' and are also placed in the top box of the operators projection Figure 6.2.

In RRG, the intervening future auxiliary can be presented as a clause tense operator. In Persian, the future auxiliary tense operator *xah* 'want' appears between the two preverbal-verbal elements in the two types of Persian nuclear junctures discussed in the previous chapters.

Another intervening element is the adjective intervention, which is applicable to two types of LVCs in Persian, namely, adjectival (discussed in Chapter 4) and nominal (Saeedi, 2009a) nuclear junctures. The flexible architecture of RRG allows the investigation of the intervening elements in LVCs, and these elements are not an indication of the dual nature of Persian as some linguists have pointed out (e.g. Megerdoomian, 2001b).

6.3.2 Relativization and focused by WH-question words

The 'relativization' and 'being focused by WH-question word' features are only applicable to the nominal nuclear junctures (Saeedi, 2009a). That is, the

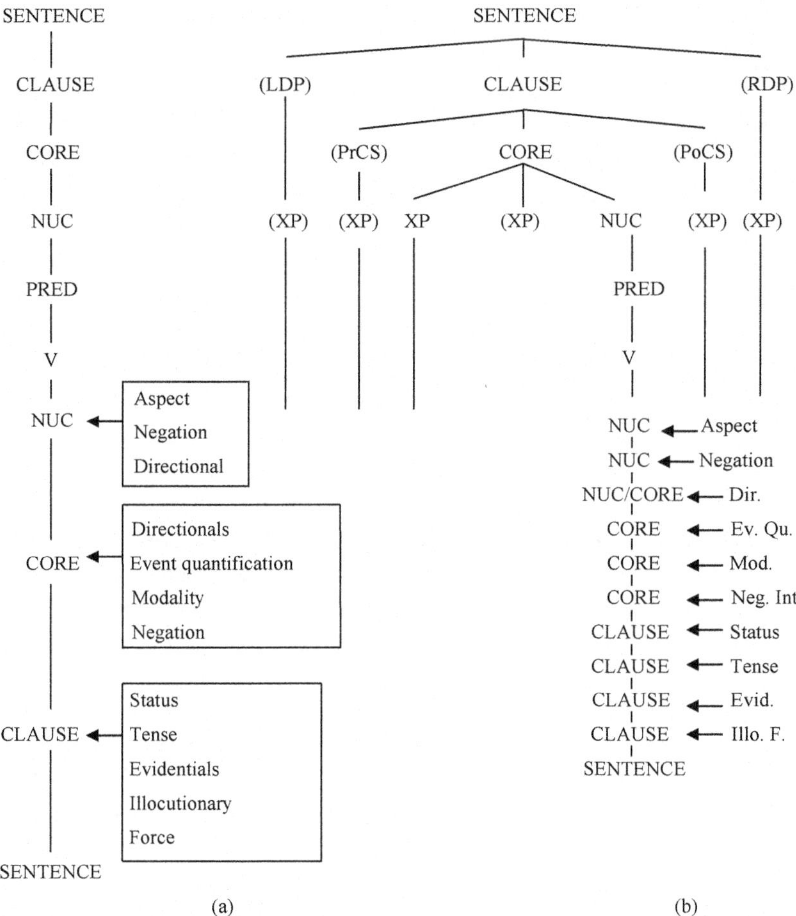

Figure 6.2 LSC with constituent and operator projections.

analysis of these two features is not applicable to the adjectival and prepositional NJs discussed in this study.

6.3.3 Coordination

The comparison of the two types of nuclear junctures (examined in this study) with regard to the next syntactic feature, i.e. 'coordination', indicates that all the preverbal elements can be coordinated with another element that belongs to the same category. In Persian, the two elements are coordinated with the conjunction *væ* 'and'. This indicates that this phenomenon along with other syntactic features, as demonstrated in this section, can adequately be accounted for within the RRG analysis.

In the literature on the Persian complex predicates it is claimed by some scholars (e.g. Karimi-Doostan, 1997) that these constructions in Persian exhibit a double or dual nature, since they have lexical as well as syntactic features such as separability of the constituents. According to Karimi-Doostan (1997), for instance, such syntactic features of these constructions as the intervention of some constituents between the two non-verbal/verbal elements create problems for the analysis of these constructions, since the syntactic features are not compatible with their lexical characteristics. In this research study, however, it is shown that these apparently problematic syntactic features are well accounted for within the RRG framework adopted in this study. In other words, the fault lies with the inability of some linguistic theoretical machineries to provide an appropriate account for analyzing such characteristics of language. That is, if a theoretical framework does not provide the necessary formal tools to account for such features as the separability of the complex predicate elements, such as takes place in Persian or German/Hungarian phrasal verb constructions (Ackerman and Webelhuth, 1998), it does not mean that these languages have a dual nature. The problem is, in fact, theory-internal.

6.4 Supporting proposition 4

RRG provides a functional account that facilitates explanation at the semantic-lexicon-morphosyntactic interfaces in terms of the nexus juncture relations and the semantic relations hierarchy. The present account demonstrates conclusively that Persian light verbs can be characterized in RRG as consisting of nuclear-cosubordination structures which contain the light verb and the pre/non-verbal element in a compound-verb derivation. The study demonstrates how this operates within the RRG layered structure of the word. In fact, lexicon plays a very important role in the RRG architecture, where the logical structure of the verb is the core of its lexical entry and the layered structure of the clause is the main machinery to present the morphological mechanism of sentences. According to RRG, it is not possible to study a language without paying serious attention to morphology (Van Valin and LaPolla, 1997, p. 2). In RRG, the morphological derivation is the key concept in creating new lexemes. In the case of Persian nuclear junctures, two elements, a pre/non-verbal element (a noun, an adjective, an adverb, a prepositional phrase) and a light verb, fuse together to create a new nucleus (NUC) or predicate. The procedure is schematized in Figure 6.3.

Along with the above line of approach in derivational morphology, Brian Nolan (forthcoming) has proposed a word layered structure of the word in a derivation, which is presented in Figure 6.4. According to Nolan (personal contact), the delta sign *(φ)* (which denotes some lexeme that is type changing and acts as the head) in his proposed model in Figure 6.4 can be replaced by an LV in the case of Persian nominal LVCs. In this word layered structure of the word, the nucleus, the nominal (NUC$_N$), the adjectival (NUC$_{ADJ}$), the adverbial (NUC$_{ADV}$), the prepositional (NUC$_{PP}$) or the argument lexeme (ARG$_{LEX}$) fuses with the verbal nucleus (NUC$_V$) or the head lexeme (Lex$_{HEAD}$) through morphological derivation to generate the new verb of the sentence or core (CORE$_V$) or (WORD$_V$) which acts as one single word or verb. This is how RRG provides a unified account for the analysis of Persian light verbal constructions.

One important point worth noticing with regard to the new predicate in Persian is that there is no difference between the behaviour of the heavy-independent full lexical verb and that of the nuclear juncture in terms of the agreement details that may be relevant in the syntax between the Privileged Syntactic Argument (PSA) (subject) and the new complex nucleus. That is, consistent with the agreement features of the Persian full lexical verbs, the light verbal constructions agree with the privileged

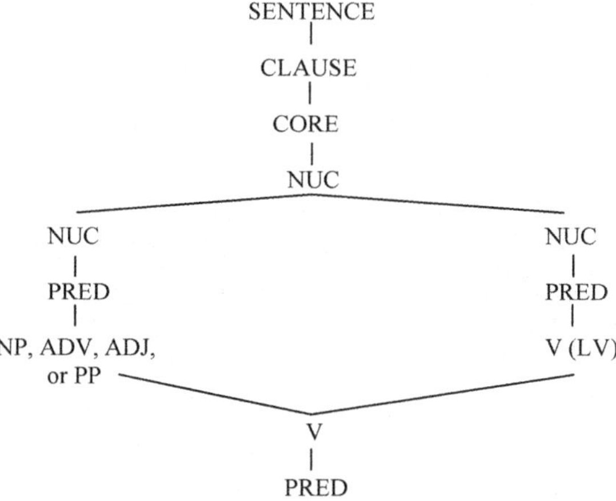

Figure 6.3 Fusion of two preverbal/light verbal elements through derivational morphology in Persian LVCs.

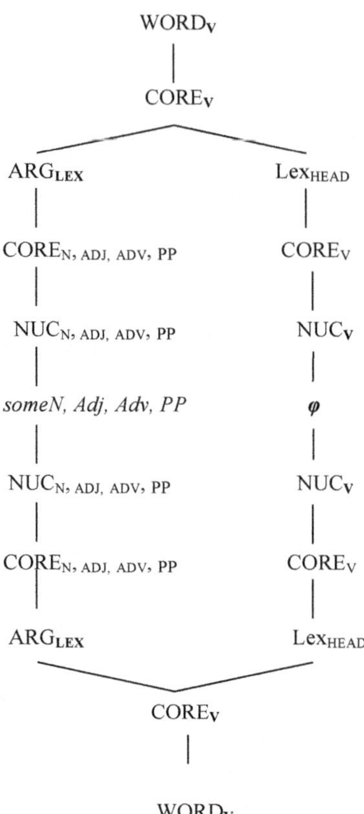

Figure 6.4 The word layered structure of the word in a derivation (Nolan, forthcoming).

syntactic argument in number and person and the PSA coded on the verb via the personal endings, even though the subject NP argument is pro-dropped. There is no gender agreement in Persian.

The formation of different types of the Persian LVCs through morphological derivation supports the idea that these constructions form in the lexicon. That is, in RRG a phenomenon is considered to be lexical if (a) it changes the aspectual properties (e.g. from achievement to accomplishment), (b) it affects the argument structure of the predicate, (c) it alters the semantic content or logical structure of the predicate, and finally (d) it affects the actor and undergoer assignment, which refers to step 1 in the semantics to syntax linking procedure presented in (10) in Section 3.4.4 of Chapter 3. On the contrary, if the phenomenon corresponds to the mapping between the macroroles and the syntactic representation, it is described as a syntactic phenomenon (e.g. passive formation as in English), since the procedure affects the selection of the PSA and the linking between macroroles and the morphosyntactically coded arguments. Since the formation of the LVCs affects all the RRG criteria (a)–(d), mentioned above, it is, in fact, a lexical phenomenon, which in RRG is distinct from the syntactic one.

In general, the RRG theoretical machinery as a lexical projectionist theory has some advantages over other lexicalist theories such as Lexical-Functional Grammar (LFG) in analyzing such language systems as Persian where there are both syntactic and lexical properties. The first advantage is that in RRG there is no rigid boundary between the two language components; that is, the bidirectional (from syntax to semantics and vice versa) linking system discussed in Chapter 3 helped the author to account for the interaction between syntactic and lexical features of Persian LVCs. Second, the RRG Layered Structure of the Clause (LSC), the linking system and the nexus-juncture architecture equipped us to schematize the morphological, syntactic and semantic-thematic features of **different types** of Persian complex predicates at a **mono**-stratal level within a **unified** framework. As discussed in each analytical chapter, this study is concerned with the first linking system, i.e. semantics to syntax.

The analysis of Persian LVCs within the RRG framework provides, in fact, a strong argument against the autonomy of lexicon and syntax. In other words, the findings contrast with what has been referred to in the literature as the 'Lexical Integrity Principle' (Bresnan and Mchombo, 1995). According to this principle, the structure of words or morphology is formed with different principles which are not visible to syntax; that is, the interaction of the two is restricted and there is a boundary between words and phrases. As Bresnan and Mchombo (1995, p. 181) put it:

> Words are built out of different structural elements and by different principles of composition than syntactic phrases. Specifically the morphological constituents of words are lexical and sublexical categories – stems and affixes – while the syntactic constituents of phrases have words as the minimal, unanalysable units; and syntactic ordering principles do not apply to morphemic structures.
> (Bresnan and Mchombo, 1995, p. 181)

Another version of this principle is the 'Atomicity of Words Thesis' posed by Di Sciullo and Williams (1987, p. 49), who maintain that 'words are "atomic" at the level of phrasal syntax and phrasal semantics. The words have "features" or properties, but these features have no structure, and the relation of these features to the internal composition of the word cannot be relevant in syntax' (Lieber and Scalise, 2007). The findings within the RRG framework, however, reject the atomicity of words and are, in fact, compatible with such theories as Construction Grammar, Cognitive Grammar and Head-driven Phrase Structure Grammar (HPSG) in that there is no rigid line between morphology and syntax. As Goldberg (2004, p.13), who analyzes Persian complex predicates within Construction Grammar, points out, 'there can be no strict division within the "construction" between words and phrasal elements'.

The RRG analysis of Persian light verbal constructions, as one of the major subcategories of complex predicates, in this research study shows that syntactic features of these constructions such as separability of the constituents do not indicate that these LVCs form in the syntax, and that there is no interaction between the two. According to Ackerman and Webelhuth (1998) the syntactic separability of some phrasal verb constructions in Hungarian and German does not indicate that they should form in the phrase structure or syntax. As pointed out by Ackerman and Webelhuth (1998), these constructions' semantic and morphological unithood is contrary to their syntactic separability if the lexicon is regarded as the source for words employed as syntactic atoms and the syntax as a system for combining and ordering them. They propose a lexicalist approach for the analysis of such phrasal verb or complex predicate constructions in a way that both predicates expressed by a single syntactic atom and predicates expressed by several such atoms form in the lexicon and are profitably associated with lexical representations. In their analysis, phrasal verbs and complex predicates are used interchangeably. In this study, the author agrees with them and believes that the formation of complex predicates takes place in the lexicon. The author further agrees that such forms as complex predicates and phrasal verbs should be placed on a continuum where the location of each language is dependent on a number of parameters, including the degree of the compositionality (e.g. Televnaja, 2005) as a criterion to categorize different types of phrasal verbs, which requires further research. The findings are compatible with Goldberg's (2004) study in that items such as Persian LVCs which have syntactic-phrasal characteristics, can be listed and formed in the lexicon. The study also agrees with such LFG research studies as Butt (1995) and Alsina (1993) in that in these constructions the argument structure of each predicating element combines together to form a composite argument structure, which provides the foundation for assigning grammatical functions to arguments of the complex predicate. As postulated by RRG, there should be a distinction between lexical and syntactic phenomena on the one hand, and lexical and syntactic rules (which involve in the formation of these phenomena) on the other. In fact, RRG avoids identifying any such problems with LVCs because it gives an independently motivated formalism that allows jointly associating the syntactically independent elements with a single lexical representation. Therefore, what would or could be a problem in some approaches is not a problem in RRG. The RRG analysis of the Persian LVCs shows the formation of these constructions occurs in the lexicon, such that the resulting predication can well be accounted in the RRG semantic-to-syntax linking system. This derivation prior to the application of the linking explains the apparent idiosyncratic behaviours of the Persian light verbal constructions. Therefore, it is a more robust and complete account than those mentioned in the literature review earlier in the present book.

In sum, an attempt was made in this study to provide a rich unified characterization of Persian light verbs and the non-verbal elements as encompassing the set of phase verbs. The present account demonstrates that the light verbs in Persian are phase verbs with a semantically bleached event structure. The non-verbal element is morphologically compounded with the LV to create a new verbal predicate available to the RRG linking system as a single predicate.

6.5 Final conclusion

In sum, the analysis of the adjectival and prepositional nuclear junctures has revealed that the preverbal elements provide the information regarding the event types and subtypes (Saeed, 2003) or attributes as mentioned above, and that they are important parameters in determining the semantic content of the whole juncture. It was found that the amount of the contribution of the preverbal/verbal constituents depends on the specific type of the preverbal element. The investigation has also revealed that the nuclear junctures in Persian belong to the nuclear cosubordination nexus-juncture, which has the tightest or strongest type of linkage.

Appendix A:
Aktionsart Diagnostic Test Application to Persian Adjectival NJs

Test 1   *dær hale* (progressive expression)

Age adjective: *pir kærdæn* 'make old'

    (22) a. an hadese dær hal-e   pir kærdæn-e   u æst.

             that accident in   process-Ez old make-INF.-Ez him be-Pres.3rd.Sg.

             'That accident is making him/her old.'

    (22′) a. u   be xatere an hadese dær hal-e   pir šodæn   æst.

             he/she to because that accident in process-Ez old become.INF. is

             'He is becaming old because of that accident.'

Dimension adjective: *kutah kædæn* 'make short'

    (23) a. Mina dær hal-e   kutah kærdæn-e   qesse-æš æst.

             Mina in   process-Ez short make.INF.-Ez story-her be-Pres.3rd.Sg.

             'Mina is making her story short.'

    (23′) a. qesse-ye Mina dær hal-e   kutah šodæn æst.

             story-Ez Mina in   process-Ez short become.INF. be-Pres.3rd.Sg.

             'Mina's story is becoming short.'

Value adjective: *bæd kærdæn* 'do wrong/bad things'

    (24) a. *Ali dær hal-e   bæd kærdæn be xod-æš æst.

             Ali in   process-Ez bad   do-INF. to self-his be-Pres.3rd.Sg.

             'Ali is doing wrong/bad (things) to himself.'

(24′) a. *nætije-ye   kar-e   Ali dær hal-e   bæd
šodæn   æst.
result-Ez (of) action-Ez Ali in   process-Ez bad
became.INF. is
'The result of Ali's action is becoming bad.'
(Note: The asterisks before the example sentences in (24a) and
(24′a) denote their ungrammaticality.)

Colour adjective: *abi kærdæn* 'make blue'
(25) a. an-ha   dær hal-e   abi   kærdæn-e   xane-ešan
hæst-ænd.
that-Pl. in   process-Ez blue make.INF.-Ez house-their
be.Pres.-Pl.3rd.
'They are making (painting) their house blue.'
(25′) a. xane-ye an-ha   dær hal-e   abi
šodæn   æst.
house-Ez that-Pl.(those) in   process-Ez blue
become.INF. be.Pres.3rd.Sg.
'Their house is becoming blue.'

Physical characteristics adjective: *sængin kærdæn* 'make heavy'
(26) a. *lebas-ha dær hal-e   sængin kærdæn-e
čæmedan hæst-ænd.
clothes-Pl. in   process-Ez heavy make.INF.-Ez
suitcase be.Pres.-Pl.3rd.
'The clothes are making the suitcase heavy.'
(26′) a. *čæmedan dær hal-e   sængin šodæn
æst.
suitcase   in   process-Ez heavy become.INF.
be-Pres.3rd.Sg.
'The suitcase is becoming heavy.'

Shape adjective: *gerd kærdæn* 'make round'
(27) a. an-ha   dær hal-e   gerd kærdæn-e   mæsir-e
mosabeqe-ye do   hæst-ænd.
that-Pl. in   process-Ez round make.INF.-Ez route-Ez
race-Ez   running be.Pres.-Pl.3rd.
'They are making the route of the running race round.'

(27′) a. mæsir-e   mosabeqe-ye do   dær hal-e   gerd
šodæn   æst.
route-Ez race-Ez   running in process-Ez round
become-INF. is
'The route of the running race is becoming round.'

Human property adjective: *xošhal kærdæn* 'make happy'
(28) a. *nomre-ye xub-æš   dær emtehan dær hal-e
xošhal kærdæn-e   u   æst.
mark-Ez   good-his/her in exam   in   process-Ez
happy   make-INF.-Ez him/her be.Pres.3rd.Sg.
'His/Her good mark in the exam is making him/her happy.'
(28′) a. *u   dær hal-e   xošhal šodæn   æst.
he/she in process-Ez happy become.INF. be.Pres.3rd.Sg.
'He/She is becoming happy.'

Speed adjective: *tond kærdæn* 'make fast/accelerate'
(29) a. dočærxe sævar dær hal-e   tond   kærdæn-e
soræt-æš æst.
bicycle   rider   in   process-Ez quick/fast make.INF.
speed-his is
'The cyclist is making his speed fast/accelerating.'
(29′) a. soræt-e   dočærxe sævar dær hal-e   tond
šodæn   æst.
speed-Ez bicycle   rider   in   process-Ez quick/fast
become.INF. is
'The speed of the cyclist is becoming fast.'

Test 2   *fæalane* 'actively'/*ba qodræt* 'with strength'

Age adjective:
(22) b. *an   hadese   u-ra   fæalane/ba qodræt   pir
kærd.
that accident him/her actively/with strength old
make-Past.3rd.Sg.
'That accident actively/strongly made him/her old.'

(22′) b. *u   be   xatere   an   hadese   fæalane/ba qodræt
       pir šod.
       he/she to   because that accident actively/with strength
       old became.
       'He actively/strongly became old because of that accident.'

Dimension adjective:

(23) b. *Mina qesse-æš-ra   fæalane kutah kærd.
       Mina story-her-DOM actively short make-Past.3ʳᵈ.Sg.
       'Mina actively made her story short/shortened her story.'

(23′) b. *qesse-ye Mina fæalane kutah šod.
       story-Ez Mina actively short become-Past.3rd.Sg.
       'Mina's story actively became short.'

Value adjective:

(24) b. *Ali fæalane be xod-æš bæd kærd.
       Ali actively to self-his bad do-Past.3ʳᵈ.Sg.
       'Ali actively did wrong/bad (things) to himself.'

(24′) b. *nætije-ye kar-e   Ali fæalane bæd
       šod.
       result-Ez (of) action-Ez Ali actively bad
       became-Past.3ʳᵈ.Sg.
       'The result of Ali's action actively became bad.'

Colour adjective:

(25) b. *an-ha xane-ešan-ra   fæalane abi kærd-ænd.
       that-Pl. house-their-DOM actively blue make.Past.3ʳᵈ.Pl.
       'They actively made their house blue.'

(25′) b. *xane an-ha fæalane/ba qodræt   abi
       šod.
       house that-Pl. actively/with strength blue
       become-Past.3ʳᵈ.Sg.
       'Their house actively/strongly became blue.'

Physical characteristics adjective:

(26) b. *lebas-ha čæmedan-ra   fæalane sængin kærd.
       clothes-Pl. suitcase-DOM actively heavy make-Past.3ʳᵈ.Pl.
       'The clothes actively made the suitcase heavy.'

(26′) b. *čæmedan fæalane/ba qodræt   sængin šod.
       suitcase   actively/with strength heavy become-Past.3rd.Sg.
       'The suitcase actively/strongly became heavy.'

Shape adjective:

(27) b. *an-ha   mæsir-e mosabeqe-ye do-ra   fæalane
       gerd   kærd-ænd.
          that-Pl. route-Ez race-Ez   running-DOM actively
       round make-Past.3rd.-Pl.
       'They actively made the route of the running race round.'

(27′) b. *mæsir-e mosabeqe-ye do   fæalane gerd
       šod.
          route-Ez race-Ez   running actively round
       become-Past.3rd.Pl.
       'The route of the running race actively became round.'

Human property adjective:

(28) b. *nomre-ye xub-æš   dær emtehan u-ra   fæalane
       xošhal kærd.
          mark-Ez good-his/her in   exam   him/her actively
       happy   make-Past.3rd.Sg.
       'His/Her good mark in the exam made him/her happy.'

(28′) b. *u   fæalane xošhal šod.
          he/she actively happy   become-Past.3rd.Sg.
       'He/She actively became happy.'

Speed adjective:

(29) b. dočærxe sævar fæalane/ba qodræt   soræt-æš-ra
       tond   kærd.
          bicycle   rider   actively/with strength speed-his/her-DOM
       quick/fast made
       'The cyclist actively/strongly made his speed fast/accelerated.'

(29′) b. *soræt-e   dočærxe sævar fæalane tond
       šod.
          speed-Ez bicycle rider   actively quick/fast
       become-Past.3rd.Sg.
       'The speed of the cyclist actively became fast.'

Test 3   *besoræt/aheste* 'quickly/slowly'

Since the adverb *aheste* 'slowly', as mentioned in Chapter 4, is preferable for some of the Aktionsart types, we use this adverb to be on the safe side.

Age adjective:
    (22) c. an   hadese   aheste u-ra   pir kærd.
              that accident slowly him/her-DOM old make-Past.3rd.Sg.
              'That accident slowly made him/her old.'
    (22′) c. *u   be xatere an   hadese   aheste pir
              šod.
              he/she to because that accident slowly old
              become-Past.3rd.Sg.
              'He slowly became old because of that accident.'

Dimension adjective:
    (23) c. Mina qesse-æš-ra   aheste kutah kærd.
              Mina   story-her-DOM slowly short make-Past.3rd.Sg.
              'Mina slowly made her story short/shortened her story.'
    (23′) c. qesse-ye Mina aheste kutah šod.
              story-Ez Mina slowly short   become-Past.3rd.Sg.
              'Mina's story slowly became short.'

Value adjective:
    (24) c. *Ali aheste be xod-æš bæd kærd.
              Ali   slowly to self-him bad   do-Past.3rd.Sg.
              'Ali slowly did wrong/bad (things) to himself.'
    (24′) c. *nætije-ye   kar-e   Ali aheste bæd
              šod.
              result-Ez (of) action-Ez Ali slowly bad
              became-Past.3rd.Sg.
              'The result of Ali's action slowly became bad.'

Colour adjective:
    (25) c. an-ha xane-ešan-ra   aheste abi   kærd-ænd.
              that-Pl. house-their-DOM slowly blue make.Past.3rd.-Pl.
              'They slowly made their house blue.'
    (25′) c. xane   an-ha   aheste abi   šod.
              house   that-Pl. slowly blue become-Past.3rd.Sg.
              'Their house slowly became blue.'

Physical characteristics adjective:

    (26) c. *lebas-ha   čæmedan-ra   aheste   sængin   kærd.

          clothes-Pl. suitcase-DOM slowly heavy   make-Past.3rd.Pl.

          'The clothes slowly made the suitcase heavy.'

    (26′) c. *čæmedan aheste   sængin   šod.

          suitcase   slowly heavy   become-Past.3rd.Sg.

          'The suitcase slowly became heavy.'

Shape adjective:

    (27) c. an-ha   mæsir-e   mosabeqe-ye do-ra   aheste
          gerd   kærd-ænd.

          that-Pl. route-Ez race-Ez   running-DOM slowly
          round make-Past.3rd.-Pl.

          'They slowly made the route of the running race round.'

    (27′) c. mæsir-e   mosabeqe-ye do   aheste   gerd
          šod.

          route-Ez race-Ez   running slowly round
          become-Past.3rd.Pl.

          'The route of the running race slowly became round.'

Human property adjective:

    (28) c. *nomre-ye xub-æš   dær emtehan u-ra   aheste
          xošhal kærd.

          mark-Ez good-his/her in   exam   him/her slowly
          happy make-Past.3rd.Sg.

          'His/Her good mark in the exam slowly made him/her happy.'

    (28′) c. *u   aheste   xošhal   šod.

          he/she   slowly happy   become-Past.3rd.Sg.

          'He/She slowly became happy.'

Speed adjective:

    (29) c. dočærxe   sævar   soræt-æš-ra   aheste   tond
          kærd.

          bicycle   rider   speed-his/her-DOM slowly quick/fast
          make-Past.3rd.Sg.

          'The cyclist slowly made his speed fast/accelerated.'

(29′) c. soræt-e   dočærxe   sævar   aheste   tond
         šod.
         speed-Ez bicycle   rider   slowly   quick/fast
         become-Past.3rd.Sg.
         'The speed of the cyclist slowly became fast.'

Test 4   *bæraye yek saæt* 'for an hour'

Age adjective:

(22) d. *an hadese   u-ra   bæraye yek saæt pir
         kærd.
          that accident him/her for   an   hour old
         make-Past.3rd.Sg.
         'That accident made him/her old for an hour.'

(22′) d. *u   be xatere   an hadese   bæraye yek saæt pir
         šod.
          he/she to because that accident for   an   hour old
         become-Past.3rd.Sg.
         'He became old for an hour because of that accident.'

Dimension adjective:

(23) d. *Mina qesse-æš-ra   bæraye yek saæt kutah
         kærd.
          Mina story-her-DOM for   an   hour short
         make-Past.3rd.Sg.
         'Mina made her story short/shortened her story.'

(23′) d. *qesse-ye Mina bæraye yek saæt kutah
         šod.
          story-Ez Mina for   an   hour short
         become-Past.3rd.Sg.
         'Mina's story became short for an hour.'

Value adjective:

(24) d. *Ali bæraye yek saæt be xod-æš bæd kærd.
          Ali for   an   hour to self-his bad do-Past.3rd.Sg.
         'Ali did wrong/bad (things) to himself for an hour.'

(24´) d. *nætije-ye   kar-e   Ali bæraye yek saæt bæd
šod.

   result-Ez (of) action-Ez Ali for   an   hour bad
became-Past.3rd.Sg.

'The result of Ali's action became bad for an hour.'

Colour adjective:

(25) d. *an-ha   xane-ešan-ra   bæraye yek saæt abi
kærd-ænd.

   that-Pl. house-their-DOM for   an   hour blue
make.Past.3rd.-Pl.

'They made their house blue for an hour.'

(25´) d. *xane   an-ha   bæraye yek saæt abi   šod.

   house that-Pl. for   an   hour blue   become-Past.3rd.Sg.

'Their house became blue for an hour.'

Physical characteristics adjective:

(26) d. *lebas-ha   čæmedan-ra   bæraye yek saæt sængin
kærd.

   clothes-Pl. suitcase-DOM for   an   hour heavy
make-Past.3rd.Pl.

'The clothes made the suitcase heavy for an hour.'

(26´) d. *čæmedan bæraye yek saæt sængin šod.

   suitcase   for   an   hour heavy   become-Past.3rd.Sg.

'The suitcase became heavy for an hour.'

Shape adjective:

(27) d. *an-ha   mæsir-e mosabeqe-ye do-ra   bæraye yek
saæt gerd   kærd-ænd.

   that-Pl. route-Ez race-Ez   running-DOM for   an
hour round make.Past.3rd.-Pl.

'They made the route of the running race round for an hour.'

(27´) d. *mæsir-e mosabeqe-ye do   bæraye yek saæt gerd
šod.

   route-Ez race-Ez   running for   an   hour round
become-Past.3rd.Pl.

'The route of the running race became round for an hour.'

Human property adjective:

    (28) d. *nomre-ye xub-æš   dær emtehan u-ra   bæraye
                  yek saæt xošhal kærd.
                  mark-Ez   good-his/her in   exam   him/her for
                  an   hour happy make-Past.3rd.Sg.
                  'His/Her good mark in the exam made him/her happy for an
                  hour.'

    (28′) d. *u   bæraye yek saæt xošhal šod.
                  he/she   for   an   hour happy   become-Past.3rd.Sg.
                  'He/She became happy for an hour.'

Speed adjective:

    (29) d. dočærxe sævar soræt-æš-ra   bæraye yek saæt
                  tond   kærd.
                  bicycle   rider speed-his/her-DOM for   an   hour
                  quick/fast make-Past.3rd.Sg.
                  'The cyclist made his speed fast/accelerated for an hour.'

    (29′) d. soræt-e   dočærxe sævar bæraye yek saæt tond
                  šod.
                  speed-Ez bicycle rider for   an   hour quick/fast
                  become-Past.3rd.Sg.
                  'The speed of the cyclist became fast for an hour.'

Test 5   *dær yek saæt* 'in an hour'

Age adjective:

    (22) e. an hadese u-ra   dær yek saæt pir kærd.
                  that accident him/her in   an   hour old make-Past.3rd.Sg.
                  'That accident made him/her old in an hour.'

    (22′) e. u   be xatere   an hadese dær yek saæt pir
                  šod.
                  he/she to   because that accident in   an   hour old
                  become-Past.3rd.Sg.
                  'He became old because of that accident in an hour.'

Dimension adjective:

(23) e. Mina qesse-æš-ra   dær yek saæt kutah
kærd.
Mina story-her-DOM in   an   hour short make-Past.3ʳᵈ.
Sg.
'Mina made her story short/shortened her story in an hour.'

(23′) e. qesse-ye Mina dær yek saæt kutah šod.
story-Ez Mina in   an   hour short become-Past.3rd.Sg.
'Mina's story became short in an hour.'

Value adjective:

(24) e. *Ali be xod-æš dær yek saæt bæd kærd.
Ali to self-his in   an   hour bad do-Past.3ʳᵈ.Sg.
'Ali did wrong/bad (things) to himself in an hour.'

(24′) e. *nætije-ye   kar-e   Ali dær yek saæt bæd
šod.
 result-Ez (of) action-Ez Ali in   an   hour bad
became-Past.3ʳᵈ.Sg.
'The result of Ali's action became bad in an hour.'

Colour adjective:

(25) e. an-ha   xane-ešan-ra   dær yek saæt abi
kærd-ænd.
that-Pl. house-their-DOM in   an   hour blue
make.Past.3ʳᵈ.-Pl.
'They made their house blue in an hour.'

(25′) e. xane   an-ha dær yak saæt abi šod.
house that-Pl. in   an   hour blue become-Past.3ʳᵈ.Sg.
'Their house became blue in an hour.'

Physical characteristics adjective:

(26) e. *lebas-ha   čæmedan-ra   dær yek saæt sængin
kærd.
 clothes-Pl. suitcase-DOM in   an   hour heavy
make-Past.3ʳᵈ.Pl.
'The clothes made the suitcase heavy in an hour.'

(26′) e. *čæmedan dær yek saæt sængin šod.
suitcase   in   an   hour heavy   become-Past.3ʳᵈ.Sg.
'The suitcase became heavy in an hour.'

Shape adjective:

(27) e. an-ha   mæsir-e   mosabeqe-ye   do-ra   dær yek
          saæt gerd   kærd-ænd.
          that-Pl. route-Ez race-Ez   running-DOM in   an
          hour round make-3ʳᵈ.Sg.
          'They made the route of the running race round in an hour.'

(27′) e. mæsir-e   mosabeqe-ye   do   dær yek saæt gerd
          šod.
          route-Ez race-Ez   running in   an   hour   round
          become-Past.3ʳᵈ.Pl.
          'The route of the running race became round in an hour.'

Human property adjective:

(28) e. *nomre-ye xub-æš   dær emtehan u-ra   dær yek
          saæt xošhal kærd.
           mark-Ez   good-his/her in   exam   him/her in   an
          hour happy made
          'His/Her good mark in the exam made him/her happy.'

(28′) e. *u   dær yek saæt xošhal šod.
           he/she in   an   hour   happy   become-Past.3ʳᵈ.Sg.
          'He/She became happy in an hour.'

Speed adjective:

(29) e. *dočærxe sævar soræt-æš-ra   dær yek saæt
          tond   kærd.
           bicycle   rider   speed-his/her-DOM in   an   hour
          quick/fast make-Past.3ʳᵈ.Sg.
          'The cyclist made his speed fast/accelerated in an hour.'

(29′) e. *soræt-e   dočærxe sævar dær yek saæt tond
          šod.
           speed-Ez bicycle   rider   in   an   hour   quick/fast
          become-Past.3ʳᵈ.Sg.
          'The speed of the cyclist became fast in an hour.'

Appendix B:
Aktionsart Diagnostic Test Application to Persian Prepositional NJs

First group: preposition (Prep.) + Prep. + light verb (LV)

1.a. *æz* 'from' + Prep. (*bær* 'on/over') + LV (*šodæn* 'become')

Test 1 *dær hal-e*

> (8) a. danešamuz-an dær hal-e   æz   bær
> šod-æn-e   hæme-ye sorud hæst-ænd.
> student-Pl.   in   process-Ez from on/over
> became-3rd.Pl.-Ez all-Ez song   be-Past.3rd.Pl.
> 'The students are memorizing the whole song.'

Test 2 *fæalane/ba qodræt*

> (8) b. *danešamuz-an fæalane hæme-ye sorud-ra   æz
> bær   šod-ænd.
> student-Pl.   actively all-Ez   song-DOM from
> on/over   became-3rd.Pl.
> 'The students actively memorized the whole song.'
>
> (Note: The asterisk before the example sentence in (8b) denotes its ungrammaticality.)

Test 3 *aheste/be soræt*

> (8) c. danešamuz-an aheste hæme-ye sorud-ra   æz   bær
> šod-ænd.
> student-Pl.   slowly all-Ez   song-DOM from on/over
> became-3rd.Pl.
> 'The students slowly memorized the whole song.'

Test 4 *bæraye yek saæt*

> (8) d. *danešamuz-an   bæraye   yek   saæt   hæme-ye   sorud-ra
> æz   bær   šod-ænd.
> student-Pl.   for   an   hour   all-Ez   song-DOM
> from   on/over   became-3rd.Pl.
> 'The students memorized the whole song for an hour.'

Test 5 *dær yek saæt*

> (8) e. danešamuz-an   dær   yek   saæt   hæme-ye   sorud-ra   æz
> bær   šod-ænd.
> student-Pl.   in   an   hour   all-Ez   song-DOM   from
> on/over   became-3rd.Pl.
> 'The students memorized the whole song in an hour.'

1.b. *æz* 'from' + Prep. (*bær* 'on/over') + LV (*kærdæn* 'make')

Test 1 *dær hal-e*

> (9) a. danešamuz-an   dær   hal-e   æz   bær
> kærd-æn-e   hæme-ye   sorud   hæst-ænd.
> student-Pl.   in   process-Ez   from   on/over
> made-3rd.Pl.-Ez   all-Ez   song   be-Past.3rd.Pl.
> 'The students are memorizing the whole song.'

Test 2 *fæalane/ba qodræt*

> (9) b. *danešamuz-an   fæalane   hæme-ye   sorud-ra   æz   bær
> kærd-ænd.
> student-Pl.   actively   all-Ez   song-DOM   from   on/over
> made-3rd.Pl.
> 'The students actively memorized the whole song.'

Test 3 *aheste/be soræt*

> (9) c. danešamuz-an   aheste   hæme-ye   sorud-ra   æz   bær
> kærd-ænd.
> student-Pl.   slowly   all-Ez   song-DOM   from   on/over
> made-3rd.Pl.
> 'The students slowly memorized the whole song.'

Test 4 *bæraye yek saæt*

    (9) d. *danešamuz-an bæraye yek saæt hæme-ye sorud-ra
            æz bær kærd-ænd.
            student-Pl. for an hour all-Ez song-DOM
            from on/over made-3rd.Pl.
            'The students memorized the whole song for an hour.'

Test 5 *dær yek saæt*

    (9) e. danešamuz-an dær yek saæt hæme-ye sorud-ra æz
            bær kærd-ænd.
            student-Pl. in an hour all-Ez song-DOM from
            on/over made-3rd.Pl.
            'The students memorized the whole song in an hour.'

1.c. *æz* 'from' + Prep. (*bær* 'on/over') + LV (*daštæn* 'have')

Test 1 *dær hal-e*

    (10) a. *danešamuz-an dær hal-e æz bær
            dašt-æn-e hæme-ye sorud hæst-ænd.
            student-Pl. in process-Ez from on/over
            have-3rd.Pl.-Ez all-Ez song be-Past.3rd.Pl.
            'The students are knowing the whole song by heart.'

Test 2 *fæalane/ba qodræt*

    (10) b. *danešamuz-an fæalane hæme-ye sorud-ra æz
            bær dašt-ænd.
            student-Pl. actively all-Ez song-DOM from
            on/over had-3rd.Pl.
            'The students actively knew the whole song by heart.'

Test 3 *aheste/be soræt*

    (10) c. *danešamuz-an aheste hæme-ye sorud-ra æz
            bær dašt-ænd.
            student-Pl. slowly all-Ez song-DOM from
            on/over had-3rd.Pl.
            'The students slowly knew the whole song by heart.'

Test 4 *bæraye yek saæt*

    (10) d. *danešamuz-an bæraye yek saæt hæme-ye sorud-ra
                æz   bær   dašt-ænd.
                student-Pl.   for   an   hour all-Ez   song-DOM
                from on/over had-3rd.Pl.
                'The students knew the whole song by heart for an hour.'

Test 5 *dær yek saæt*

    (10) e. *danešamuz-an dær yek saæt hæme-ye sorud-ra
                æz   bær   dašt-ænd.
                student-Pl.   in   an   hour all-Ez   song-DOM
                from on/over had-3rd.Pl.
                'The students knew the whole song by heart in an hour.'

The summary of the test application to the three NJs with *æz bær* 'from on/over' is presented in Table 1.

Table 1 Results of the five Aktionsart tests applied to the PNJs with the prepositions *æz* and *bær* and the three light verbs *šodæn*, *kærdæn* and *daštæn*

	Prepositional NJ		
Tests	***æz bær šodæn*** **'memorize'**	***æz bær kærdæn*** **'memorize'**	***æz bær daštæn*** **'know by heart/** **have memorized'**
1. dær hal-e	Yes	Yes	No
2. fæalane/ba qodræt	No	No	No
3. aheste/be soræt	Yes	Yes	No
4. bæraye yek saæt	No	No	No
5. dær yek saæt	Yes	Yes	No
Aktionsart type	Accomplishment	Accomplishment	Achievement

1.d. *æz* 'from' + Prep. (*beyn* 'between') + LV (*ræftæn* 'go')

Test 1 *dær hal-e*

    (11) a. tæmam-e šæhr dær hal-e   æz   beyn   ræftæn æst.
                all-ez   city   in   process-Ez from between go.INF. is
                'The whole city is being wiped out.'

Test 2   *fæalane/ba qodræt*

   (11) b. *tæmam-e   šæhr   fæalane   æz   beyn   ræft.
             all-ez   city   actively   from between   went
             'The whole city was actively wiped out.'

Test 3   *aheste/be soræt*

   (11) c. tæmam-e   šæhr   aheste   æz   beyn   ræft.
             all-ez   city   slowly   from between   went
             'The whole city was slowly wiped out.'

Test 4   *bæraye yek saæt*

   (11) d. *tæmam-e   šæhr   bæraye   yek   saæt   æz   beyn   ræft.
             all-ez   city   for   an   hour   from between   went
             'The whole city was wiped out for an hour.'

Test 5   *dær yek saæt*

   (11) e. tæmam-e   šæhr   dær   yek   saæt   æz   beyn   ræft.
             all-ez   city   in   an   hour   from between   went
             'The whole city was wiped out in an hour.'

1.e.   *æz* 'from' + Prep. (*beyn* 'between') + LV (*bordæn* 'take')

Test 1   *dær hal-e*

   (12) a. seyl   dær hal-e   æz   beyn   bordæn-e
             tæmam-e šæhr æst.
             flood   in   process-Ez from between take.INF-Ez
             all-Ez   city   is
             'The flood is wiping out the whole city.'

Test 2   *fæalane/ba qodræt*

   (12) b. *seyl   fæalane tæmam-e šæhr-ra   æz   beyn
             bord.
              flood   actively all-Ez   city-DOM from between
              took/carried
             'The flood actively wiped out the whole city.'

Test 3   *aheste/be soræt*

(12)   c.   seyl   aheste   tæmam-e   šæhr-ra   æz   beyn
bord.
flood   slowly   all-Ez   city-DOM   from   between
took/carried
'The flood slowly wiped out the whole city.'

Test 4   *bæraye yek saæt*

(12)   d.   *seyl   bæraye   yek   saæt   tæmam-e   šæhr-ra   æz
beyn   bord.
flood   for   an   hour   all-Ez   city-DOM   from
between   took/carried
'The flood wiped out the whole city for an hour.'

Test 5   *dær yek saæt*

(12)   e.   seyl   dær   yek   saæt   tæmam-e   šæhr-ra   æz   beyn
bord.
flood   in   an   hour   all-Ez   city-DOM   from   between
took/carried
'The flood wiped out the whole city in an hour.'

Table 2 Results of the five Aktionsart tests applied to the two PNJs *æz beyn ræftæn* and *æz beyn bordæn*

| | Prepositional NJ | |
| | --- | --- |
Tests	*æz beyn raftæn* 'be wiped out'	*æz beyn bordæn* 'wipe out'
1. dær hal-e	Yes	Yes
2. fæalane/ba qodræt	No	No
3. aheste/be soræt	Yes	Yes
4. bæraye yek saæt	No	No
5. dær yek saæt	Yes	Yes
Aktionsart type	Accomplishment	Accomplishment

1.f. æz 'from' + Prep. (*piš* 'before/front')

Test 1 *dær hal-e*

(13) a. *an vækil   dær hal-e   æz   piš
          bordæn-e   kar-ha   ba-deqqæt æst.
          that barrister in   process-Ez from before/front
          take.INF-Ez work-Pl. with-care is
          'That barrister is managing all the work carefully.'
      (Note that in the second and third tests below, since along with the
      adverbs of *fæalane* 'actively' and *aheste* 'slowly' there is already
      another adverb of manner in the sentence, namely, the adverb
      be-deqqæt 'carefully', the word *væ* 'and' is added to the sentence.)

Test 2 *fæalane/ba qodræt*

(13) b. *an   vækil   kar-ha-ra   fæalane   væ   ba-deqqæt
          æz   piš   bord.
          that   barrister work-Pl.-DOM   actively   and   with-care
          from before/front   took
          'That barrister actively and carefully managed all the work.'

Test 3 *aheste/be soræt*

(13) c. *an   vækil   kar-ha-ra   aheste   væ   ba-deqqæt
          æz   piš   bord.
          that   barrister work-Pl.-DOM   slowly   and   with-care
          from before/front took
          'That barrister slowly and carefully managed all the work.'

Test 4 *bæraye yek saæt*

(13) d. *an   vækil   bæraye yek saæt kar-ha-ra
          ba-deqqæt æz   piš   bord.
          that   barrister for   an   hour   work-Pl.-DOM
          with-care   from before/front took
          'That barrister managed all the work carefully for an hour.'

Test 5 *dær yek saæt*

(13) e. *an   vækil   dær yek saæt kar-ha-ra   ba-deqqæt
      æz   piš   bord.
      that barrister in   an   hour work-Pl.-DOM with-care
      from before/front took
      'That barrister managed all the work carefully in an hour.'

Table 3 Results of the five Aktionsart tests applied to the PNJ with the prepositions *æz* and *piš* and the light verb *bordæn*

	Prepositional NJ
Tests	*æz piš bordæn* **'manage'**
1. dær hal-e	No
2. fæalane/ba qodræt	No
3. aheste/be soræt	No
4. bæraye yek saæt	No
5. dær yek saæt	No
Aktionsart type	Achievement

1.g. *æz* 'from' + Prep. (*miyan* 'among') + LV (*bordæn* 'take')

Test 1 *dær hal-e*

(14) a. seyl   dær hal-e   æz   miyan bordæn-e
      tæmam-e šæhr æst.
      flood in   process-Ez from among take.INF-Ez
      all-Ez   city   is
      'The flood is wiping out the whole city.'

Test 2 *fæalane/ba qodræt*

(14) b. *seyl   fæalane tæmam-e šæhr-ra   æz   miyan
      bord.
      flood actively all-Ez   city-DOM from among
      took/carried
      'The flood actively wiped out the whole city.'

Test 3   *aheste/be soræt*

(14)   c.   seyl   aheste   tæmam-e   šæhr-ra   æz   miyan
bord.
flood   slowly   all-Ez   city-DOM   from   among
took/carried
'The flood slowly wiped out the whole city.'

Test 4   *bæraye yek saæt*

(14)   d.   *seyl   bæraye   yek   saæt   tæmam-e   šæhr-ra   æz
miyan   bord.
flood   for   an   hour   all-Ez   city-DOM   from
among   took/carried
'The flood wiped out the whole city for an hour.'

Test 5   *dær yek saæt*

(14)   e.   seyl   dær   yek   saæt   tæmam-e   šæhr-ra   æz   miyan
bord.
flood   in   an   hour   all-Ez   city-DOM   from   among
took/carried
'The flood wiped out the whole city in an hour.'

Table 4 Results of the five Aktionsart tests applied to the PNJ with the prepositions *æz* and *miyan* and the light verb *bordæn*

	Prepositional NJ
Tests	*æz miyan bordæn* **'wipe out'**
1. dær hal-e	Yes
2. fæalane/ba qodræt	No
3. aheste/be soræt	Yes
4. bæraye yek saæt	No
5. dær yek saæt	Yes
Aktionsart type	Accomplishment

Second group: Prep. + NP + LV

1.a. æz 'from' + NP (concrete noun dæst 'hand' + LV (ræftæn 'go')

Test 1 *dær hal-e*

(15) a. *forsæt-e   tælayee-e   mæn   dær   hal-e   æz
dæst   ræftæn   æst.
opportunity-Ez   golden-Ez   me/I/my   in   process-Ez   from
hand   go.INF   is
'My golden opportunity is being lost.'

Test 2 *fæalane/ba qodræt*

(15) b. *forsæt-e   tælayee-e   mæn   fæalane   æz   dæst
ræft.
opportunity-Ez   golden-Ez   me/I/my   actively   from   hand
went
'My golden opportunity was actively lost.'

Test 3 *aheste/be soræt*

(15) c. *forsæt-e   tælayee-e   mæn   aheste   æz   dæst
ræft.
opportunity-Ez   golden-Ez   me/I/my   slowly   from   hand
went
'My golden opportunity was slowly lost.'

Test 4 *bæraye yek saæt*

(15) d. *forsæt-e   tælayee-e   mæn   bæraye yek saæt
æz   dæst   ræft.
opportunity-Ez   golden-Ez   me/I/my   for   an   hour
from   hand   went
'My golden opportunity was lost for an hour.'

Test 5 *dær yek saæt*

(15) e. *forsæt-e   tælayee-e   mæn   dær yek saæt æz
dæst   ræft.
opportunity-Ez   golden-Ez   me/I/my   in   an   hour   from
hand   went
'My golden opportunity was lost in an hour.'

1.b. æz 'from' + NP (abstract noun *huš* 'consciousness') + LV (*ræftæn* 'go')

Test 1 *dær hal-e*

(16) a. *u   dær hal-e   æz   huš   ræftæn dær
xiyaban æst.
he/she in   process-Ez from consciousness go.INF. in
street   is
'He/She is losing his/her consciousness/fainting in the street.'

Test 2 *fæalane/ba qodræt*

(16) b. *u   dær xiyaban fæalane æz   huš   ræft.
he/she in   street   actively from consciousness went
'He/She actively lost his/her consciousness/fainted in the
street.'

Test 3 *aheste/be soræt*

(16) c. *u   dær xiyaban aheste æz   huš   ræft.
he/she in   street   slowly from consciousness went
'He/She slowly lost his/her consciousness/fainted in the street.'

Test 4 *bæraye yek saæt*

(16) d. *u   dær xiyaban bæraye yek saæt æz
huš   ræft.
he/she in   street   for   an   hour from
consciousness went
'He/She lost his/her consciousness/fainted in the street for an
hour.'

Test 5 *dær yek saæt*

(16) e. *u   dær xiyaban dær yek saæt æz   huš
ræft.
he/she in   street   in   an   hour from consciousness
went
'He/She lost his/her consciousness/fainted in the street in an
hour.'

Table 5 Results of the five Aktionsart tests applied to the two PNJs *æz dæst ræftæn* (with the concrete N *dæst*) and *æz huš bordæn* (with the abstract N *huš*)

Tests	Prepositional NJ	
	æz dæst raftæn 'be lost'	*æz huš ræftæn* 'lose consciousness'
1. dær hal-e	No	No
2. fæalane/ba qodræt	No	No
3. aheste/be soræt	No	No
4. bæraye yek saæt	No	No
5. dær yek saæt	No	No
Aktionsart type	Achievement	Achievement

1.c. *æz* 'from' + NP (abstract noun *yad* 'remembrance') + LV (*bordæn* 'take')

Test 1 *dær hal-e*

    (17)   a. *pedær-æm   dær   hal-e   æz   yad
                    bordæn-e   xatere-ye   an   hadese   æst.
                    father-my   in   process-Ez   from   remembrance
                    take.INF-Ez memory-Ez   that   accident   is
                    'My father is forgetting the memory of that accident.'

Test 2 *fæalane/ba qodræt*

    (17)   b. *pedær-æm   xatere-ye   an   hadese-ra   fæalane
                    æz   yad   bord.
                    father-my   memory-Ez   that   accident-DOM   actively
                    from   remembrance   took
                    'My father actively forgot the memory of that accident.'

Test 3 *aheste/be soræt*

    (17)   c. *pedær-æm   xatere-ye   an   hadese-ra   aheste   æz
                    yad   bord.
                    father-my   memory-Ez   that   accident-DOM   slowly   from
                    remembrance   took
                    'My father slowly forgot the memory of that accident.'

Test 4   *bæraye yek saæt*

> (17)   d. *pedær-æm   xatere-ye   an   hadese-ra   bæraye   yek
>   saæt   æz   yad   bord.
>   father-my   memory-Ez   that   accident-DOM   for   an
>   hour   from   remembrance   took
>   'My father forgot the memory of that accident for an hour.'

Test 5   *dær yek saæt*

> (17)   e. *pedær-æm   xatere-ye   an   hadese-ra   dær   yek
>   saæt   æz   yad   bord.
>   father-my   memory-Ez   that   accident-DOM   in   an
>   hour   from   remembrance   took
>   'My father forgot the memory of that accident in an hour.'

Table 6 Results of the five Aktionsart tests applied to the PNJ with the prepositions *æz* and NP *yad* and the light verb *bordæn*

| | Prepositional NJ |
| | *æz yad bordæn* |
Tests	**'forget'**
1. dær hal-e	No
2. fæalane/ba qodræt	No
3. aheste/be soræt	No
4. bæraye yek saæt	No
5. dær yek saæt	No
Aktionsart type	Achievement

1.d. *æz* 'from' + NP (concrete noun *sær* 'head') + LV (*gereftæn* 'take')

Test 1   *dær hal-e*

> (18)   a. *kudæk   dær   hal-e   æz   sær   gereftæn-e   gerye
>   æst.
>   child   in   process-Ez   from   head   take.INF-Ez   crying
>   is
>   'The child is starting crying all over again.'

Test 2 *fæalane/ba qodræt*

    (18) b. *kudæk fæalane gerye-ra   æz   sær   gereft.
                  child   actively crying-DOM from head took
                  'The child actively started crying all over again.'

Test 3 *aheste/be soræt*

    (18) c. *kudæk aheste gerye-ra   æz   sær   gereft.
                  child   slowly crying-DOM from head took
                  'The child slowly started crying all over again.'

Test 4 *bæraye yek saæt*

    (18) d. *kudæk bæraye yek saæt gerye-ra   æz   sær
                  gereft.
                  child   for   an hour crying-DOM from head
                  took
                  'The child started crying all over again for an hour.'

Test 5 *dær yek saæt*

    (18) e. *kudæk dær yek saæt gerye-ra   æz   sær   gereft.
                  child   in   an hour crying-DOM from head took
                  'The child started crying all over again in an hour.'

Table 7 Results of the five Aktionsart tests applied to the PNJ with the prepositions *æz* and NP *sær* and the light verb *gereftæn*

	Prepositional NJ
Tests	***æz sær gereftæn*** **'do all over again'**
1. dær hal-e	No
2. fæalane/ba qodræt	No
3. aheste/be soræt	No
4. bæraye yek saæt	No
5. dær yek saæt	No
Aktionsart type	Achievement

2.a. *ba* 'with' + NP + LV (*šodæn* 'become')

Test 1 *dær hal-e*

> (19) a. *pedær-æm dær hal-e   ba   xæbær   šodæn
>   æz   hadesc   æst.
>   father-my   in   process-Ez   with   news   become.INF
>   from   accident   is
>   'My father is becoming informed of the accident.'

Test 2 *fæalane/ba qodræt*

> (19) b. *pedær-æm   æz   hadese   fæalane   ba   xæbær   šod.
>   father-my   from   accident   actively   with   news   became
>   'My father actively became informed of the accident.'

Test 3 *aheste/be soræt*

> (19) c. *pedær-æm   æz   hadese   aheste   ba   xæbær   šod.
>   father-my   from   accident   slowly   with   news   became
>   'My father slowly became informed of the accident.'

Test 4 *bæraye yek saæt*

> (19) d. *pedær-æm   æz   hadese   bæraye   yek   saæt   ba
>   xæbær   šod.
>   father-my   from   accident   for   an   hour   with
>   news   became
>   'My father became informed of the accident for an hour.'

Test 5 *dær yek saæt*

> (19) e. *pedær-æm   æz   hadese   dær   yek   saæt   ba   xæbær
>   šod.
>   father-my   from   accident   in   an   hour   with   news
>   became
>   'My father became informed of the accident in an hour.'

2.b. *ba* 'with' + NP + LV (*kærdæn* 'make')

Test 1 *dær hal-e*

> (20) a. *Hamid dær hal-e   ba   xæbær kærdæn-e
>   pedær-æm æz   hadese   æst.
>   Hamid in   process-Ez with news   make.INF-Ez
>   father-my from accident is
>   'Hamid is informing my father of the accident.'

Test 2 *fæalane/ba qodræt*

> (20) b. *Hamid fæalane pedær-æm-ra   æz   hadese   ba
>   xæbær kærd.
>   Hamid actively father-my-DOM   from accident with
>   news   made
>   'Hamid actively informed my father of the accident.'

Test 3 *aheste/be soræt*

> (20) c. *Hamid aheste pedær-æm-ra   æz   hadese   ba
>   xæbær kærd.
>   Hamid slowly father-my-DOM from accident with
>   news   made
>   'Hamid slowly informed my father of the accident.'

Test 4 *bæraye yek saæt*

> (20) d. *Hamid bæraye yek saæt pedær-æm-ra   æz
>   hadese   ba   xæbær kærd.
>   Hamid for   an   hour father-my-DOM   from
>   accident with news   made
>   'Hamid informed my father of the accident for an hour.'

Test 5 *dær yek saæt*

> (20) e. *Hamid dær yek saæt pedær-æm-ra   æz   hadese
>   ba   xæbær kærd.
>   Hamid in   an   hour father-my-DOM   from accident
>   with news   made
>   'Hamid informed my father of the accident in an hour.'

Table 8 Results of the five Aktionsart tests applied to the two PNJs *ba xæbær šodæn* and *ba xæbær kærdæn* (both with the same preposition + N)

| | Prepositional NJ | |
Tests	*ba xæbær šodæn* 'become informed'	*ba xæbær kærdæn* 'inform'
1. dær hal-e	No	No
2. fæalane/ba qodræt	No	No
3. aheste/be soræt	No	No
4. bæraye yek saæt	No	No
5. dær yek saæt	No	No
Aktionsart type	Achievement	Achievement

3.a. *bær* 'on/over' + NP + LV (*ræftæn* 'go')

Test 1 *dær hal-e*

(21) a. hæme-ye pul-ha-yæš   dær hal-e   bær   bad
      ræftæn   æst.
      all-Ez   money-Pl-his/her in   process-Ez on/over wind
      go.INF   is
      'All his/her money is being squandered.'

Test 2 *fæalane/ba qodræt*

(21) b. *hæme-ye pul-ha-yæš   fæalane bær   bad   ræft.
         all-Ez   money-Pl-his/her actively on/over wind went
         'All his/her money was actively squandered.'

Test 3 *aheste/be soræt*

(21) c. hæme-ye pul-ha-yæš   aheste bær   bad   ræft.
         all-Ez   money-Pl-his/her slowly on/over wind went
         'All his/her money was slowly squandered.'

Test 4 *bæraye yek saæt*

(21) d. *hæme-ye pul-ha-yæš   bæraye yek saæt bær
         bad   ræft.
         all-Ez   money-Pl-his/her for   an   hour on/over
         wind   went
         'All his/her money was squandered for an hour.'

Test 5 *dær yek saæt*

> (21) e. hæme-ye pul-ha-yæš   dær yek saæt bær   bad
> ræft.
> all-Ez   money-Pl-his/her in   an   hour on/over wind
> went
> 'All his/her money was squandered in an hour.'

3.b. *bær* 'on/over' + NP + LV (*dadæn* 'give')

Test 1 *dær hal-e*

> (22) a. u   dær hal-e   bær   bad dadæn-e
> hæme-ye pul-ha-yæš   æst.
> he/she in   process-Ez on/over wind give.INF.-Ez
> all-Ez   money-Pl-his/her is
> 'He/She is squandering all his/her money.'

Test 2 *fæalane/ba qodræt*

> (22) b. *u   fæalane hæme-ye pul-ha-yæš-ra   bær
> bad   dad.
> he/she actively all-Ez   money-Pl.-his/her-DOM on/over
> wind gave
> 'He/She actively squandered all his/her money.'

Test 3 *aheste/be soræt*

> (22) c. u   aheste hæme-ye pul-ha-yæš-ra   bær
> bad   dad.
> he/she slowly all-Ez   money-Pl.-his/her-DOM on/over
> wind gave
> 'He/She slowly squandered all his/her money.'

Test 4 *bæraye yek saæt*

> (22) d. *u   bæraye yek saæt hæme-ye
> pul-ha-yæš-ra   bær   bad dad.
> he/she for   an   hour all-Ez
> money-Pl.-his/her-DOM on/over wind gave
> 'He/She squandered all his/her money for an hour.'

Test 5 *dær yek saæt*

   (22) e. u   dær yek saæt hæme-ye pul-ha-yæš-ra
                 bær   bad   dad.
                 he/she in   an   hour all-Ez   money-Pl.-his/her-DOM
                 on/over wind gave
                 'He/She squandered all his/her money in an hour.'

Table 9 Results of the five Aktionsart tests applied to the two PNJs *bær bad ræftæn* and *bær bad dadæn* (both with the same preposition + N)

	Prepositional NJ	
Tests	***bær bad ræftæn*** **'be squandered'**	***bær bad dadæn*** **'squander'**
1. dær hal-e	Yes	Yes
2. fæalane/ba qodræt	No	No
3. aheste/be soræt	Yes	Yes
4. bæraye yek saæt	No	No
5. dær yek saæt	Yes	Yes
Aktionsart type	Accomplishment	Accomplishment

4.a. *be* 'to' + Prep. (*miyan* 'among') + LV (*aværdæn* 'bring')

Test 1 *dær hal-e*

   (23) a. *modir   dær hal-e   be miyan aværdæn-e
               mozu-e   pul   æst.
               manager in   process-Ez to among bring.INF-Ez
               subject-Ez money is
               'The manager is broaching/bringing up the subject of money.'

Test 2 *fæalane/ba qodræt*

   (23) b. *modir   fæalane mozu-e   pul-ra   be miyan
               aværd.
               manager actively subject-Ez money-DOM to among
               brought
               'The manager actively broached/brought up the subject of
               money.'

Test 3   *aheste/be soræt*

    (23) c. *modir   aheste   mozu-e   pul-ra   be   miyan aværd.
                manager slowly   subject-Ez money-DOM to   among brought
                'The manager slowly broached/brought up the subject of money.'

Test 4   *bæraye yek sæt*

    (23) d. *modir   bæraye yek sæt mozu-e   pul-ra   be miyan   aværd.
                manager for   an   hour   subject-Ez money-DOM to among brought
                'The manager broached/brought up the subject of money for an hour.'

Test 5   *dær yek sæt*

    (23) e. *modir   dær   yek   sæt mozu-e   pul-ra   be miyan   aværd.
                manager in   an   hour   subject-Ez money-DOM to among brought
                'The manager broached/brought up the subject of money in an hour.'

Table 10 Results of the five Aktionsart tests applied to the PNJ with the two prepositions *be* and *miyan* and the light verb *aværdæn*

	Prepositional NJ
Tests	*be miyan aværdæn* **'broach/bring up'**
1. dær hal-e	No
2. fæalane/ba qodræt	No
3. aheste/be soræt	No
4. bæraye yek sæt	No
5. dær yek sæt	No
Aktionsart type	Achievement

4.b. *be* 'to' + NP (concrete noun *dæst* 'hand') + LV (*amædæn* 'come')

Test 1 *dær hal-e*

> (24) a. *pul-e   ziyad-i   dær hal-e   be dæst
> amædæn   dær in   moamele æst.
> money many-Ind.A. in   process-Ez to hand
> come.INF. in   this   deal   is
> 'A lot of money is being obtained in the deal.'

Test 2 *fæalane/ba qodræt*

> (24) b. *pul-e   ziyad-i   dær in   moamele fæalane be
> dæst amæd.
> money many-Ind.A. in   this   deal   actively to
> hand came
> 'A lot of money was actively obtained in the deal.'

Test 3 *aheste/be soræt*

> (24) c. *pul-e   ziyad-i   dær in   moamele aheste be dæst
> amæd.
> money many-Ind.A. in   this   deal   slowly to hand
> came
> 'A lot of money was slowly obtained in the deal.'

Test 4 *bæraye yek saæt*

> (24) d. *pul-e   ziyad-i   bæraye yek saæt dær in
> moamele be dæst amæd.
> money many-Ind.A. for   an   hour in   this
> deal   to hand came
> 'A lot of money was obtained in the deal for an hour.'

Test 5 *dær yek saæt*

> (24) e. *pul-e   ziyad-i   dær yek saæt dær in   moamele
> be dæst amæd.
> money many-Ind.A. in   an   hour in   this deal
> to hand came
> 'A lot of money was obtained in the deal in an hour.'

4.c. *be* 'to' + NP (abstract noun *huš* 'consciousness') + LV (*amædæn* 'come')

Test 1   *dær hal-e*

(25) a. *saeed dær hal-e   be huš   amædæn   æst.
       Saeed in   process-Ez to consciousness come.INF. is
       'Saeed is gaining his consciousness.'

Test 2   *fæalane/ba qodræt*

(25) b. *saeed fæalane be huš   amæd.
       Saeed actively to consciousness came
       'Saeed actively gained his consciousness.'

Test 3   *aheste/be soræt*

(25) c. *saeed bæraye yek saæt be huš   amæd.
       Saeed for   an   hour to consciousness came
       'Saeed slowly gained his consciousness.'

Test 4   *bæraye yek saæt*

(25) d. *saeed bæraye yek saæt be huš   amæd.
       Saeed for   an   hour to consciousness came
       'Saeed gained his consciousness for an hour.'

Test 5   *dær yek saæt*

(25) e. *saeed dær yek saæt be huš   amæd.
       Saeed in   an   hour to consciousness came
       'Saeed gained his consciousness in an hour.'

Table 11 Results of the five Aktionsart tests applied to the two PNJs *be dæst amædæn* and *be huš amædæn* (both with the same preposition + LV)

| | Prepositional NJ | |
Tests	*be dæst amædæn* 'be obtained'	*be huš amædæn* 'gain consciousness'
1. dær hal-e	No	No
2. fæalane/ba qodræt	No	No
3. aheste/be soræt	No	No
4. bæraye yek saæt	No	No
5. dær yek saæt	No	No
Aktionsart type	Achievement	Achievement

4.d. *be* 'to' + NP (abstract noun *yad* 'remembrance') + LV (*aværdæn* 'bring')

Test 1 *dær hal-e*

> (26) a. *mæn   dær   hal-e   be   yad   aværdæn-e
>   esm-æš   hæst-æm.
>   I   in   process-Ez   to   remembrance   bring.INF-Ez
>   name-his/her   be-1st.Sg.
>   'I am remembering his/her name.'

Test 2 *fæalane/ba qodræt*

> (26) b. *mæn   fæalane   esm-æš-ra   be   yad
>   aværd-æm.
>   I   actively   name-his/her-DOM   to   remembrance
>   brought-1st.Sg.
>   'I actively remembered his/her name.'

Test 3 *aheste/be soræt*

> (26) c. *mæn   aheste   esm-æš-ra   be   yad
>   aværd-æm.
>   I   slowly   name-his/her-DOM   to   remembrance
>   brought-1st.Sg.
>   'I slowly remembered his/her name.'

Test 4 *bæraye yek saæt*

> (26) d. *mæn   bæraye   yek   saæt   esm-æš-ra   be
>   yad   aværd-æm.
>   I   for   an   hour   name-his/her-DOM   to
>   remembrance   brought-1st.Sg.
>   'I remembered his/her name for an hour.'

Test 5 *dær yek saæt*

> (26) e. *mæn   dær   yek   saæt   esm-æš-ra   be
>   yad   aværd-æm.
>   I   in   an   hour   name-his/her-DOM   to
>   remembrance   brought-1st.Sg.
>   'I remembered his/her name in an hour.'

4.e. *be* 'to' + NP (abstract noun *yad* 'remembrance') + LV (*daštæn* 'have')

Test 1   *dær hal-e*

> (27)   a. *mæn   dær   hal-e   be   yad   daštæn-e
>   esm-æš   hæst-æm.
>   I   in   process-Ez   to   remembrance   have.INF-Ez
>   name-his/her   be-1ˢᵗ.Sg.
>   'I am remembering his/her name.'

Test 2   *fæalane/ba qodræt*

> (27)   b. *mæn   fæalane   esm-æš-ra   be   yad
>   dar-æm.
>   I   actively   name-his/her-DOM   to   remembrance
>   have-1ˢᵗ.Sg.
>   'I actively remember his/her name.'

Test 3   *aheste/be soræt*

> (27)   c. *mæn   aheste   esm-æš-ra   be   yad
>   dar-æm.
>   I   slowly   name-his/her-DOM   to   remembrance
>   have-1ˢᵗ.Sg.
>   'I slowly remember his/her name.'

Test 4   *bæraye yek saæt*

> (27)   d. *mæn   bæraye   yek   saæt   esm-æš-ra   be
>   yad   dar-æm.
>   I   for   an   hour   name-his/her-DOM   to
>   remembrance   have-1ˢᵗ.Sg.
>   'I remember his/her name for an hour.'

Test 5   *dær yek saæt*

> (27)   e. *mæn   dær   yek   saæt   esm-æš-ra   be
>   yad   dar-æm.
>   I   in   an   hour   name-his/her-DOM   to
>   remembrance   have-1ˢᵗ.Sg.
>   'I remember his/her name in an hour.'

Table 12 Results of the five Aktionsart tests applied to the two prepositional NJs *be yad aværdæn* and *be yad daštæn* (both with the same preposition + N)

	Prepositional NJ	
Tests	***be yad aværdæn*** 'remember'	***be yad daštæn*** 'remember'
1. dær hal-e	No	No
2. fæalane/ba qodræt	No	No
3. aheste/be soræt	No	No
4. bæraye yek saæt	No	No
5. dær yek saæt	No	No
Aktionsart type	Achievement	Achievement

4.f.   *be* 'to' + NP (action noun *kar* 'work') + LV (*bordæn* 'take')

Test 1   *dær hal-e*

    (28) a. an-ha   dær hal-e   be kar   bordæn-e
                 æslæhe-ye   jædid dær jæng hæst.ænd.
                 that-Pl. in   process-Ez to work take.INF-Ez
                 weapon_Ez new   in   war   be.1st.Pl.
                 'They are using the new weapon in the war.'

Test 2   *fæalane/ba qodræt*

    (28) b. *an-ha   fæalane   æslæhe-ye jædid-ra   dær jæng be
                 kar   bord-ænd.
                 that-Pl. actively weapon-Ez new-DOM in   war   to
                 work   took/carried-1st.Pl.
                 'They actively used the new weapon in the war.'

Test 3   *aheste/be soræt*

    (28) c. an-ha   aheste   æslæhe-ye jædid-ra   dær jæng be
                 kar   bord-ænd.
                 that-Pl. slowly weapon-Ez new-DOM in   war   to
                 work   took/carried-3rd.Pl
                 'They slowly used the new weapon in the war.'

Test 4 *bæraye yek saæt*

(28) d. *an-ha   bæraye yek   saæt   æslæhe-ye   jædid-ra   dær
      jæng be kar   bord-ænd.
      that-Pl. for   an   hour weapon-Ez new-DOM in
      war   to work took/carried-1st.Sg.
      'They used the new weapon in the war for an hour.'

Test 5 *dær yek saæt*

(28) e. an-ha   dær yek saæt æslæhe-ye   jædid-ra   dær jæng
      be kar   bord-ænd.
      that-Pl. in   an   hour weapon-Ez new-DOM in   war
      to   work took/carried-1st.Sg.
      'They used the new weapon in the war in an hour.'

4.g. *be 'to'* + NP (action noun *kar* 'work') + LV (*gereftæn* 'take')

Test 1 *dær hal-e*

(29) a. an-ha   dær hal-e   be kar   gereftæn-e   æslæhe-ye
      jædid dær jæng hæst.ænd.
      that-Pl. in   process-Ez to work take.INF-Ez weapon_Ez
      new   in   war   be.1st.Pl.
      'They are using the new weapon in the war.'

Test 2 *fæalane/ba qodræt*

(29) b. *an-ha   fæalane æslæhe-ye   jædid-ra   dær jæng be
      kar   gereft-ænd.
      that-Pl. actively weapon-Ez new-DOM   in   war   to
      work took/caught-1st.Sg.
      'They actively used the new weapon in the war.'

Test 3 *aheste/be soræt*

(29) c. an-ha   aheste æslæhe-ye   jædid-ra   dær jæng be
      kar   gereft-ænd.
      that-Pl. slowly weapon-Ez new-DOM   in   war   to
      work took/caught-3rd.Pl.
      'They slowly used the new weapon in the war.'

Test 4   *bæraye yek saæt*

> (29) d. *an-ha   bæraye   yek   saæt   æslæhe-ye   jædid-ra   dær
>   jæng   be   kar   gereft-ænd.
>   that-Pl.   for   an   hour   weapon-Ez   new-DOM   in
>   war   to   work   took/caught-1ˢᵗ.Sg.
>   'They used the new weapon in the war for an hour.'

Test 5   *dær yek saæt*

> (29) e. an-ha   dær   yek   saæt   æslæhe-ye   jædid-ra   dær   jæng
>   be   kar   gereft-ænd.
>   that-Pl.   in   an   hour   weapon-Ez   new-DOM   in   war
>   to   work   took/caught-1ˢᵗ.Sg.
>   'They used the new weapon in the war in an hour.'

Table 13 Results of the five Aktionsart tests applied to the two PNJs *be kar bordæn* and *be kar gereftæn* (both with the same preposition + N)

	Prepositional NJ	
Tests	*be kar bordæn* 'use'	*be kar gereftæn* 'use'
1. dær hal-e	Yes	Yes
2. fæalane/ba qodræt	No	No
3. aheste/be soræt	Yes	Yes
4. bæraye yek saæt	No	No
5. dær yek saæt	Yes	Yes
Aktionsart type	Accomplishment	Accomplishment

4.h. *be* 'to' + NP (concrete noun *pa* 'foot') + LV (*kærdæn* 'make')

Test 1   *dær hal-e*

> (30) a. an   bačče   xod-æš   dær   hal-e   be   pa
>   kærdæn-e   kæfš   æst.
>   that   child   self-his/her   in   process-Ez   to   foot
>   make.INF-Ez   shoe   is
>   'That child is putting on the shoes on his/her own.'

Test 2 *fæalane/ba qodræt*

> (30) b. *an bačče xod-æš fæalane kæfš-ra be pa kærd.
>   that child self-his/her actively shoe-DOM to foot made
>   'That child actively put on the shoes on his/her own.'

Test 3 *aheste/be soræt*

> (30) c. an bačče xod-æš aheste kæfš-ra be pa kærd.
>   that child self-his/her slowly shoe-DOM to foot made
>   'That child slowly put on the shoes on his/her own.'

Test 4 *bæraye yek saæt*

> (30) d. *an bačče xod-æš bæraye yek saæt kæfš-ra be pa kærd.
>   that child self-his/her for an hour shoe-DOM to foot made
>   'That child put on the shoes on his/her own for an hour.'

Test 5 *dær yek saæt*

> (30) e. an bačče xod-æš dær yek saæt kæfš-ra be pa kærd.
>   that child self-his/her in an hour shoe-DOM to foot made
>   'That child put on the shoes on his/her own in an hour.'

Table 14 Results of the five Aktionsart tests applied to the PNJ with the prepositions *be* and NP *pa* and the light verb *kærdæn*

	Prepositional NJ
Tests	*be pa kærdæn* 'put on/ wear (on the foot)'
1. dær hal-e	Yes
2. fæalane/ba qodræt	No
3. aheste/be soræt	Yes
4. bæraye yek saæt	No
5. dær yek saæt	Yes
Aktionsart type	Accomplishment

4.i.   *be* 'to' + NP (abstract noun *dærd* 'pain') + LV (*xordæn* 'eat')

Test 1 *dær hal-e*

> (31) a. *an ačar-e   kohne dær hal-e   be dærd
>   xordæn æst.
>   that spanner-Ez old   in   process-Ez to pain
>   eat.INF   is
>   'That old spanner is being useful.'

Test 2 *fæalane/ba qodræt*

> (31) b. *an ačar-e   kohne fæalane be dærd xord.
>   that spanner-Ez old   actively to pain ate
>   'That old spanner was actively useful.'

Test 3 *aheste/be soræt*

> (31) c. *an ačar-e   kohne aheste be dærd xord.
>   that spanner-Ez old   slowly to pain ate
>   'That old spanner was slowly useful.'

Test 4 *bæraye yek saæt*

> (31) d. *an ačar-e   kohne bæraye yek saæt be dærd
>   xord.
>   that spanner-Ez old   for   an   hour to pain
>   ate
>   'That old spanner was useful for an hour.'

Test 5 *dær yek saæt*

> (31) e. *an ačar-e   kohne dær yek saæt be dærd xord.
>   that spanner-Ez old   in   an   hour to pain ate
>   'That old spanner was useful in an hour.'

Table 15 Results of the five Aktionsart tests applied to the PNJ with the prepositions *be* and NP *dærd* and the light verb *xordæn*

Tests	Prepositional NJ
	be dærd xordæn 'be useful'
1. dær hal-e	No
2. fæalane/ba qodræt	No
3. aheste/be soræt	No
4. bæraye yek saæt	No
5. dær yek saæt	No
Aktionsart type	Achievement

4.j. *be* 'to' + NP (concrete noun *jib* 'pocket') + LV (*zædæn* 'hit/strike')

Test 1 *dær hal-e*

    (32) a. *agha-ye Tæmæddon dær hal-e   be jib
              zædæn-e   sæhm-e šoræka-ye xod æst.
              Mr.-Ez Tæmæddon in   process-Ez to pocket
              hit/strike.INF-Ez share-Ez   partner-Ez self is
              'Mr. Tæmæddon is pocketing his own partners' shares too.'

Test 2 *fæalane/ba qodræt*

    (32) b. *agha-ye Tæmæddon fæalane sæhm-e šoræka-ye
              xod-ra   hæm be jib   zæd.
              Mr.-Ez   Tæmæddon actively share-Ez partner-Ez
              self-DOM too   to pocket hit/struck
              'Mr. Tæmæddon actively pocketed his own partners' shares
              too.'

Test 3 *aheste/be soræt*

    (32) c. *agha-ye Tæmæddon aheste sæhm-e   šoræka-ye
              xod-ra   hæm be jib   zæd.
              Mr.-Ez   Tæmæddon slowly share-Ez partner-Ez
              self-DOM too   to   pocket hit/struck
              'Mr. Tæmæddon slowly pocketed his own partners' shares too.'

Test 4 *bæraye yek saæt*

 (32) d. *agha-ye Tæmæddon bæraye yek saæt sæhm-e
     šoræka-ye xod-ra hæm be jib zæd.
     Mr.-Ez Tæmæddon for an hour share-Ez
     partner-Ez self-DOM too to pocket hit/struck
     'Mr. Tæmæddon pocketed his own partners' shares for an hour
     too.'

Test 5 *dær yek saæt*

 (32) e. *agha-ye Tæmæddon dær yek saæt sæhm-e šoræka-ye
     xod-ra hæm be jib zæd.
     Mr.-Ez Tæmæddon in an hour share-Ez partner-Ez
     self-DOM too to pocket hit/struck
     'Mr. Tæmæddon pocketed his own partners' shares in an hour
     too.'

Table 16 Results of the five Aktionsart tests applied to the PNJ with the prepositions *be* and NP *jib* and the light verb *zædæn*

	Prepositional NJ
Tests	***be jib zædæn*** **'pocket'**
1. dær hal-e	No
2. fæalane/ba qodræt	No
3. aheste/be soræt	No
4. bæraye yek saæt	No
5. dær yek saæt	No
Aktionsart type	Achievement

4.k. *be* 'to' + NP (the concrete nouns *xak* 'soil' and *xun* 'blood') + LV (*kešidæn* 'pull')

Test 1 *dær hal-e*

 (33) a. eskændær dær hal-e be xak væ xun
     kešidæn-e mærdom-e ziyad-I æst.
     Alexander in process-Ez to soil and blood
     pull.INF-Ez people-Ez many-Ind.A. is
     'Alexander is killing many people.'

Test 2 *fæalane/ba qodræt*

    (33) b. *eskændær fæalane mærdom-e ziyad-i-ra   be
                    xak væ xun   kešid.
                    Alexander actively people-Ez many-Ind.A.-DOM to
                    soil and blood pulled
                    'Alexander actively killed many people.'

Test 3 *aheste/be soræt*

    (33) c. eskændær aheste mærdom-e ziyad-i-ra   be xak
                    væ xun   kešid.
                    Alexander slowly people-Ez many-Ind.A.-DOM to soil
                    and blood pulled
                    'Alexander slowly killed many people.'

Test 4 *bæraye yek saæt*

    (33) d. *eskændær bæraye yek saæt mærdom-e
                    ziyad-i-ra   be xak væ xun   kešid.
                    Alexander for   an hour people-Ez
                    many-Ind.A.-DOM to soil and blood pulled
                    'Alexander killed many people for an hour.'

Test 5 *dær yek saæt*

    (33) e. eskændær dær yek saæt mærdom-e ziyad-i-ra
                    be xak væ xun   kešid.
                    Alexander in an hour people-Ez many-Ind.A.-DOM
                    to soil and blood pulled
                    'Alexander killed many people in an hour.'

Table 17 Results of the five Aktionsart tests applied to the PNJ with the prepositions *be* and the two NPs *xak* and *xun* and the light verb *kešidæn*

	Prepositional NJ
Tests	*be (xak væ) xun* *kešidæn* 'kill'
1. dær hal-e	Yes
2. fæalane/ba qodræt	No
3. aheste/be soræt	Yes
4. bæraye yek saæt	No
5. dær yek saæt	Yes
Aktionsart type	Accomplishment

5.a. *bi* 'without' + NP (abstract noun *hes* 'feeling') + LV (*šodæn* 'become')

Test 1 *dær hal-e*

    (34) a. *dæst-æm dær hal-e   bi   hes   šodæn
                  æst.
                  hand-my in   process-Ez without feeling become.INF
                  is
                  'My hand is becoming numb/anaesthetized.'

Test 2 *fæalane/ba qodræt*

    (34) b. *dæst-æm fæalane bi   hes   šod.
                  hand-my actively without feeling became
                  'My hand actively became numb/anaesthetized.'

Test 3 *aheste/be soræt*

    (34) c. *dæst-æm aheste bi   hes   šod.
                  hand-my slowly without feeling became
                  'My hand slowly became numb/anaesthetized.'

Test 4 *bæraye yek saæt*

    (34) d. *dæst-æm bæraye yek saæt bi   hes   šod.
                  hand-my for   an   hour without feeling became
                  'My hand became numb/anaesthetized for an hour.'

Test 5 *dær yek saæt*

    (34) e. *dæst-æm dær yek saæt bi   hes   šod.
                      hand-my in an hour without feeling became
                      'My hand became numb/anaesthetized in an hour.'

5.b. *bi* 'without' + NP (abstract noun *hes* 'feeling') + LV (*kærdæn* 'make')

Test 1 *dær hal-e*

    (35) a. *doktor dæ hal-e   bi   hes   kærdæn-e
                      dæst-æm æst.
                      doctor in   process-Ez without feeling make.INF-Ez
                      hand-my is
                      'The doctor is numbing/anaesthetizing my hand.'

Test 2 *fæalane/ba qodræt*

    (35) b. *doktor fæalane dæst-æm-ra   bi   hes   kærd.
                      doctor actively hand-my-DOM without feeling made
                      'The doctor actively numbed/anaesthetized my hand.'

Test 3 *aheste/be soræt*

    (35) c. *doktor aheste dæst-æm-ra   bi   hes   kærd.
                      doctor slowly hand-my-DOM without feeling made
                      'The doctor slowly numbed/anaesthetized my hand.'

Test 4 *bæraye yek saæt*

    (35) d. *doktor bæraye yek saæt dæst-æm-ra   bi
                      hes   kærd.
                      doctor for   an hour hand-my-DOM without
                      feeling made
                      'The doctor numbed/anaesthetized my hand for an hour.'

Test 5 *dær yek saæt*

    (35) e. *doktor dær yek saæt dæst-æm-ra   bi   hes
                      kærd.
                      doctor in   an hour hand-my-DOM without feeling
                      made
                      'The doctor numbed/anaesthetized my hand in an hour.'

Table 18 Results of the five Aktionsart tests applied to the two PNJs *bi hes šodæn* and *bi hes kærdæn* (both with the same preposition + N)

| | Prepositional NJ | |
| | --- | --- |
Tests	*bi hes šodæn* 'become numb/ anaesthetized'	*bi hes kærdæn* 'make numb/ anaesthetize'
1. dær hal-e	No	No
2. fæalane/ba qodræt	No	No
3. aheste/be soræt	No	No
4. bæraye yek saæt	No	No
5. dær yek saæt	No	No
Aktionsart type	Achievement	Achievement

6.a. *dær* 'in' + Prep. (*bær* 'on/over') + LV (*daštæn* 'have'): (Prep./Prep./LV)

Test 1 *dær hal-e*

> (36) a. *saxt-e   in   sæd   dær   hal-e   dær   bær
>   daštæn-e   hæzine-ha-ye   ziyadi dašt.
>   building-Ez this dam in   process-Ez in   on/over
>   have.INF-Ez expenses-Pl-Ez   much   is
>   'The building of this dam incurred large expenses.'

Test 2 *fæalane/ba qodræt*

> (36) b. *saxt-e   in   sæd   fæalane hæzine-ha-ye   ziyadi dær
>   bær   dašt.
>   building-Ez this dam   actively expense-Pl.-Ez much   in
>   on/over had.
>   'The building of this dam actively incurred large expenses.'

Test 3 *aheste/be soræt*

> (36) c. *saxt-e   in   sæd   aheste   hæzine-ha-ye   ziyadi dær
>   bær   dašt.
>   building-Ez this dam   slowly   expense-Pl.-Ez much   in
>   on/over had
>   'The building of this dam slowly incurred large expenses.'

Test 4 *bæraye yek saæt*

(36) d. *saxt-e   in   sæd   bæraye yek saæt hæzine-ha-ye
ziyadi dær bær   dašt.
building-Ez this dam for   an   hour expense-Pl.-Ez
much in   on/over had
'The building of this dam incurred large expenses for an hour.'

Test 5 *dær yek saæt*

(36) e. *saxt-e   in   sæd dær yek saæt hæzine-ha-ye
ziyadi dær bær   dašt.
building-Ez this dam in   an   hour expense-Pl.-Ez
much in   on/over had
'The building of this dam incurred large expenses in an hour.'

Table 19 Results of the five Aktionsart tests applied to the PNJ with the two prepositions *dær* and *bær* and the light verb *daštæn*

	Prepositional NJ
Tests	***dær bær daštæn*** **'incur'**
1. dær hal-e	No
2. fæalane/ba qodræt	No
3. aheste/be soræt	No
4. bæraye yek saæt	No
5. dær yek saæt	No
Aktionsart type	Achievement

6.b. *dær* 'in' + Prep. (*bær* 'on/over') + LV (*gereftæn* 'take')

Test 1 *dær hal-e*

(37) a. seyl   dær hal-e   dær bær   gereftæn-e
hæme-ye   šæhr æst.
flood in   process-Ez in   on/over take.INF.-Ez
whole/all-Ez city is
'The flood is surrounding the whole city.'

Test 2 *fæalane/ba qodræt*

(37) b. seyl   fæalane   hæme-ye   šæhr-ra   dær   bær
gereft.
flood   actively   all/whole-Ez   city-DOM   in   on/over
took
'The flood actively surrounded the whole city.'

Test 3 *aheste/be soræt*

(37) c. seyl   aheste   hæme-ye   šæhr-ra   dær   bær
gereft.
flood   slowly   all/whole-Ez   city-DOM   in   on/over
took
'The flood slowly surrounded the whole city.'

Test 4 *bæraye yek saæt*

(37) d. seyl   hæme-ye   šæhr-ra   bæraye yek saæt dær
bær   gereft.
flood   all/whole-Ez   city-DOM   for   an   hour in
on/over   took
'The flood surrounded the whole city for an hour.'

Test 5 *dær yek saæt*

(37) e. seyl   hæme-ye   šæhr-ra   dær yek saæt dær
bær   gereft.
flood   all/whole-Ez   city-DOM   in   an   hour in
on/over   took
'The flood surrounded the whole city in an hour.'

Table 20 Results of the five Aktionsart tests applied to the PNJ with the two prepositions *dær* and *bær* and the light verb *gereftæn*

Tests	Prepositional NJ *dær bær gereftæn* 'surround'
1. dær hal-e	Yes
2. fæalane/ba qodræt	No
3. aheste/be soræt	Yes
4. bæraye yek saæt	No
5. dær yek saæt	Yes
Aktionsart type	Accomplishment

7.a. *dær* 'in' + NP (concrete noun *dæst* 'hand' and abstract noun *extiyar* 'authority') + LV (*daštæn* 'have')

Test 1 *dær hal-e*

(38) a. *u   dær hal-e   dær dæst daštæn-e
          edare-ye   šerkæt   æst.
          he/she in   process-Ez in   hand   have.INF.-Ez
          running-Ez company is
          'He/She is having/exercising authority over the company.'

(38′) a. *u   dær hal-e   dær extiyar   daštæn-e
           edare-ye   šerkæt   æst.
           he/she in   process-Ez in   authority have.Inf.-Ez
           running-Ez company is
           'He/She is having/exercising authority over the company.'

Test 2 *fæalane/ba qodræt*

(38) b. *u   fæalane edare-ye   šerkæt-ra   dær dæst
          dašt.
          he/she actively running-Ez company-DOM in   hand
          had
          'He/She actively had/exercised authority over the company.'

(38′) b. *u   fæalane edare-ye   šerkæt-ra   dær extiyar
           dašt.
           he/she actively running-Ez company-DOM in   authority
           had
           'He/She actively had/exercised authority over the company.'

Test 3 *aheste/be soræt*

(38) c. *u   aheste edare-ye   šerkæt-ra   dær dæst
dašt.
  he/she slowly running-Ez company-DOM in   hand
had
'He/She slowly had/exercised authority over the company.'

(38′) c. *u   aheste edare-ye   šerkæt-ra   dær extiyar
dašt.
  he/she slowly running-Ez company-DOM in   authority
had
'He/She slowly had/exercised authority over the company.'

Test 4 *bæraye yek saæt*

(38) d. *u   bæraye yek saæt edare-ye   šerkæt-ra
dær dæst dašt.
  he/she for   an   hour running-Ez company-DOM
in   hand had
'He/She had/exercised authority over the company for an hour.'

(38′) d. *u   bæraye yek saæt edare-ye   šerkæt-ra
dær extiyar   dašt.
  he/she for   an   hour running-Ez company-DOM
in   authority had
'He/She had/exercised authority over the company for an hour.'

Test 5 *dær yek saæt*

(38) e. *u   dær yek saæt edare-ye   šerkæt-ra   dær
dæst dašt.
  he/she in   an   hour running-Ez company-DOM in
hand had
'He/She had/exercised authority over the company in an hour.'

(38′) e. *u   dær yek saæt edare-ye   šerkæt-ra   dær
extiyar   dašt.
  he/she in   an   hour running-Ez company-DOM in
authority had
'He/She had/exercised authority over the company in an hour.'

Table 21 Results of the five Aktionsart tests applied to the two PNJs *dær dæst daštæn* and *dær extiyar daštæn* (both with the same preposition + LV, but the former with concrete N and the latter with abstract N)

	Prepositional NJ	
Tests	*dær dæst daštæn* 'have/exercise authority over'	*dær extiyar daštæn* 'have/exercise authority over'
1. dær hal-e	No	No
2. fæalane/ba qodræt	No	No
3. aheste/be soræt	No	No
4. bæraye yek saæt	No	No
5. dær yek saæt	No	No
Aktionsart type	Achievement	Achievement

7.b. *dær* 'in' + NP (*dæst* 'hand' and *extiyar* 'authority') + LV (*gereftæn* 'take')

Test 1 *dær hal-e*

(39) a. *u   dær hal-e   dær dæst   gereftæn-e
           edare-ye   šerkæt   æst.
           he/she in   process-Ez in   hand   take.INF-Ez
           running-Ez company is
           'He/She is taking charge of the company.'

(39′) a. *u   dær hal-e   dær extiyar   gereftæn-e
            edare-ye   šerkæt   æst.
            he/she in   process-Ez in   authority take.Inf-Ez
            running-Ez company is
            'He/She is taking charge of the company.'

Test 2 *fæalane/ba qodræt*

(39) b. *u   fæalane edare-ye   šerkæt-ra   dær   dæst
           gereft.
           he/she actively running-Ez company-DOM in   hand
           took
           'He/She actively took charge of the company.'

(39′) b. *u   fæalane edare-ye   šerkæt-ra   dær extiyar
gereft.
he/she actively running-Ez company-DOM in   authority
took
'He/She actively took charge of the company.'

Test 3 *aheste/be soræt*

(39) c. *u   aheste edare-ye   šerkæt-ra   dær dæst
gereft.
he/she slowly running-Ez company-DOM in   hand
took
'He/She slowly took charge of the company.'
(39′) c. *u   aheste edare-ye   šerkæt-ra   dær extiyar
gereft.
he/she slowly running-Ez company-DOM in   authority
took
'He/She slowly took charge of the company.'

Test 4 *bæraye yek saæt*

(39) d. *u   bæraye yek saæt edare-ye   šerkæt-ra   dær
dæst gereft.
he/she for   an hour running-Ez company-DOM in
hand took
'He/She took charge of the company for an hour.'
(39′) d. *u   bæraye yek saæt edare-ye   šerkæt-ra   dær
extiyar   gereft.
he/she for   an hour running-Ez company-DOM in
authority took
'He/She took charge of the company for an hour.'

Test 5 *dær yek saæt*

(39) e. *u   dær yek saæt edare-ye   šerkæt-ra   dær
dæst gereft.
he/she in   an hour running-Ez company-DOM in
hand took
'He/She took charge of the company in an hour.'

(39′) e. *u   dær yek saæt edare-ye   šerkæt-ra   dær
extiyar   gereft.
he/she in   an   hour running-Ez company-DOM in
authority took
'He/She took charge of the company in an hour.'

Table 22 Results of the five Aktionsart tests applied to the two PNJs *dær dæst gereftæn* and *dær extiyar gereftæn* (both with the same preposition + LV, but the former with concrete N and the latter with abstract N)

| | Prepositional NJ | |
| | --- | --- |
Tests	*dær dæst gereftæn* 'take charge of'	*dær extiyar gereftæn* 'take charge of'
1. dær hal-e	No	No
2. fæalane/ba qodræt	No	No
3. aheste/be soræt	No	No
4. bæraye yek saæt	No	No
5. dær yek saæt	No	No
Aktionsart type	Achievement	Achievement

Bibliography

Ackerman, F. (2000). 'Syntactic expression as morphological exponence'. Talk given at the Chicago Linguistics Society Meeting. Available at: http://idiom.ucsd.edu/~acherman/clspaperweb.pdf.

Ackerman, F. and P. Lesourd (1997). Toward a lexical representation of phrasal predicates. In A. Alsina, J. Bresnan and P. Sells (eds), *Complex Predicates*. Stanford, California: CSLI Publications, pp. 67–106.

Ackerman, F. and Gert Webelhuth (1998). The composition of (dis)continuous predicates: Lexical or syntactic? *Acta Linguistica Hungarica* 44: 317–340.

Aissen, J. (1983). Indirect object advancement in Tzotzil. In D. Perlmutter (ed.), *Studies in Relational Grammar 1*. Chicago: University of Chicago Press, pp. 272–302.

Aissen, J. and D. Perlmutter (1976). Clause reduction in Spanish. *Proceedings of the 2nd Annual Meeting of the Berkeley Linguistics Society*, pp. 1–30.

Aissen, J. and D. Perlmutter (1983). Clause reduction in Spanish. In David Perlmutter (ed.), *Studies in Relational Grammar 1*. Chicago: University of Chicago Press, pp. 360–403.

Allen, Keith (2001). *Natural Language Semantics*. Oxford and New York: Blackwell Publishers.

Alsina, A. (1993). *Predicate Composition: A Theory of Syntactic Function Alternations*. PhD thesis, Stanford University.

Alsina, A. (1997). Causatives in Bantu and Romance. In A. Alsina, J. Bresnan and P. Sells (eds), *Complex Predicates*. Stanford, California: CSLI Publications, pp. 204–247.

Alsina, A., J. Bresnan and P. Sells (eds) (1997). *Complex Predicates*. Stanford, California: CSLI Publications.

Anderson, Mona (1983). Prenominal genitive NPs. *The Linguistic Review* 3: 1–24.

Andrews, A.D. and C.D. Manning (1999). *Complex Predicates and Information Spreading in LFG*. Stanford, California: CSLI Publications.

Assi, S.M. (1997). Farsi Linguistic Database (FLDB). Institute for Humanity and Cultural Studies in Tehran, Iran.

Baker, M. (1988). *Incorporation: A Theory of Grammatical Function Changing*. Chicago: Chicago University.

Baker, M. (1997). Complex predicates and agreement in polysynthetic languages. In A. Alsina, J. Bresnan and P. Sells (eds), *Complex Predicates*. Stanford, California: CSLI Publications, pp. 247–288.

Baldi, Philip (1983). *An Introduction to Indo-European Languages*. Illinois: Southern Illinois University Press.

Barjesteh, D. (1983). *Morphology, Syntax, and Semantics of Persian Compound Verb: A Lexical Approach*. PhD thesis, Unversity of Illinois.

Bashiri, I. (1981). *Persian Syntax*. Minneapolis: Burgess Publishing Company.

Bickel, Balthasar (2003). Referential density in discourse and syntactic typology. *Language* 79: 708–736.

Bijankhan, M. (1994). Bijankhan Corpus. Data Base Research at the University of Tehran: Iran.

Bjerre, Tavs (2003). The semantics of locative prepositions and adverbs in Danish. *Nordlyd* 31(1): 1–12.

Bolinger, D. (1971). *The Phrasal Verb in English*. Cambridge, Massachusetts: Harvard University Press.

Bolkestein, A. Machtelt, Henk A. Combe, Simon C. Dik, Casper de Groot, Jadranka Gvozdanovic, Albert Rijksbaron and Co Vet (1981). *Predication and Expression in Functional Grammar*. London: Academic Press Inc. (London) Ltd.

Borer, H. (2000). *The Forming, the Formation and the Form of Nominals*. Manuscript, University of Southern California.

Borik, Olga. (2006). *Aspect and Reference Time*. Oxford: Oxford University Press.

Bresnan, J. (1982). *The Mental Representation of Grammatical Relations*. Cambridge, Massachusetts: MIT Press.

Bresnan, J. (1997). 'Mixed categories as head sharing constructions'. Talk presented at Lexical Functional Grammar 1997, 19–21 June, University of California San Diego.

Bresnan, Joan and Sam A. Mchombo (1995). The lexical integrity principle: Evidence from Bantu. *Natural Language and Linguistic Theory* 13(2): 181–254.

Burzio, L. (1986). *Italian Syntax: A Government and Binding Approach*. Dordrecht: D. Reidel.

Butt, Miriam (1995). *The Structure of Complex Predicates in Urdu*. Dissertations in Linguistics. Stanford, California: CSLI Publications.

Butt, M. (1997). Complex predicates in Urdu. In A. Alsina, J. Bresnan and P. Sells (eds), *Complex Predicates*. Stanford, California: CSLI Publications, pp. 10–150.

Butt, Miriam and Wilhelm Geuder (2001). Light verbs in Urdu and grammaticalization. In Christopher Schwarze, Regine Eckardt and Klaus Von Heusinger (eds), *Words in Time: Diachronic Semantics from Different Points of View*. Stanford, California: CSLI Publications. Under Review.

Cain, Bruce and James Gair (2000). *Dhivehi (Maldivian)*. Languages of the World/ Materials 63. Munich: Lincom Europa.

Cattell, R. (1984). *Composite Predicates in English*. Orlando, Florida: Academic Press.

Choi, Incheol and Stephen Wechsler (2001). Mixed categories and argument transfer in the Korean light verb construction. *Proceedings of the 8th International HPSG Conference*, Norwegian University of Science and Technology, pp. 103–120.

Chomsky, N. (1977). *Essays on Form and Interpretation*. New York: North-Holland.

Chomsky, N. (1982). *Noam Chomsky on the Generative Enterprise. A Discussion with Riny Huybregts and Henk van Riemsdijk*. Dordrecht: Foris Publications.

Chomsky, N. (1986). *Barriers*. Cambridge, Massachusetts: MIT Press.

Chomsky, N. (1995). *The Minimalist Program*. Cambridge, Massachusetts: MIT Press.

Comrie, B. (1976). *Aspect: An Introduction to the Study of Verbal Aspect and Related Problems*. Cambridge: Cambridge University Press.

Coseriu, E. and Horst Geckeler (1981). *Trends in Structural Semantics*. Tübingen, Germany: Gunter Narr Verlag.

Croft, W. (1995). Autonomy and functionalist linguistics. *Language* 71: 490–532.

Croft, William (1999). What (some) functionalists can learn from (some) formalists. In Michael Darnell, Edith Moravcsik, Frederick Newmeyer, Michael Noonan and Kathleen Wheatley (eds), *Functionalism and Formalism in Linguistics, Vol. 1: General Papers*. Amsterdam: John Benjamins, pp. 85–108.

Dabir-Moghaddam, M. (1982). *Syntax and Semantics of Causative Constructions in Persian*. PhD thesis.

Dabir-Moghaddam, M. (1997). Compound verbs in Persian. *Studies in the Linguistic Sciences* 27(2): 25–59.

Dabir-Moghaddam, M. (1998). 'Compound verbs in Persian'. Paper presented at the Third Linguistics Conference in Iran, ed. by Y. Modarres and M. Dabir-Moghaddam, pp. 67–122.

Dehé, N. (2002). *Particle Verbs in English*. Amsterdam and Philadelphia: John Benjamins.

Dik, Simon C. (1980). *Studies in Functional Grammar*. Amsterdam: North-Holland.

Dik, Simon C. (1991). Functional grammar. In F.G. Droste and J.E. Joseph (eds), *Linguistic Theory and Grammatical Description: Nine Current Approaches*. Amsterdam and Philadelphia: John Benjamins, pp. 247–247.

Di Sciullo, A.M. and E. Williams (1987). *On the Definition of Words*. Cambridge, Massachusetts: MIT Press.

Dowty, D. (1979). *Word Meaning and Montague Grammar*. Dordrecht: D. Reidel.

Dowty, D. (1991). Thematic proto-roles and argument selection. *Language* 67: 547–619.

Emonds, Joseph. (1985). *A Unified Theory of Syntactic Categoriers*. Dordrecht: Foris Publications.

Engerer, Volkmar (2007). *Phasal Verbs*. Available at: http://www.statsbiblioteket.dk/forskning/volkmar-engerer/Final-Phase%20Verbs%20-%20vers01.pdf.

Everett, D.L. (2002). 'Asymmetrical clause linking in Wari and the theory of phrase structure'. Paper presented at 2001 RRG Conference, University of California, Santa Barbara.

Fillmore, Charles J. (1963). The position of embedding transformations in a grammar. *Word* 19: 208–231.

Fillmore, Charles J. (1968). The case for case. In Emmon Bach and Robert Harms (eds), *Universals in Linguistic Theory*. New York: Holt, Reinhart and Winston, pp. 1–88.

Foley, W.A. and Robert D. Van Valin, Jr. (1984). *Functional Syntax and Universal Grammar*. Cambridge: Cambridge University Press.

Folli, R., H. Harley and S. Karimi (2005). Determinants of event type in Persian complex predicates. *Lingua* 115: 1365–1401.

Gholam-Alizadeh, Khosro (1996). *Sâxt-e Zabân-e Fârsi* (The Structure of Farsi). Tehran: Ehya Ketab.

Ghomeshi, J. (2002). 'Determination of event type in Persian complex predicates'. New Trends in Linguistics Workshop, University of Toronto.

Ghomeshi, J. and D. Massam (1994). Lexical/syntactic relations without projection. *Linguistic Analysis* 23(3–4): 175–217.

Gil, David (2003). *Word Order without Syntactic Categories: How Riau Indonesian Does It*. Available at: http://linguistics.arizona.edu/carnie/papers/v1volume/Gil.pdf.

Givon, Talmy (1984). *Syntax: A Functional-Typological Introduction*, vol. I. Amsterdam and Philadelphia: John Benjamins.

Goldberg, A.E. (1996). Words by default: Optimizing constraints and the Persian complex predicate. *Annual Proceedings of the Berkeley Linguistic Society*, p. 22.

Goldberg, Adele E. (2004). Words by default: The Persian complex predicate construction. In Elaine Francis and Laura Michaelis (eds), *Linguistic Mismatches*. Stanford, California: CSLI Publications.

Gries, S. (2000). *Multifactorial Analysis in Corpus Linguistics*. New York: Continuum.

Grimshaw, J. (1990). *Argument Structure*. Cambridge, Massachusetts: MIT Press.

Grimshaw, Jane and Armin Mester (1988). Light verbs and θ-theory. *Linguistic Inquiry* 19: 205–232.

Groot, Casper de (1989). *Predicate Structure in a Functional Grammar of Hungarian*. Dordrecht: Foris Publications.

Guerrero, Lilian (2007). 'Aspect shift: Phase verbs and quantitative aspect in Spanish'. International Conference on Role and Reference Grammar, 6–10 August, Mexico City, Mexico.

Gustavsson, Sven (1976). *Predicative Adjectives with the Copula byt' in Modern Russian*. Stockholm, Sweden: Almqwist & Wiksel International.

Hale, K. and J. Keyser (1991). *On the Syntax of Argument Structure*. Lexicon Project Working Papers, Centre for Cognitive Science: MIT Press.

Hale, K. and J. Keyser (1993). On argument structure and lexical expression of syntactic relations. In K. Hale and J. Keyser (eds), *A View from Building 20, Festschrift for Sylvain Bromberger.* Cambridge, Massachusetts: MIT Press.

Hale, K. and J. Keyser (1996). On the complex nature of simple predicators. In A. Alsina, J. Bresnan and P. Sells, *Complex Predicates.* Stanford, California: CSLI Publications, pp. 29–66.

Hale, M. and A. Marantz (1993). Distributed morphology and the pieces of inflection. In K. Hale and S.J. Keyser (eds), *A View from Building 20, Festschrift for Sylvain Bromberger*. Cambridge, Massachusetts: MIT Press, pp. 53–110.

Halliday, Michael A.K. (1994). *An Introduction to Functional Grammar* (2nd edn). London: Edward Arnold.

Hamshahri online newspaper in Iran. Available at: http://en.wikipedia.org/wiki/Hamshahri_Corpus.

Hengeveld, Kees. (1992). *Non-Verbal Predication: Theory, Typology, Diachrony*. Berlin, New York: Mouton de Gruyter.

Higgins, F. R. (1974). *The Pseudo-Cleft Construction in English*. Doctoral dissertation. Cambridge, Massachusetts: MIT Press.

Jackendoff, Ray S. (1972). *Semantic Interpretation in Generative Grammar*. Cambridge, Massachusetts: MIT Press.

Jackendoff, R. (1974). A Deep Structure Projection Rule. *Linguistic Inquiry* 5(4): 481–506.

Jackendoff, Ray S. (1976). Toward an explanatory semantic representation. *Linguistic Inquiry* 7(1): 89–150.

Jackendoff, Ray S. (2002). English Particle Constructions, the Lexicon, and Autonomy of Syntax. In N. Dehé, R. Jackendoff, A. McIntyre and S. Urban (eds), *Verb-Particle Explanations. Interface Explanations, 1*. Berlin, New York: Mouton de Gruyter, pp. 67–95.

Jespersen, O. (1954). *A Modern English Grammar on Historical Principles*. London: Allen and Unwin.

Johnson, Mark (1987). A new approach to clause structure in Role and Reference Grammar. *Davis Working Papers in Linguistics* 2: 55–9. University of California: Davis.

Jolly, Julia (1991). Prepositional analysis within the framework of Role and Reference Grammar. New York: Peter Lang.

Jolly, Julia (1993). Preposition assignment in English. In R.D. Van Valin (ed.), *Advances in Role and Reference Grammar*. Amsterdam: John Benjamins, pp. 275–310.

Junger, Judith (1987). *Predication Formation in the Verbal System of Modern Hebrew*. Dordrecht: Foris Publications.

Kahnemuyipour, Arsalan (2001). 'Persian stress revisited'. Paper presented at the Workshop on Issues in Farsi Linguistics, Isfahan, Azad University at Khorasgan (available on Iranian Linguist Website).

Karimi, Simin (1997). Persian complex verbs: Idiomatic or compositional. *Lexicology* 3(2): 273–318.

Karimi-Doostan, G. (1997). *Light Verb Constructions in Persian*. PhD thesis, University of Essex.

Karimi-Doostan, G. (2005). Light verbs and structural case. *Lingua* 115: 1737–1756.

Khanlari, P.N. (1979). *A History of the Persian Language, vol. 1*. Trans. by N.H. Ansari. Delhi, India: Idarah-i Adabiyat-i Delli.

Lambrecht, Kund (1986). *Topic, Focus and the Grammar of Spoken French*. PhD dissertation, University of California Berkeley.

Lambrecht, Kund (1987). Sentence focus, information structure, and the thetic-categorial distinction. *Berkeley Linguistic Society* 13: 366–382.

Lambrecht, Kund (1994). *Information Structure and Sentence Form*. Cambridge: Cambridge University Press.

Lambrecht, Kund (2000). When subjects behave like objects: A markedness analysis of sentence focus constructions across languages. *Studies in Language* 24: 611–682.

Lambton, A.K.S. (1984 [1953]). *Persian Grammar.* Cambridge: Cambridge University Press.

Larson, Robert (1988). On the double object construction. *Linguistic Inquiry* 19: 335–391.

Lazard, G. (1957). *Grammaire du Persan Contemporain*. Paris: Klincksieck.

Levin, Beth and Malka R. Hovav (2005). *Argument Realization*. Cambridge: Cambridge University Press.

Lieber, Rochelle and Sergio Scalise (2007). The lexical integrity hypothesis in a new theoretical universe. In G. Booij *et al.* (eds), *Online Proceedings of the Fifth Mediterranean Morphology Meeting (MMM5)*, Fréjus, 15–18 September 2005, University of Bologna. Available at: http://mmm.lingue.unibo.it.

Lyons, John (1977). *Semantics*. Cambridge: Cambridge University Press.

Mahootian, Shahrzad (1997). *Persian*. London: Routledge.

Manning, C.D. (1997). *Romance Complex Predicates. In Defence of the Right-Branching Structure*. Available at: http://www-nlp.stanford.edu/manning/papers/right-paper.pdf.

Marantz, A. (1997). No escape from syntax: Don't try morphological analysis in the privacy of your own lexicon. In A. Demitriadis *et al.* (eds), *University of Pennsylvania Working Pages in Linguistics*, vol. 4(2). Philadelphia, Pennsylvania: Pennsylvania State University, pp. 201–225.

Megerdoomian, K. (2001a). 'Complex predicates in Persian: Verb-formation and the syntax-lexicon interface'. Talk presented at the USC Student Workshop, Los Angeles, 30 April, 2001.

Megerdoomian, K. (2001b). Event structure and complex predicates in Persian. *Canadian Journal of Linguistics* 46(1/2): 97–125.

Megerdoomian, K. (2001c). 'Complex predicates in Persian'. Paper presented at the Trends in Linguistics Workshop, Isfahan, Iran.

Megerdoomian, K. (2002). *Beyond Words and Phrases: A Unified Theory of Predicate Composition*. PhD dissertation, University of Southern California.

Milsark, Gary (1977). Towards an Explanation of Certain Peculiarities of the Existential Construction in English. *Linguistic Analysis* 3: 1–29.

Mithun, Marianne (1984). The evolution of noun incorporation. *Language* 60: 847–894.

Miyamoto, Tadao (1999). *The Light Verb Constructions in Japanese: The Role of the Verbal Noun*. Amsterdam and Philadelphia: John Benjamins.

Mohammad, J. and Simin Karimi (1992). Light verbs are taken over: Complex verbs in Persian. *Proceedings of the Western Conference in Linguistics* 5: 195–212.

Mohanan, T. (1990). *Argument Structure in Hindi*. PhD thesis, Stanford University. Dissertations in Linguistics Series. Stanford, California: CSLI Publications.

Mohanan, T. (1997). Multidimensionality of representation: NV complex predicates in Hindi. In A. Alsina, J. Bresnan and P. Sells (eds), *Complex Predicates*. Stanford CA: CSLI Publications, pp. 431–472.

Müller, Stefen (2002). *Complex Predicates: Verbal Complexes, Resultative Constructions, and Particle Verbs in German*. Stanford, California: CSLI Publications.

Napoli, Donna Jo (1989). *Predication Theory: A Case Study for Indexing Theory*. Cambridge: Cambridge University Press.

Newmeyer, F.J. (1998). *Language Form and Language Function*. Cambridge, Massachusetts: MIT Press.

Nichols, Johanna (1981). *Predicate Nominals: A Partial Surface Syntax of Russian*. University of California Press.

Nolan, Brian (forthcoming). *The Layered Structure of the Word: Motivating an RRG Theory of Morphology*. Blanchardstown, Dublin: Institute of Technology.

O'Dowd, E.M. (1998). *Prepositions and Particles in English*. Oxford: Oxford University Press.

Payne, Thomas E. (1997). *Describing Morphology*. Cambridge: Cambridge University Press.

Perlmutter, D. and P. Postal (1983). Some proposed laws of basic clause structure. In D. Perlmutter (ed.), *Studies in Relational Grammar 1*. Chicago: University of Chicago Press, pp. 81–128.

Pustejovsky, James J. (1991). The generative lexicon. *Computational Linguistics* 17: 409–441.

Pustejovsky, James J. (1995). *The Generative Lexicon*. Cambridge. Massachusetts: MIT Press.

Pustet, Regina (2003). *Copulas: Universals in the Categorization of the Lexicon*. Oxford: Oxford University Press.

Rastorgueva, V.S. (1964). *A Short Sketch of the Grammar of Persian*. Trans. by S.P. Hill and ed. by H.H. Paper. Bloomington: Indiana University Research Centre in Anthropology, Folklore, and Linguistics.

Rezai, Mohammad Javad (2006). L2 acquisition of English 'verb + prepositional phrase' and 'verb + particle' constructions by Persian speakers. In Mary Grantham O'Brien, Christine Shea and John Archibald (eds), *Proceedings of the 8th Generative Approaches to Second Language Acquisition Conference (GASLA 2006)*. Somerville, Massachusetts: Cascadilla Proceedings Project, pp. 114–123. Available at: http://www.lingref.com, document #1493.

Rezai, Vâli (2003). *A Role and Reference Grammar Analysis of Simple Sentences in Farsi (Modern Persian)*. PhD thesis. Iran: Isfahan University.

Rijkhoft, Jan (2003). When can a language have nouns and verbs? *Acta-Linguistica-Hafuiensa* 35: 7–38.

Rizzi, L. (1982). *Issues in Italian Syntax*. Dordrecht: Foris Publications.

Rodriguez, Francisco J.C. (2006). Derivational morphology in Role and Reference Grammar: A new proposal. *RESLA* 19, 41–66.

Rosen, S. (1989). *Argument Structure and Complex Predicates*. PhD thesis, Brandeis University.

Saeed, John I. (2003). *Semantics*, 2nd edn. Oxford: Blackwell.

Saeedi T., Zari (2009a). *Persian Light Verb Constructions: A Role and Reference Grammar Account*. PhD dissertation, Trinity College, Dublin.

Saeedi T., Zari (2009b). Adjectival nuclear junctures in Persian. *Institute of Technology Blanchardstown (ITB)* 18: 5–26. Available at: http://www.itb.ie/ResearchatITB/itbjournal.html.

Saeedi T., Zari (2010). Event structure of prepositional nuclear junctures. *Institute of Technology Blanchardstown (ITB)* 19: 5–19. Available at: http://www.itb.ie/ResearchatITB/itbjournal.html.

Saeedi T., Zari (2012).'Adverbial nuclear junctures in Persian'. Paper published in the Proceedings of the 8th Linguistics Conference on Linguistics, held at Allame Tabataba'i University.

Saksena, A. (1982). Contact in causation. *Language* 58: 820–831.

Samvelian, Pollet (2005). 'The Ezafe construction in Iranian languages'. Paper presented at the First International Conference on Iranian Linguistics, 17–19 June, Leipzig, Germany.

Shamisa, Soroush (2001). *Dastoor-e Zaban-e Panj Ostad* (Five Professors' Persian Language Grammar). Tehran: Ferdos Press.

Shibatani, Masayoshi and P. Pardeshi (2002). The causative continuum. In M. Shibatani (ed.), *The Grammar of Causation and Interpersonal Manipulation*. Amsterdam: John Benjamins, pp. 85–126.

Song, J.J. (1996). *Causative and Causation: A Universal-Typological Perspective*. Longman: New York.

Spencer, Andrew (1995). Incorporation in Chukchi. *Language* 71(3): 439–489.

Tabaian, H. (1979). Persian compound verbs. *Lingua* 47: 189–208.

Televnaja, Julia (2005). Representation of English phrasal verbs in ontological semantics. *Kalbotyra* 55(3): 74–80.

Thompson, Sandra A. (1988). A discourse approach to the cross-linguistic category 'adjective'. In John A. Hawkins (ed.), *Explaining Language Universals*. Oxford and New York: Blackwell, pp. 167–185.

Toratani, Kiyoko (2002). *The Morphosyntactic Structure and Logical Structure of Compound Verbs in Japanese*. PhD thesis. State University of New York at Buffalo.

Vahedi-Langrudi, M.M. (1996). *The Syntax, Semantics and Argument Structure of Complex Predicates in Modern Farsi*. PhD thesis, University of Ottawa.

Vahidian, K. Taghi and G.R. Emrani (2000). *Dastur-e Zaban-e Farsi* (Farsi Grammar). Tehran: SAMT.

Van Valin, Robert D. (1993). *Advances in Role and Reference Grammar*. Amsterdam and Philadelphia: John Benjamins.

Van Valin, Robert D. (1999). A typology of the interaction of focus structure and syntax. In E. Raxilina and J. Testelec (eds), *Typology a Linguistic Theory: From Description to Explanation*, pp. 511–524. Moscow: Languages of Russian Culture. Available on RRG website.

Van Valin, Robert D. (2001a). The acquisition of complex sentences: A case study in the role of theory in the study of language development. *Chicago Linguistic Society* 36(2): 511–531.

Van Valin, Robert D. (2001b). A brief overview of Role and Reference Grammar. Available on RRG website: http://linguistics.buffalo.edu/people/faculty/vanvalin/rrg.html.

Van Valin, Robert, D. (2005). *Exploring the Syntax-Semantics Interface*. Cambridge: Cambridge University Press.

Van Valin, Robert D. and William Foley (1980). Role and Reference Grammar. In E.A. Moravcsik and J.R. Wirth (eds), *Syntax and Semantics, vol. XIII: Current Approaches to Syntax*. New York: Academic Press, pp. 329–352.

Van Valin, Robert D. and Randy J. LaPolla (1997). *Syntax: Structure, Meaning and Function*. Cambridge: Cambridge University Press.

Vendler, Zeno (1957 [1967]). *Linguistics in Philosophy*. Ithaca: Cornell University Press.

Vergnaud, Jean-Roger (2000). 'Primitive aspects of the syntactic code'. Paper presented at Université Deloris VII, Paris.

Williams, Edwin (1980). Predication. *Linguistic Inquiry* 11: 203–238.

Zand, H. (1991). *Aspects of Persian Intransitive Verbs*. PhD thesis, University of Kansas.

Index

CPSIA information can be obtained at www.ICGtesting.com
Printed in the USA
BVOW06*1856150216

436792BV00001B/3/P